SUPERSIMPLE
CHEMISTRY

Senior editor Mani Ramaswamy
Senior art editor Michelle Staples
Project editors Francesco Piscitelli, Bharti Bedi
US editors Jenny Wilson, Lori Hand
Project art editors Jessica Tapolcai,
Mary Sandberg, Heena Sharma
Designer Sifat Fatima
Design assistant Lauren Quinn
CGI artist Adam Brackenbury
Illustrator Gus Scott
Managing editor Lisa Gillespie
Managing art editor Owen Peyton Jones
Producer, preproduction Andy Hilliard
Senior producer Meskerem Berhane
Jacket designer Akiko Kato
Jackets design development manager Sophia MTT
Publisher Andrew Macintyre
Art director Karen Self
Publishing director Jonathan Metcalf
Authors Nigel Saunders, Kat Day, Iain Brand, Anna Claybourne
Consultants Ian Stanbridge, Emily Wren, John Firth, Douglas Stuart

First American Edition, 2020
Published in the United States by DK Publishing
1450 Broadway, Suite 801, New York, NY 10018

Copyright © 2020 Dorling Kindersley Limited
DK, a Division of Penguin Random House LLC
21 22 23 24   10 9 8 7 6 5 4 3 2
005–315038–May/2020

A catalog record for this book
is available from the Library of Congress.
ISBN 978-1-4654-9323-1

DK books are available at special discounts when purchased in bulk for sales promotions, premiums,
fund-raising, or educational use. For details, contact: DK Publishing Special Markets, 1450 Broadway,
Suite 801, New York, NY
SpecialSales@dk.com

Printed and bound in China

A WORLD OF IDEAS:
SEE ALL THERE IS TO KNOW

www.dk.com

Smithsonian

Established in 1846, the Smithsonian is the world's largest museum and research complex,
dedicated to public education, national service, and scholarship in the arts, sciences, and history.
It includes 19 museums and galleries and the National Zoological Park. The total number of artifacts,
works of art, and specimens in the Smithsonian's collection is estimated at 154 million.

SUPERSIMPLE
CHEMISTRY

THE ULTIMATE BITESIZE STUDY GUIDE

Contents

The Scientific Method

Basic Chemistry

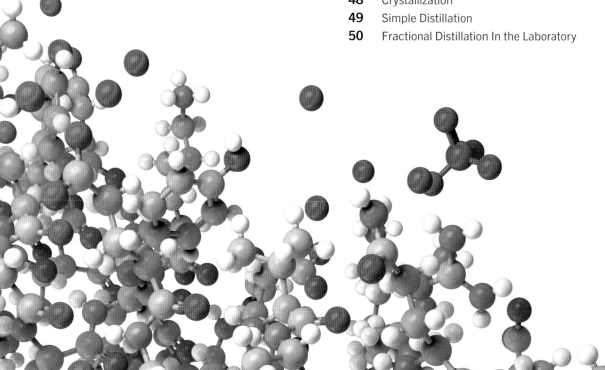

Elements

Structure and Bonding

States of Matter

Nanoscience and Smart Materials

Quantitative Chemistry

The Chemistry of Acids

Metals and Their Reactivity

Energy Changes

The Rate and Extent of Chemical Change

Organic Chemistry

Chemical Analysis

Chemistry of the Earth

Using Resources

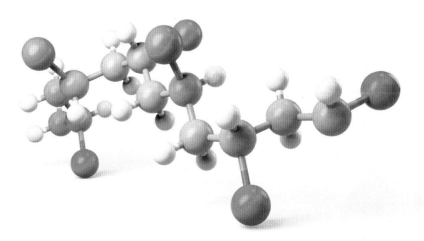

Using
Resources

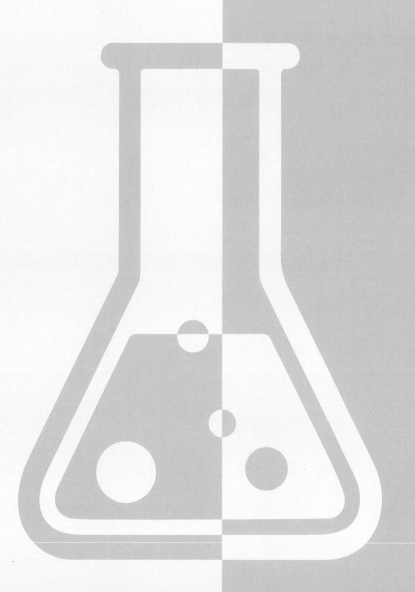

The Scientific Method

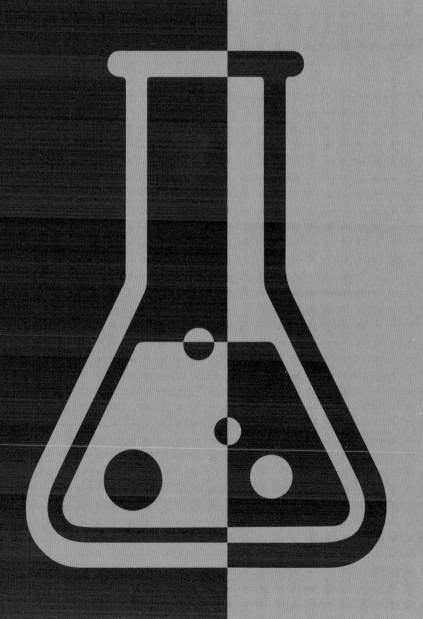

How Science Works

Scientists want to explain how and why things happen using facts—such as what happens when two elements react together, or when atoms bond. They do this by thinking logically in a step-by-step process called the scientific method. This method is used in all fields of science, including chemistry, biology, and physics.

Key Facts

✓ Scientists have a testable idea called a hypothesis.

✓ Scientists predict what may happen during an experiment.

✓ If a hypothesis is supported by an experiment's conclusion, it is accepted as fact.

✓ Scientists present their discoveries, however the media may present their own theories on the same subject in a different way.

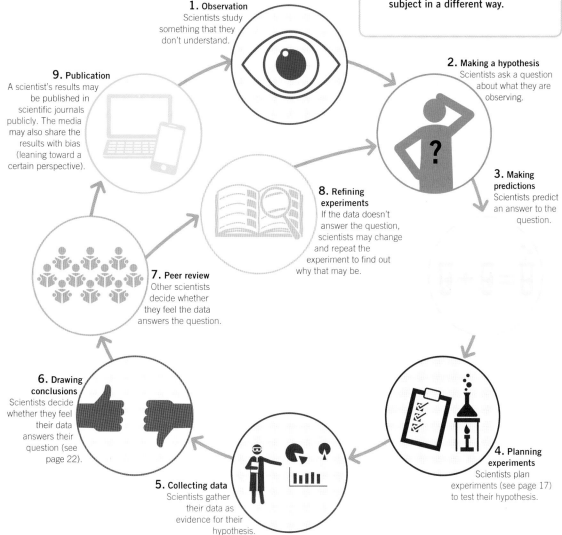

1. Observation
Scientists study something that they don't understand.

9. Publication
A scientist's results may be published in scientific journals publicly. The media may also share the results with bias (leaning toward a certain perspective).

2. Making a hypothesis
Scientists ask a question about what they are observing.

8. Refining experiments
If the data doesn't answer the question, scientists may change and repeat the experiment to find out why that may be.

3. Making predictions
Scientists predict an answer to the question.

7. Peer review
Other scientists decide whether they feel the data answers the question.

6. Drawing conclusions
Scientists decide whether they feel their data answers their question (see page 22).

5. Collecting data
Scientists gather their data as evidence for their hypothesis.

4. Planning experiments
Scientists plan experiments (see page 17) to test their hypothesis.

Scientific Issues

Science can improve our lives, from finding new ways to generate energy to creating new medicine to help the sick. This new knowledge can lead to positive developments; however, they may also raise issues that may not have been obvious at first. It's important to be aware of these issues so we can understand the full impact of new scientific discoveries on the world.

Key Facts

✓ New scientific discoveries may raise unexpected concerns.

✓ These concerns need to be understood by people who are affected by the scientific discovery.

✓ Science may raise moral issues to which it can't provide answers for.

Building dams

Dams are designed to provide us with easy access to water, as well as many other benefits. However, their creation has led to unexpected issues.

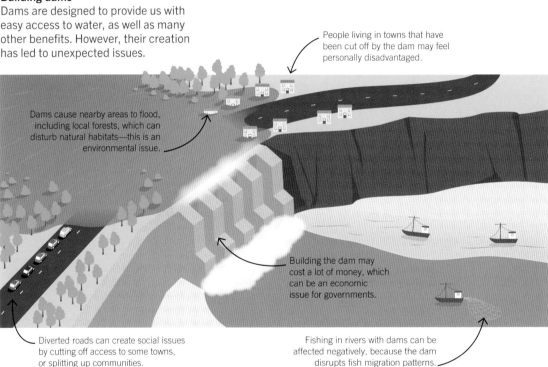

People living in towns that have been cut off by the dam may feel personally disadvantaged.

Dams cause nearby areas to flood, including local forests, which can disturb natural habitats—this is an environmental issue.

Building the dam may cost a lot of money, which can be an economic issue for governments.

Diverted roads can create social issues by cutting off access to some towns, or splitting up communities.

Fishing in rivers with dams can be affected negatively, because the dam disrupts fish migration patterns.

🔍 Ethical Issues in Science

Science aims to provide answers to questions, but there are some questions that can't be answered by science. Some scientific developments present ethical issues—whether something is right or wrong. For example, the field of genetics can provide cures for diseases, but some people believe that modifying life in this way is wrong.

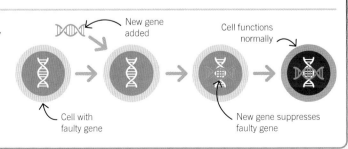

New gene added

Cell functions normally

Cell with faulty gene

New gene suppresses faulty gene

Scientific Risk

There is a chance that scientific discoveries may be dangerous or cause harm—this is called risk. This is measured by how likely the negative effects are to happen and how serious they can be if they do. Risk can be obvious, such as coming into contact with a toxic substance. Risk may also be hard to foresee, such as a product containing a new substance that has properties we are not sure about.

Key Facts

✓ Hazards may cause harm to others or the environment

✓ The chance that hazards cause harm is called risk.

✓ People assess for themselves how risky a certain scientific development might be in their life.

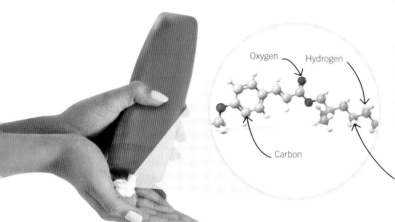

Oxygen   Hydrogen

Carbon

Substances in sunscreen

Formulations (see page 39) such as some sunscreens can contain a harmful substance called octinoxate. This is an artificial compound that blocks harmful radiation from the Sun.

Octinoxate is a long chain of molecules.

Unforeseen hazard of octinoxate

The use of sunscreens that contain octinoxate is very risky for health and for the environment. Recent studies have shown that it disrupts hormone production in the thyroid gland, and it can wash off a swimmer's skin into the ocean, bleaching coral, and harming the environment.

Thyroid gland

Strands of sunscreen

Bleached coral

Healthy coral

Validity

Scientists won't trust a experiment's findings if the experiment produces different results when repeated, or if the experiment can't be conducted by other scientists.
If an experiment is repeatable and reproducible, and the results answer the hypothesis, then the experiment is considered valid.

Key Facts

✓ An experiment is repeatable if the same person recreated the experiment using the same equipment and they collected similar results.

✓ An experiment is reproducible if different people conducted the same experiment with different equipment and similar results were collected.

✓ If an experiment is repeatable and reproducible, and the results answer the hypothesis, then the experiment is considered valid.

	First try	Second try
Repeatable If the same person repeated the experiment using the same equipment and collected similar results, the experiment is repeatable.		
Reproducible If a different person conducted the experiment using different equipment and observed similar results, the experiment is reproducible.	30 ml	30 ml
Same results? If the experiment is repeated and reproduced and produces the same results, then the experiment is valid.	12/13/14	12/13/14

⚙ Precise Equipment

It's important to use equipment that can measure quantities precisely. For example, a pipette where you can clearly see measurements in increments of 1 ml along the side (rather than a measuring cylinder with increments of 5 ml) will ensure that you can measure the same quantity when you repeat your experiment, so your results are likely to be the same.

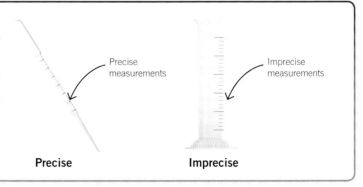

Precise measurements

Imprecise measurements

Precise   **Imprecise**

Experiment Variables

When testing a hypothesis, scientists conduct experiments by changing one thing and seeing how it will influence something else. Sometimes, they need to keep some things the same so they can understand how one thing affects the other. These things are called variables, and by identifying them, scientists ensure their experiments are fair.

Examples of variables

This simple experiment involves hydrochloric acid reacting with iron sulfide to create hydrogen sulfide, and has an independent, dependent, and controlled variable.

The amount of hydrochloric acid is the independent variable.

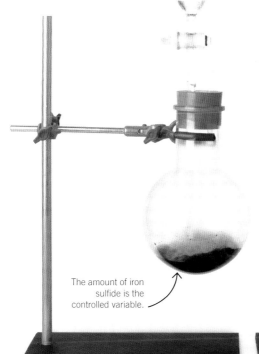

The amount of iron sulfide is the controlled variable.

Key Facts

✓ Variables are things that can affect the results of your experiment.

✓ The independent variable is the thing that you change during an experiment.

✓ The dependent variable is the thing that you measure when you change the independent variable during an experiment.

✓ The controlled variables are the things that you try and keep the same during an experiment.

⚙ Control Experiments

There are things that may be impossible to control, such as the temperature of the room or the time of day. A control experiment is the same experiment, but where nothing is changed. The results of this are compared with your original experiments so you can see the effects of things outside your control.

The amount of hydrogen sulfide produced is the dependent variable.

Safe Experiments

It's important to conduct experiments safely to avoid any accidents happening. Sometimes, chemistry experiments can involve corrosive acids or heating substances, so there's a risk of being injured or burned. The safety equipment shown here helps make experiments safer.

Key Facts

✓ Experiments can be unsafe.
✓ Equipment or procedures should be planned for to keep experiments as safe as possible.

Protecting your eyes
Glasses protect your eyes from small particles during explosive chemical reactions.

Protecting your hands
Gloves protect your skin from accidental spills of corrosive substances.

Safe heating
Water baths are a safer, and more efficient, way of heating substances by submerging them in hot water instead of using an open flame from a Bunsen burner.

Preventing fires
Heatproof mats prevent fires from starting in the laboratory.

Heatproof mat

Protecting your body
Lab coats protect your body from harmful substances.

🔍 Dangerous Chemicals

Some chemical substances can be dangerous. Look out for labels on bottles that provide different types of warnings.

Flammable   Corrosive   Toxic

Equipment

When conducting an experiment, choosing the right equipment is important to collect the results you need appropriately and safely.

Chemistry equipment

Beakers, test tubes, gauze, tripods, heatproof mats, and Bunsen burners are some of the most common equipment used in chemistry experiments.

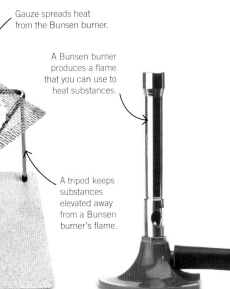

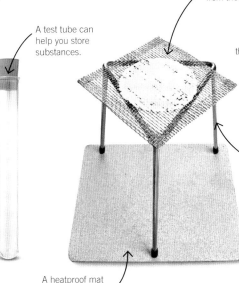

Key Facts

✓ It's important to understand each piece of the equipment's function.

✓ It's important to be able to draw each piece of equipment as a simple line drawing.

A glass beaker can help you heat substances safely.

A test tube can help you store substances.

Gauze spreads heat from the Bunsen burner.

A Bunsen burner produces a flame that you can use to heat substances.

A tripod keeps substances elevated away from a Bunsen burner's flame.

A heatproof mat helps stop fires.

▤ Drawing Equipment

Sometimes, you may also need to draw your experiment in an exam. Simple line drawings of each piece of equipment are shown below.

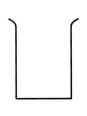

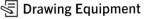

Gauze

Tripod

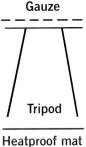

Heatproof mat

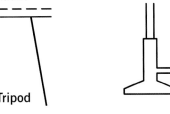

Beaker   **Test tube**   **Bunsen burner**

Planning Experiments

Every stage of an experiment must be carefully planned out. You may need to carry out experiments in the classroom or explain how you would conduct an experiment for an exam. Every experiment is different, but there are six common stages. Most of these stages involve choosing your variables (see page 14), which is very important.

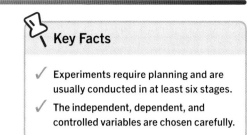

Key Facts

✓ Experiments require planning and are usually conducted in at least six stages.

✓ The independent, dependent, and controlled variables are chosen carefully.

Neutralization reaction
This experiment involves adding hydrochloric acid to sodium hydroxide and measuring the temperature.

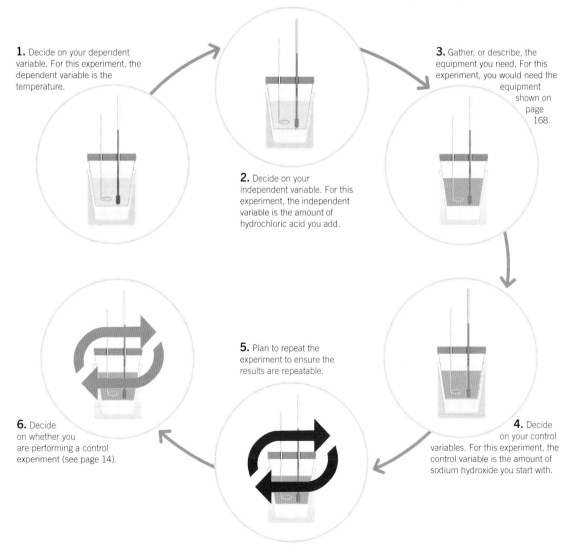

1. Decide on your dependent variable. For this experiment, the dependent variable is the temperature.

2. Decide on your independent variable. For this experiment, the independent variable is the amount of hydrochloric acid you add.

3. Gather, or describe, the equipment you need. For this experiment, you would need the equipment shown on page 168.

4. Decide on your control variables. For this experiment, the control variable is the amount of sodium hydroxide you start with.

5. Plan to repeat the experiment to ensure the results are repeatable.

6. Decide on whether you are performing a control experiment (see page 14).

Organizing Data

Data is the information that you collect from your experiment. Data is usually numbers or measurements, such as the volume of liquid collected. Data is collected using your equipment. Organizing data into tables helps you to make sense of it.

 Key Facts

✓ Data is the information collected from experiments.

✓ Data must be organized so that it can be easily reviewed.

✓ Calculating the mean of a data set can help you to get an average.

Anomalous results are pieces of data that are very different from the rest and are not close to the mean.

Inaccurate data are ranges of data that are very different from the rest.

Data set 1	Data set 2	Data set 3	Data set 4
22	20	(27)	35
21	21	21	34
22	22	22	35
22	**21**	**22**	**35**

Calculate the mean from each data set to find the average. Anomalous results are not included when calculating the mean.

📑 Significant Figures

Some numbers in your data may include many decimal points, such as 24.823. In an exam, you may be asked to round your answers to a certain number of significant figures, such as two significant figures. In this example, you would give your answer as 25.

This number gives five significant figures.

24.823
1 2 3 4 5

This number gives two significant figures.

25
1 2

Math and Science

Chemistry sometimes involves a bit of simple mathematics. It's worth brushing up on your multiplication and division skills, as well as what's listed here.

How to rearrange an equation

The subject of a formula is what is being figured out. You can change the subject by performing the opposite calculation on what you want the new subject to be.

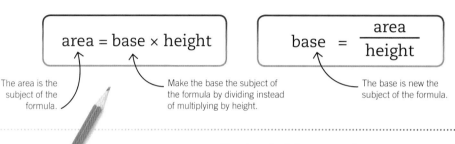

$$\text{area} = \text{base} \times \text{height}$$

$$\text{base} = \frac{\text{area}}{\text{height}}$$

The area is the subject of the formula.

Make the base the subject of the formula by dividing instead of multiplying by height.

The base is new the subject of the formula.

How to calculate a percentage

A percentage is a way of expressing how much a value is of the total, which is represented as 100%. Calculate this by dividing the value by the total, and then multiply this by 100.

Relative atomic mass of sodium is 23, and there are two atoms of sodium in sodium carbonate. 23 multiplied by 2 is 46. This is the value.

$$\frac{46}{106} \times 100 = 43\%$$

Percentage of sodium by mass in sodium carbonate.

The relative formula mass of the compound that contains sodium carbonate is 106. This is the total.

How to calculate ratios

The ratio is a number representing the proportion of something in relation to something else. For example, here is the ratio of hydrogen atoms in an ammonia molecule to the number in hydrogen molecules.

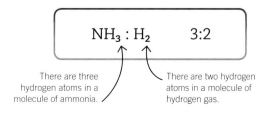

$$\text{NH}_3 : \text{H}_2 \qquad 3:2$$

There are three hydrogen atoms in a molecule of ammonia.

There are two hydrogen atoms in a molecule of hydrogen gas.

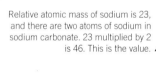

Units of Measurement

Standard units are a universal set of measurements that help scientists measure things in the same way, allowing everybody to understand and compare collected data. One unit describes one measurement of a particular quantity. Here are some metric units.

📌 **Key Facts**

✓ Units help scientists measure things using certain equipment.

✓ Using the same units helps scientists compare data with each other.

✓ Different pieces of equipment measure things using different units.

Weight
Scales are used to measure something's weight in grams or kilograms.

Quantity	Base unit	
weight	gram (g)	kilogram (kg)

Length
Rulers are used to measure how long something is in centimeters or meters.

Quantity	Base unit	
length	centimeter (cm)	meter (m)

Volume
Beakers are used to measure the volume of liquids in cubic centimeters or cubic meters.

Quantity	Base unit	
volume	cubic centimeter (cm³)	cubic meter (m³)

Time
Stopwatches and timers can be used to measure time in seconds, minutes, or hours.

Quantity	Base unit	
time	seconds (s)	minutes (m)

Mole
Unique beakers are used to measure the mole, which is both the mass and volume of substances (see page 109).

Quantity	Base unit
mole	mole (mol)

🗒 Converting Units

Units can be converted between different levels using a number called a conversion factor.

×1,000 →

g	kg
mm	m
m³	dm³
mol/dm³	mol/cm³

← ÷1,000

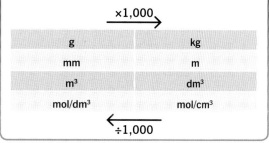

Charts and Graphs

On its own, data may not tell you enough about what you've found. Charts and graphs are a visual way of representing your data, and certain graphs are more useful than others, depending on your data.

Key Facts

✓ Charts and graphs are a clear, visual way of representing your data.

✓ Bar charts are useful for presenting data that is in categories.

✓ Line graphs are useful for presenting data with variables that changed.

Bar charts

A bar chart is used for discontinuous data (such as data collected in categories), such as shoe size, eye color, or relative atomic masses of elements.

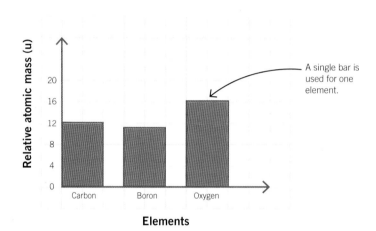

A single bar is used for one element.

Line graphs

Line graphs are useful for continuous data (or data collected over time), such as the volume of liquid produced over time. This line graph is showing a positive correlation (rising trend from left to right).

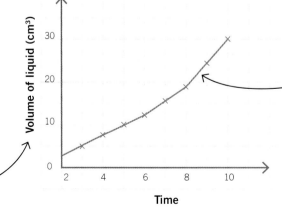

Linear scales are chosen to fill the graph paper.

Data is plotted on the graph, and a line is drawn to connect the data together.

Conclusions

Reviewing your data can help you make a clear statement about what happened in your experiment—this is a conclusion. Identifying patterns, such as, over time, higher temperatures evaporate more liquid, can help form these conclusions. However, you can't assume why this is. It's important to check whether your conclusion supports your hypothesis.

Hypothesis
For the below flame test, the hypothesis is that a metal will turn a Bunsen burner's flame yellow.

Key Facts

✓ It's important to make concise conclusions about your data.

✓ Only comment on what the data is showing, not why you think that may be.

✓ A pattern in your data doesn't mean something is causing something else.

Hypothesis supported

Hypothesis unsupported

You can conclude that the flame turned yellow, so this conclusion supports your hypothesis.

You can conclude that the flame did not turn yellow, so this conclusion does not support your hypothesis.

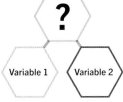

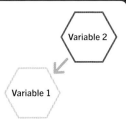

🔍 What Conclusions Can't Tell You

Even though you can conclude that the flame turned yellow in the presence of a metal, you can't assume why that is in your conclusion. This may inspire you to do more experiments to find out more.

The relationship between two variables may be up to chance—one does not affect the other.

The relationship between two variables may be influenced by an unknown third variable.

Your data may show that one variable directly influences another.

Errors and Uncertainty

There is always uncertainty around your data. Uncertainty represents whether your data were collected accurately and precisely. Two factors influence uncertainty: the limits of your equipment (quantitative error), and poor planning (qualitative error).

Choosing equipment
Quantitative errors can be avoided by choosing equipment that can measure things as precisely as possible. A piece of equipment's ability to measure precisely is called its resolution. For example, if you need to measure liquids in quantities of 1 ml, choose a pipette that can measure amounts in single milliliters.

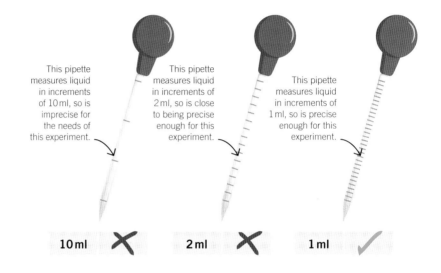

This pipette measures liquid in increments of 10 ml, so is imprecise for the needs of this experiment.

This pipette measures liquid in increments of 2 ml, so is close to being precise enough for this experiment.

This pipette measures liquid in increments of 1 ml, so is precise enough for this experiment.

10 ml ✗   2 ml ✗   1 ml ✓

Avoiding random errors
You may accidentally measure a liquid inaccurately, especially if the measurements are very small. This might mean your results are slightly different each time you take a measurement, and is unavoidable.

1ml

First try

1ml

Second try

Uncertainty formula

$$\text{uncertainty} = \frac{\text{range}}{2}$$

Accounting for uncertainty
If you measure 1 ml of liquid with a measuring cylinder, the range of possible values may be anything between 1.5 and 0.5 ml. The uncertainty formula takes this into account.

$$\pm\, 0.5 = \frac{1.5 - 1}{2}$$

Evaluations

Reflecting back over an experiment helps you understand what may have gone wrong and how things could be improved. There are six stages to carrying out an evaluation, and they can be used to plan further experiments.

Key Facts

✓ Evaluations can be done to highlight what could be improved about the experiment.

✓ Further experiments may be conducted after evaluations have been made.

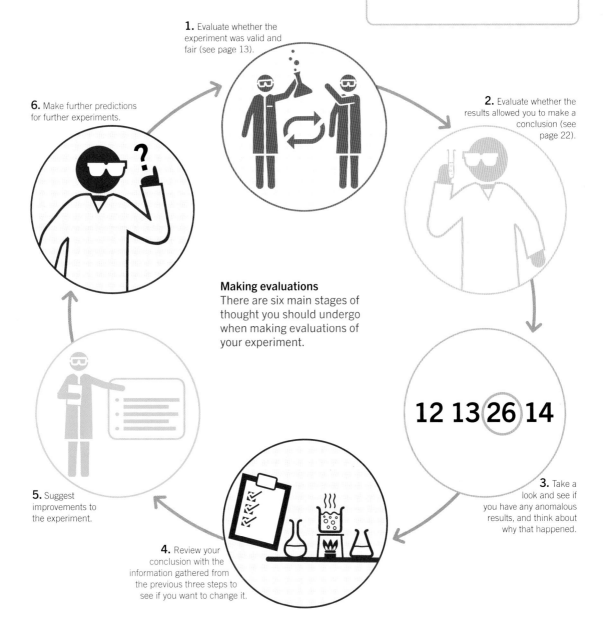

1. Evaluate whether the experiment was valid and fair (see page 13).

6. Make further predictions for further experiments.

2. Evaluate whether the results allowed you to make a conclusion (see page 22).

Making evaluations
There are six main stages of thought you should undergo when making evaluations of your experiment.

12 13 26 14

3. Take a look and see if you have any anomalous results, and think about why that happened.

5. Suggest improvements to the experiment.

4. Review your conclusion with the information gathered from the previous three steps to see if you want to change it.

Basic Chemistry

Atoms

Everything in the Universe is made of atoms. They are the smallest unit of elements (see page 30), such as gold, carbon, or oxygen, and all matter is made of elements. All atoms are microscopically small. They vary in size, but a typical atom is one-ten-millionth of a millimeter. A piece of paper is about one million atoms thick.

Key Facts

✓ All matter is composed of atoms.

✓ Atoms are very small and have a radius of 0.1 nanometers.

✓ Atoms are made up of even smaller subatomic particles called protons, neutrons, and electrons.

Atomic structure

All atoms are made of subatomic particles called protons, neutrons, and electrons. Each atom has a nucleus in the middle with electrons orbiting around it.

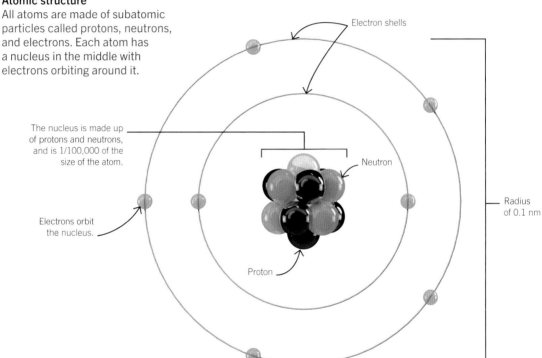

Electron shells

The nucleus is made up of protons and neutrons, and is 1/100,000 of the size of the atom.

Neutron

Electrons orbit the nucleus.

Proton

Radius of 0.1 nm

🔎 What's Inside an Atom?

Protons and neutrons have the same mass, and together they make up the atom's total mass. Electrons are much lighter, smaller, and have almost no mass. Protons have a positive electric charge, neutrons have no charge, and electrons have a negative electric charge.

		Charge	Mass
➕	**Proton**	+1	1
⚪	**Neutron**	0	1
⊖	**Electron**	−1	0

The charges and the masses given here are all relative to one another, and are not exact measurements.

History of the Atom

In the 5th century BCE, ancient Greek philosopher Democritus thought that matter was made from tiny particles called atoms. In 1803, British chemist John Dalton suggested that each element is made of different atoms, based on the way different gases react with one another.

Changing atom models
Scientists created many different models of how atoms were structured. Over time, these models were revised and updated by other scientists.

Key Facts

✓ The concept of atoms dates from around 500 BCE in ancient Greece.

✓ Ideas about what atoms are made of have changed over time.

✓ Scientists including John Dalton, J.J. Thomson, Ernest Rutherford, Neils Bohr, James Chadwick, and many others contributed to how atoms are understood.

1. Spherical model
The first model of the atom was theorized by John Dalton in 1803. Dalton suggested atoms were solid particles that could not be divided into smaller parts.

2. Plum pudding model
J.J. Thomson discovered electrons in 1904. He suggested the Plum pudding model, in which negatively charged electrons are embedded in a positively charged ball.

The gold foil experiment
In 1909, New Zealand scientist Ernest Rutherford performed the gold foil experiment. He fired tiny positively charged alpha particles at a sheet of gold foil. The results revealed the existence of a positively charged nucleus in the center of all atoms.

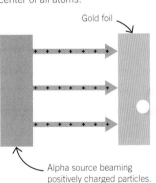

Gold foil

Alpha source beaming positively charged particles.

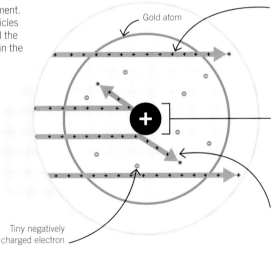

Gold atom

Beam of positively charged particles passed straight through some areas of atoms.

Positively charged nucleus repels positively charged particles because they have the same charge.

Tiny negatively charged electron

Beam of positively charged particles deflected by positively charged central nucleus.

3. Nuclear model
Ernest Rutherford proposed an atomic model of a positive nucleus in the center of a scattered cloud of electrons. He later discovered the proton as the positive charge in the nucleus.

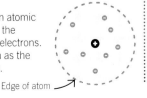

Edge of atom

4. Modern nuclear model
Neils Bohr found that electrons orbit the nucleus. Later, James Chadwick discovered neutral (no charge) neutrons in the nucleus. This led to the latest atomic model used today.

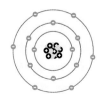

Electron Shells

Electrons are small particles of an atom. They orbit around the atom's nucleus in pathways called shells. A small atom, with only a few electrons, only has one or two shells. Larger atoms, such as radium, have lots of electrons, and need more shells to hold them all. Chemists draw shells as rings around the nucleus.

Key Facts

✓ Electrons orbit the nucleus in shells.

✓ Each shell can hold a fixed maximum number of electrons.

✓ Electrons must fill their innermost shells first before filling their outer shells.

Electron shell rules
In atoms with 20 electrons or fewer, such as aluminum atoms, each shell can hold a fixed number of electrons.

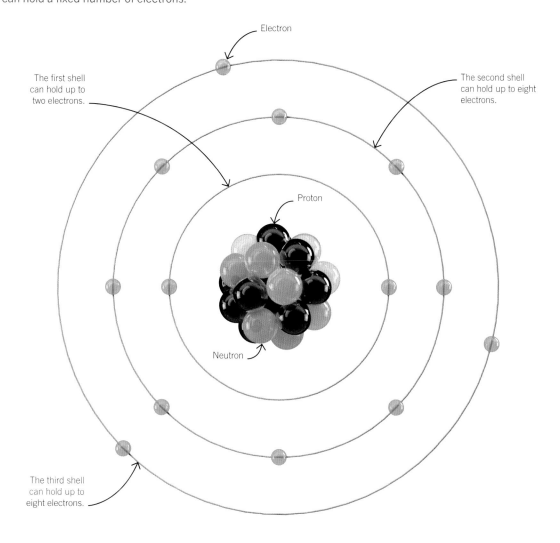

Electron

The first shell can hold up to two electrons.

The second shell can hold up to eight electrons.

Proton

Neutron

The third shell can hold up to eight electrons.

Electronic Structure

You can use information found on the periodic table (see pages 52–53) to calculate the electronic structure of an atom. Scientists can display an atom's electronic structure by using drawings (see page 28) or list the numbers of electrons held in each shell—for example: 2, 8, 3.

Method one: using the atomic number
Take the atomic number (total number of electrons) and share out the electrons between the shells until they are filled (following the rules on page 28) to work out the electronic structure.

Key Facts

✓ An atom's electronic structure lists the number of electrons in each of its shells.

✓ An electronic structure can be calculated if you know the number of electrons and shells within each atom.

✓ The electronic structure can be calculated for 20 elements using two methods.

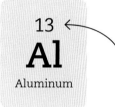

1. Look up aluminum's atomic number on the periodic table. Aluminum's atomic number is 13.

2. Follow the electron shell rules on page 28. You have 13 electrons to share out between three shells.

3. Aluminum's electronic structure is 2, 8, 3.

Method two: using periods and rows
An element's period number is equal to the number of shells its atoms have. An element's group number is equal to how many electrons are in the outermost shell.

1. Aluminum is in period 3, so its atoms have three shells.

2. Aluminum is in group 3, so its atoms have three electrons in their outermost shells.

3. Aluminum's inner two shells must be full because inner shells must be filled first.

4. If aluminum's inner shell has two electrons and its outer shell has three electrons, there are eight electrons left for its middle shell. So, aluminum's electronic structure is 2, 8, 3.

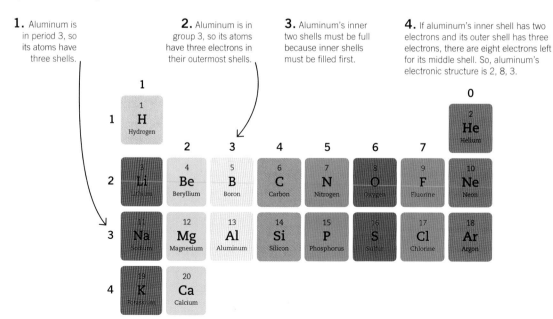

Elements

Elements are pure substances that cannot be broken down into simpler substances. Each one has unique physical and chemical properties. The number of protons in an atom determines the element, and this number is known as the element's atomic number.

Key Facts

✓ Elements contain one type of atom.

✓ The number of protons in an atom's nucleus determines the element.

✓ 118 different elements have been discovered so far.

Inside elements
Pure samples of each element have one type of atom.

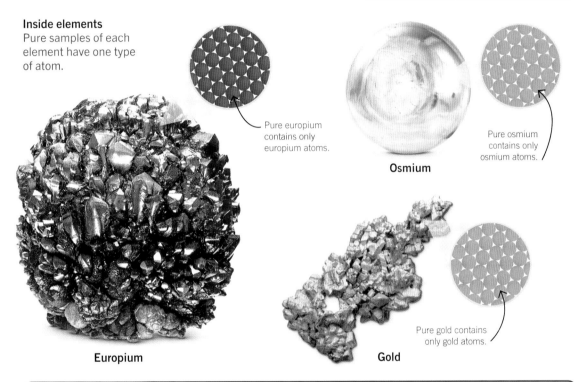

Pure europium contains only europium atoms.

Osmium

Pure osmium contains only osmium atoms.

Pure gold contains only gold atoms.

Europium

Gold

🔍 The Periodic Table

Scientists arrange all the elements in order of atomic number into a chart called the periodic table. Elements are grouped together depending on their properties, often as varying choices of colors. Read more about the periodic table on pages 52–53.

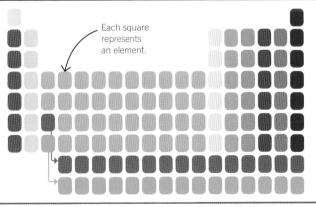

Each square represents an element.

Isotopes

Isotopes are different forms of the same element, where the atoms have the same number of protons but a different number of neutrons. For example, a typical magnesium atom has 12 protons, 12 neutrons, and 12 electrons. But some magnesium atoms have more neutrons. They are still magnesium atoms, just a different isotope of magnesium.

📌 **Key Facts**

✓ Isotopes are forms of an element.

✓ The number of neutrons in an atom's nucleus determines the isotope.

✓ Elements can have multiple isotopes.

✓ Isotope names are written as the element name followed by the total number of protons and neutrons.

Isotopes of magnesium
Magnesium has three isotopes; magnesium-24, magnesium-25, and magnesium-26. Their abundance is how common they are on Earth, and is given as a percentage.

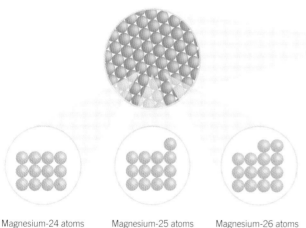

Magnesium-24 atoms have 12 neutrons in their nuclei, and an abundance of 78.99%.

Magnesium-25 atoms have 13 neutrons in their nuclei, and an abundance of 10%.

Magnesium-26 atoms have 14 neutrons in their nuclei, and an abundance of 11.01%.

Magnesium

📑 **Measuring Isotopes**

You can use this formula to calculate the average mass of all isotopes of an element, which is known as the relative atomic mass (A_r). If you know the isotope mass numbers (their total amount of protons and neutrons) and abundances, you can calculate the A_r for any element.

Relative atomic mass formula:

Isotope 1   Isotope 2

$$A_r = \frac{(\text{mass number} \times \text{abundance}) + (\text{mass number} \times \text{abundance})}{100}$$

This is the sum of all abundances and is always 100.

Mixtures

Sometimes, elements can be mixed or combined together, but they do not react or bond to form new compounds. This type of combination of two or more elements or compounds is called a mixture. For example, air is a mixture of oxygen, nitrogen, and other gases.

Key Facts

✓ A mixture is made up of two or more different elements or compounds.

✓ Mixtures contain elements and/or compounds that are not chemically bonded together.

✓ The elements or compounds keep the properties they had before they were mixed.

✓ Elements in a mixture can be separated from one another without using chemical reactions.

Iron and sulfur mixture
This mixture is made of sulfur powder and iron filings. The two elements do not react or bond when they are mixed, and can be easily separated using a magnet.

Iron   Sulfur   Iron and sulfur mixture

🔍 Atoms in Mixtures

As the different elements in a mixture are not chemically bonded, their atoms do not mix in a regular pattern or shape. Instead, they form a random pattern.

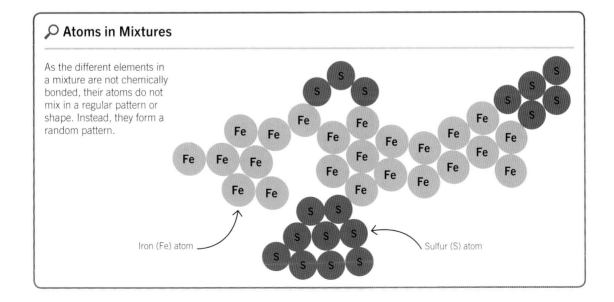

Iron (Fe) atom   Sulfur (S) atom

Compounds

Different elements can react with one another to chemically bond together, making new structures called compounds. Most substances around us are made up of different compounds.

Key Facts

✓ Most elements can undergo a reaction to form compounds.

✓ Compounds are made of atoms of one or more elements that are bonded together.

✓ The properties of a compound are different from the properties of the separate elements it's made of.

✓ Elements in a compound can only be separated using chemical reactions.

Iron and sulfur compound
The elements iron and sulfur react and bond together to form the compound pyrite. Iron is magnetic, sulfur is brittle, but pyrite is neither magnetic nor brittle.

Iron and sulfur undergo a reaction.

Iron

Sulfur

Iron and sulfur compound

🔍 Atoms in Compounds

When atoms bond together to make a compound, they create a new structure. This gives the compound new physical and chemical properties. For example, in pyrite, iron and sulfur atoms bond together in a regular three-dimensional arrangement.

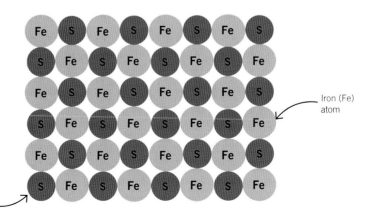

Iron (Fe) atom

Sulfur (S) atom

Formulas

Formulas are a simple and quick way of writing out what elements are in a compound. They use words or symbols (see page 53), and sometimes numbers. There are many different types of formulas. Below are four formulas for sodium chloride.

Word formula
The names of the elements in the compound are listed in full, instead of using their symbols.

Chemical formula
The symbols for each element are used. There is no space between each symbol.

Sodium chloride

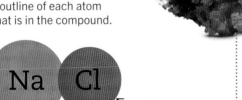

NaCl

Na is the symbol for sodium.

Cl is the symbol for chlorine.

Atomic formula
The symbols for each element and the outline of each atom show what is in the compound.

Na Cl

Cl atom

Structural formula
The symbols for each element are connected by a dash that represents a bond between each atom.

Na – Cl

The dash represents a bond between an Na atom and a Cl atom.

🔍 **Common Formulas**

Familiarize yourself with these common chemical compounds. A formula may have small numbers next to the symbols. This tells you how many atoms of this element are in a molecule of this compound.

Carbon dioxide	CO_2	Carbon monoxide	CO	
Ammonia	NH_3	Hydrochloric acid	HCl	There are two chlorine atoms in a molecule of calcium chloride.
Water	H_2O	Calcium chloride	$CaCl_2$	
Methane	CH_4	Sulfuric acid	H_2SO_4	

Deducing Formulas

Atoms bond with each other so they can fill their outer shells with electrons. Each element has a valence, which shows how many electrons an atom of that element will gain, lose, or share when it bonds with another atom or atoms.

Key Facts

✓ Valence is a number that relates to how an atom will bond with other atoms.

✓ A valence chart lists valences for elements in groups.

✓ The "drop and swap" method allows you to figure out formulas for compounds made of elements using valences.

Figuring out valences

Elements in the same group on the periodic table have the same valence, listed in a valence chart. Formulas for compounds such as water can be determined using a valence chart and the drop and swap method.

Group	1	2	3	4	5	6	7	0
Valence	1	2	3	4	−3	−2	−1	0

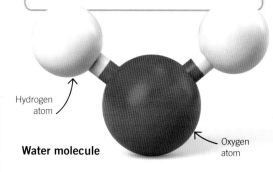

Hydrogen atom

Water molecule

Oxygen atom

For example:

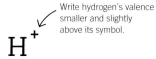

Write hydrogen's valence smaller and slightly above its symbol.

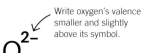

Write oxygen's valence smaller and slightly above its symbol.

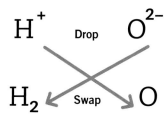

H^+ Drop O^{2-}

H_2 Swap O

1. Hydrogen (H) is in Group 1, so its valence is one. Hydrogen atoms may lose one electron, giving it a positive charge. The "one" isn't written. Instead, write a plus sign to indicate the positive charge.

2. Oxygen (O) is in Group 6, so its valence is minus two. Oxygen atoms gain two electrons to fill their outer shell, giving them a negative charge of 2. In this instance, the number and the charge sign is added to the symbol.

3. Drop the valences from above the symbol to below. Swap the valences to the other element. This provides the formula for when hydrogen and oxygen combine: H_2O, or water.

🔍 Transition Metals

The transition metals (see pages 62–63) fill in the middle part of the periodic table, between Group 2 and Group 3. You can't tell what their valence is by looking at the table. Transition metals often have more than one valence. For example, iron (Fe) can have a valence of either 2 or 3. These valences are written using Roman numerals, such as Iron II and Iron III.

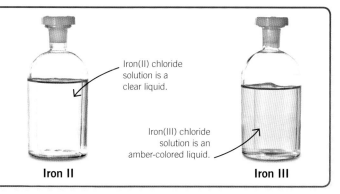

Iron(II) chloride solution is a clear liquid.

Iron(III) chloride solution is an amber-colored liquid.

Iron II   **Iron III**

Equations

Equations use symbols (see page 53) and formulas (see page 34) to show the changes that happen to substances during a chemical reaction. The substances that react together are called reactants. The chemical reaction is represented by an arrow. The new substances that form after the reaction has taken place are called products.

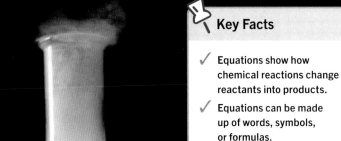

Sodium chloride
These equations show the elements sodium and chlorine (reactants) reacting to form sodium chloride (product).

This reaction is often contained within a flask because it produces a lot of heat and light.

Word equation	Sodium + chlorine	$\longrightarrow$	Sodium chloride
Formula equation	$2Na + Cl_2$	$\longrightarrow$	$2NaCl_2$
	Reactants	The reaction is represented by an arrow.	**Product**

State symbols
Equations may also contain state symbols (see page 98). These are in parentheses that show the states of matter of the substances.

Sodium and chlorine atoms bond to make a solid substance; sodium chloride.

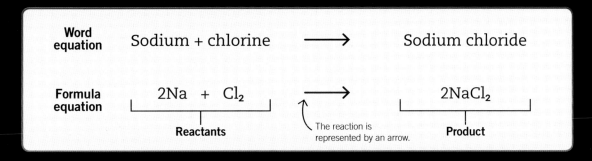

Sodium atom

Chlorine atom

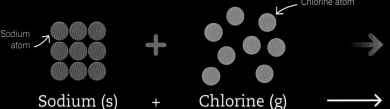

Sodium (s)   +   Chlorine (g) $\longrightarrow$ Sodium chloride (s)

This state symbol (g) shows that chlorine is a gas.

This state symbol (s) shows that sodium chloride is a solid.

Balancing Equations

During chemical reactions, atoms (see page 26) of different elements (see page 30) rearrange to form new products. To reflect this, the two sides of a chemical equation must be balanced so they both have an equal number of atoms. If an equation is unbalanced, numbers can be added to balance it. Charges must also balance (see page 151).

see page 26

see page 30

see page 151

Key Facts

✓ Equations must be balanced, with the same number of atoms on both sides, because atoms are never lost or gained during reactions.

✓ Unbalanced equations can be balanced by adding numbers in front of the formulas, until both sides have the same number of atoms.

An unbalanced equation
This equation shows the elements hydrogen and oxygen reacting to make water. It is an unbalanced equation, because it has two oxygen atoms on the left but only one on the right.

This "H" is the formula for hydrogen.

This small "2" represents two hydrogen atoms.

This "O" is the formula for oxygen.

This is the formula for water.

$$H_2 + O_2 \longrightarrow H_2O$$

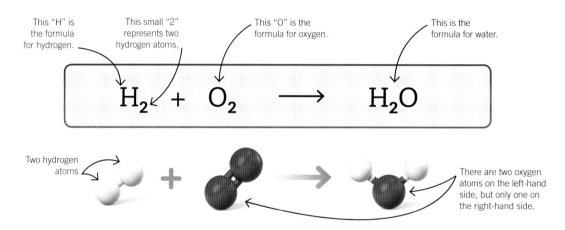

Two hydrogen atoms

There are two oxygen atoms on the left-hand side, but only one on the right-hand side.

How to balance an equation
Keep adding numbers to the equation until it is balanced.

1. Add a big "2" to the left-hand side next to hydrogen. This doubles the number of hydrogen atoms.

2. Add a big "2" to the right-hand side. This adds another water molecule. Recount. This now matches the number of atoms on the left-hand side.

$$2H_2 + O_2 \longrightarrow 2H_2O$$

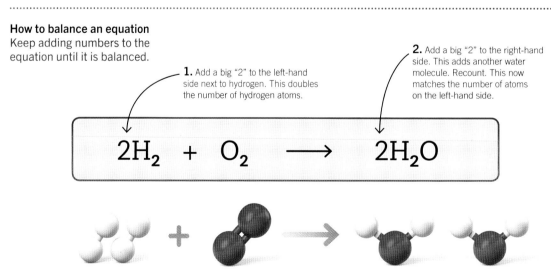

Purity

Pure substances contain only one type of element (see page 30) or compound (see page 33). For example, pure water contains only water molecules, a compound of hydrogen and oxygen. However, substances are rarely completely pure. They usually have other elements or compounds mixed into them that we can't see.

Checking for purity

Pure substances have fixed melting and boiling points. For example, water melts at 32°F (0°C) and boils at 212°F (100°C). Impure water will melt or boil over a range of temperatures.

Key Facts

✓ A pure substance contains only one type of element or compound.

✓ Purity can be tested by checking when a substance will melt or boil.

✓ Impurities in a substance usually lower the melting point and increase the boiling point.

✓ The closer a substance's boiling and melting points are to the pure substance's boiling and melting points, the purer it is.

🔍 Key

—————— solid
—————— liquid
—————— gas

Pure water melts from a solid into a liquid at 32°F.

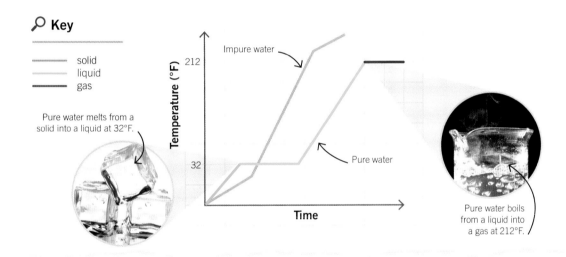

Impure water

Pure water

Pure water boils from a liquid into a gas at 212°F.

⚙ Useful Impurities

Impurities aren't always bad—they can be useful. For example, dissolving salt in water increases the water's boiling point, making food cook faster. Adding salt to icy roads makes the ice melt much quicker so that roads are safer to drive on during the cold months.

Salt and water

Salt and ice

Formulations

A formulation is a type of mixture (see page 32) that is made for a specific use. Each ingredient added to the formulation gives it a specific property. Formulations can be everyday substances, such as nail polish, medicine, laundry detergent, and paint.

Key Facts

✓ Formulations are mixtures that contain exact amounts of specific ingredients.

✓ Formulations are made for a purpose and work in a particular way.

✓ Chemists working in different industries often create and test formulations.

Paint

Paint is an example of a formulation. Three of its ingredients have useful functions. The four chemicals in paint are added in carefully measured amounts so that it works at its best. Any more or less of one chemical and the paint may be too runny or too thick.

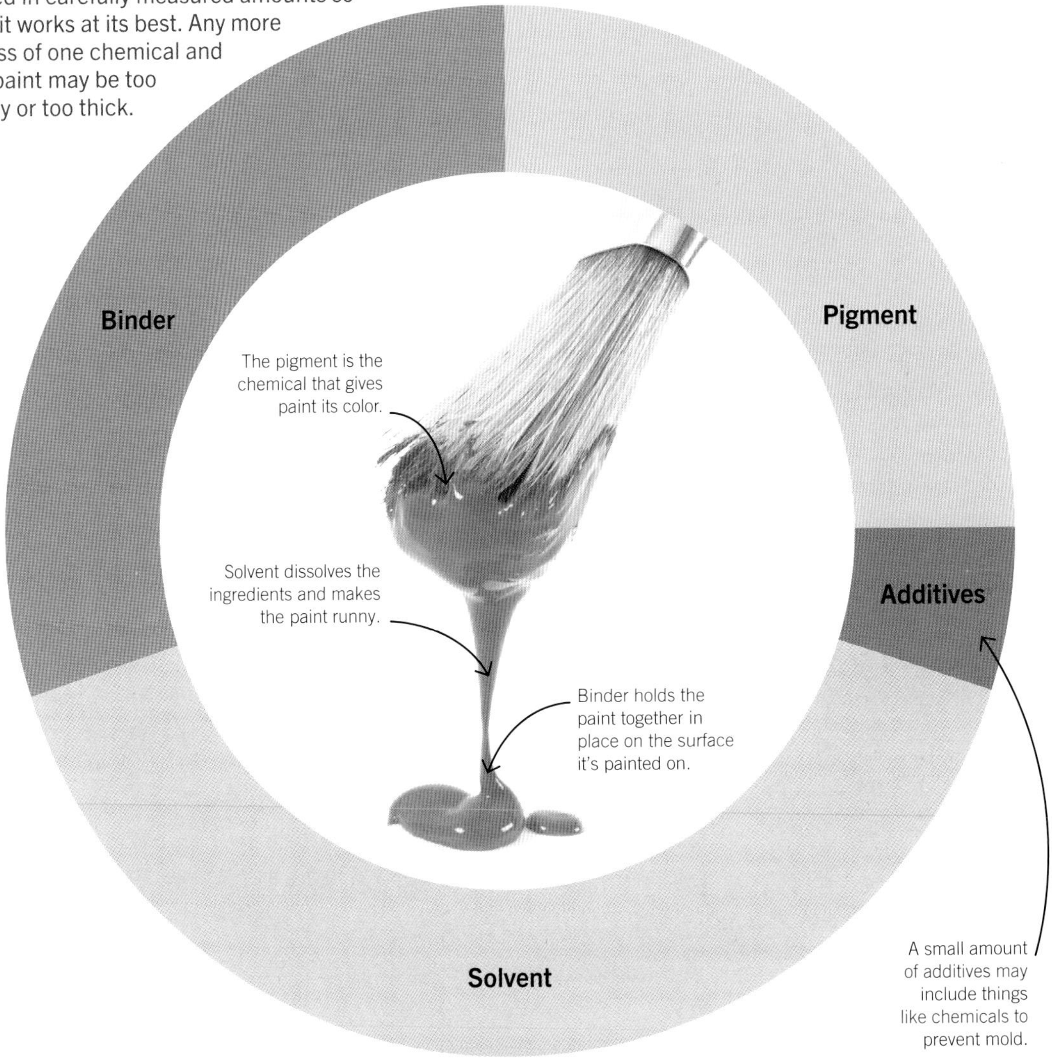

Binder

Pigment

The pigment is the chemical that gives paint its color.

Solvent dissolves the ingredients and makes the paint runny.

Additives

Binder holds the paint together in place on the surface it's painted on.

Solvent

A small amount of additives may include things like chemicals to prevent mold.

Dissolving

Dissolving happens when one substance breaks apart into tiny particles and becomes completely mixed throughout another. Substances that dissolve, such as sugar, salt, or tablets, are called solutes. Substances that can dissolve solutes, such as water or ethanol, are called solvents. Together, they form a solution.

Dissolving sugar
Sugar dissolves easily in water. Once dissolved, the sugar can no longer be seen.

Sugar is a solute

Water is a solvent

Key Facts

✓ Solutes are substances that are being dissolved.

✓ Solvents are liquids that dissolve solutes.

✓ Solutions are created when solutes dissolve in solvents.

✓ Not all substances can dissolve.

⚙ Molecules Separate

Many substances dissolve in water. Water molecules are attracted to many different kinds of molecules and atoms, breaking them apart easily. You can make solutes dissolve faster by heating and stirring mixtures.

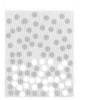

1. At first, the solute, such as salt, holds together because of the bonds between its atoms or molecules.

2. Gradually, water molecules surround the salt particles, breaking them away from each other.

3. When the solute is completely dissolved, it is evenly spread out through the solvent.

Grinding

Grinding breaks down large chunks of a solid, such as rocks or crystals, into a fine powder. This helps the powder dissolve in a liquid much quicker. Grinding can also speed up a reaction by increasing a reactant's surface area.

Key Facts

✓ Grinding breaks substances into smaller particles.

✓ Grinding helps substances dissolve in liquids quicker.

✓ Grinding helps speed up reactions.

Separating compounds
A mortar and pestle can be used to grind rock salt into smaller pieces.

Mortar

Smaller pieces of rock salt crystals

Pestle

Rock salt crystal chunks.

⚙ Increasing Surface Area

Chemical reactions happen much quicker if the surface area of a solid reactant increases. For example, grinding a 8 cm³ cube of rock salt with a surface area of 24 cm² breaks into lots of 1 cm³ cubes with a total surface area of 48 cm². This provides double the surface area for the reactant to react with, speeding up the reaction.

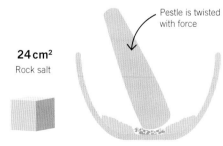

Pestle is twisted with force

24 cm²
Rock salt

48 cm²
Fine salt

1. The surface area of a rock salt cube may measure about 24 cm².

2. Take a mortar and pestle and grind it into smaller chunks.

3. Now, the combined surface area of the rock salt is about 48 cm².

Solubility

The solubility of a substance is a measure of how much of it can be dissolved in a solvent (see page 40). Usually, the higher the temperature it is heated to, the higher its solubility. Solubility is measured in grams per solute per 100 grams of solvent (g/100 g).

Key Facts

✓ Solubility is a measure of how much solute will dissolve in a solvent.

✓ The solubility of most solids increases as you raise the temperature.

✓ You can measure solubility by evaporating the solvent away from a solution and measuring the mass of the remaining solute.

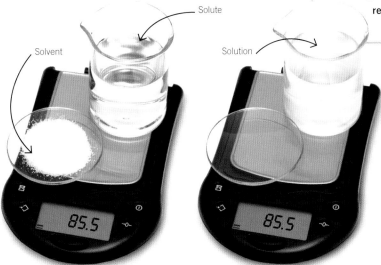

Solute

Solvent

Solution

Mass stays the same
A solution's mass is the same as the combined mass of the solute and solvent before it has been dissolved.

Different temperatures, different rates

The higher the temperature, the more solvent can be dissolved in a solute. You can conduct a simple experiment by varying the temperature and measuring the mass of salt dissolved in water. You should keep the mass of water and number of stirs the same.

10g of salt dissolved in water	**50g of salt dissolved in water**	**100g of salt dissolved in water**

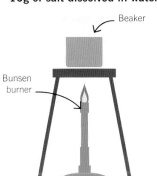

Beaker

Bunsen burner

Water temperature at 50°F (10°C)   Water temperature at 68°F (20°C)   Water temperature at 86°F (30°C)

Calculating Solubility

The solubility of a substance can be measured precisely, and you can calculate it if you know the mass of the solvent (such as water), and the mass of the maximum amount of solute (such as salt) that will dissolve in it.

How to calculate solubility
Weigh the solution. Then, evaporate the solvent from the solution and weigh the solute left behind. Subtract that from the mass of the solution to get the mass of the solvent.

Solution

Solute after solvent
has evaporated

$$\text{solubility (g per 100g of solvent)} = \frac{\text{mass of solid (g)}}{\text{mass of water removed (g)}} \times 100$$

Solubility curves
The solubility of a substance at different temperatures can be marked on a graph, known as a solubility curve. Different substances will have unique solubility curves.

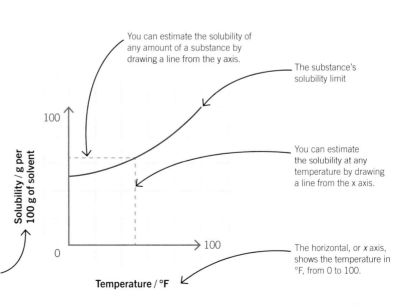

You can estimate the solubility of any amount of a substance by drawing a line from the y axis.

The substance's solubility limit

You can estimate the solubility at any temperature by drawing a line from the x axis.

The vertical, or *y* axis, shows the solubility in g/100g, from 0 to 100.

The horizontal, or *x* axis, shows the temperature in °F, from 0 to 100.

Solubility / g per 100 g of solvent

Temperature / °F

Chromatography

Chromatography is a process that separates compounds (see page 33, such as dyes) from a mixture (see page 32, such as ink). There are two parts, or phases. The stationary phase is the paper, as this does not move. The mobile phase is the liquid or gas that flows through the stationary phase, separating the mixture. The compounds are separated because they have different solubilities (see page 42).

Key Facts

✓ Chromatography is a way of separating compounds from mixtures.

✓ Chromatography involves a stationary phase and a mobile phase.

✓ Some chemicals move further through the stationary phase than others.

✓ The R_f value shows how far the chemicals move compared to the mobile phase.

Making a chromatogram

All you need to make a chromatogram is filter paper, a pencil, a selection of inks, some water, and a container to keep the water in. Follow these steps to create a chromatogram. A chromatogram is the physical result of chromatography.

2. The mobile phase (water) rises up the stationary phase (paper), carrying the ink with it. The more soluble a solute is, the higher it will rise.

1. Use a pencil to draw a line near the bottom of the paper. Add spots of ink to the line. Hang the paper above a dish of water, with the paper's edge in the water.

Clip suspended on rod holds the paper in place.

Ensure you use pencil, not pen, to draw the baseline—if you use pen, its ink will interfere with the experiment.

Place water below the baseline so the inks are not washed away.

The paper is the stationary phase.

The water is the mobile phase.

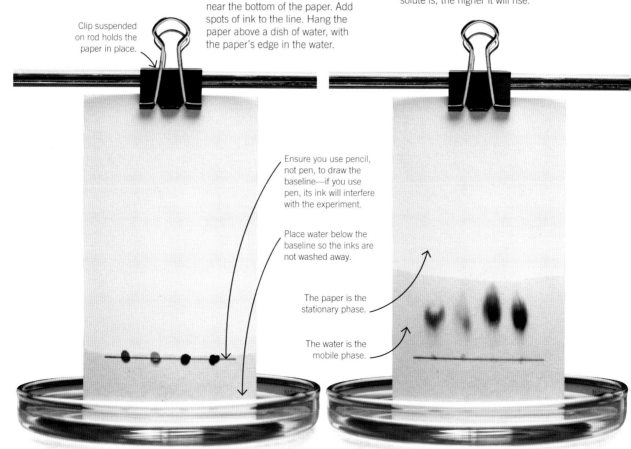

🗐 Calculating R_f Value

The R_f value is a measurement of how far a substance travels through the stationary phase (paper), compared to how far the mobile phase (water) travels. If the chromatogram is repeated using ink with the same dye, and the R_f value is the same, the substances are pure.

$$R_f = \frac{\text{Distance traveled by one dye (cm)}}{\text{Solvent front (cm)}}$$

Example for purple dye: $0.9 = \dfrac{4.5\,\text{cm}}{5\,\text{cm}}$

3. The inks collect in spots at different distances up the paper. The resulting pattern is called a chromatogram.

4. Use a ruler to measure the distance each dye has traveled from the baseline. The furthest distance the mobile phase has traveled is called the solvent front. Use a pencil to mark the solvent front on the paper.

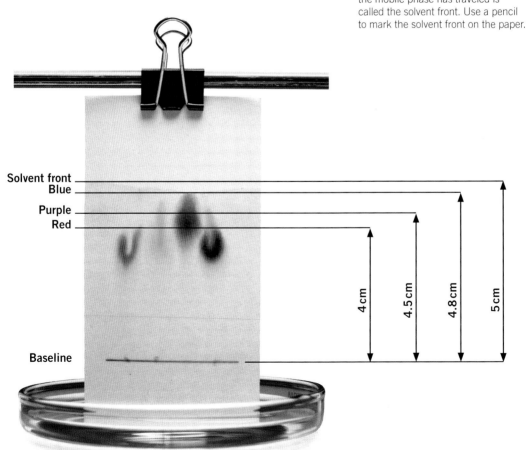

Solvent front
Blue
Purple
Red

4 cm   4.5 cm   4.8 cm   5 cm

Baseline

Filtration

Filtration is used to separate a liquid from an insoluble solid. An insoluble solid is one that doesn't dissolve (see page 40) in a particular liquid (solvent), such as water. The mixture is poured though filter paper, which has tiny holes in it. Water molecules are small enough to pass through the tiny holes, but the larger insoluble solid particles are caught by the paper.

Key Facts

✓ Filtration separates insoluble solvents from liquids.

✓ Filtration is one of several methods of separating mixtures.

✓ If a solid can't dissolve in a particular solvent, it is said to be insoluble in that solvent.

Filtering sand
Sand is an insoluble solid in water. Filtration can be used to separate sand from water.

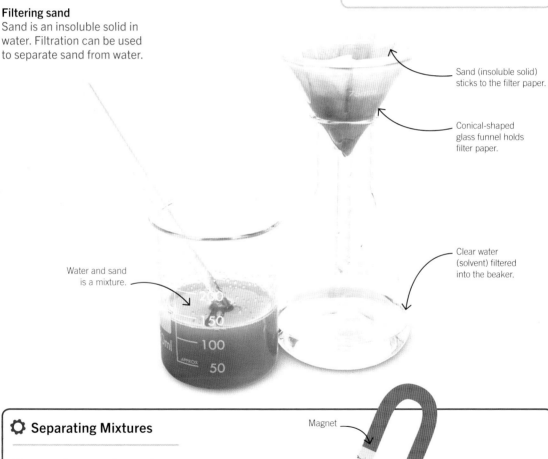

Sand (insoluble solid) sticks to the filter paper.

Conical-shaped glass funnel holds filter paper.

Clear water (solvent) filtered into the beaker.

Water and sand is a mixture.

⚙ Separating Mixtures

There are other ways of separating mixtures, depending on the properties of the substances they contain. For example, a magnet can be used to separate a mixture of magnetic iron filings and nonmagnetic sand.

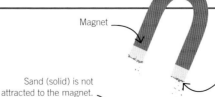

Magnet

Sand (solid) is not attracted to the magnet.

Iron filings (solid) are attracted to the magnet.

Evaporation

Evaporation happens when liquid molecules break their bonds to become a gas. Water slowly evaporates at room temperature—that's why wet clothes dry when hung up. Heating water makes the water evaporate faster.

Boiling water
If you heat a liquid to its boiling point, it boils—all the liquid evaporates quickly into a gas.

Steam
(water vapor)

Bubbles of gas rise to the surface.

Separating Mixtures

Evaporation can be used to separate a solvent from a solute dissolved in it (see page 40). They can be separated because the solvent has a higher boiling point than the solute.

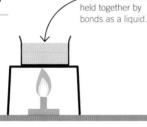

Water molecules are held together by bonds as a liquid.

1. A solution of copper sulfate in water is heated.

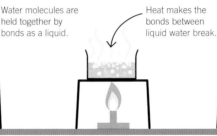

Heat makes the bonds between liquid water break.

2. The solution starts to boil, forming water vapor.

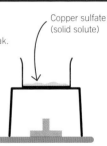

Copper sulfate (solid solute)

3. The water turns into a gas, leaving copper sulfate behind.

Crystallization

Crystals are solid structures with atoms (see page 26) that form a regular three-dimensional lattice pattern. Solutions (see page 40) that are gently heated and left to cool may form crystals—this process is called crystallization. The longer it takes to cool, the larger the crystals that form, in most cases.

Copper sulfate crystals
When a solution containing copper sulfate is slowly heated and then left to cool, navy-blue crystals form.

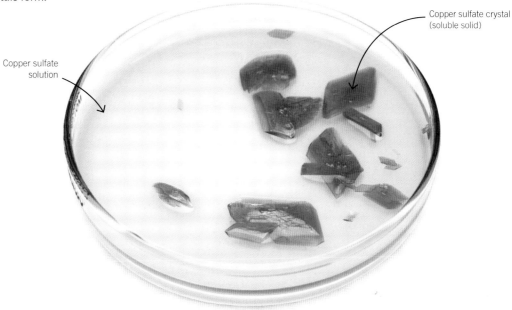

Copper sulfate solution

Copper sulfate crystal (soluble solid)

Key Facts

✓ Crystallization separates a solute from a solution.

✓ Crystallization involves slowly heating to dissolve the solute, and then cooling, a solution to cause the solute to crystallize.

✓ The crystal's size, and sometimes the shape, depend on how quickly the solid cooled.

⚙ How Crystals Form

When solutions with dissolved solids are heated, the liquid evaporates and the solute's molecular structure becomes more rigid. If the solution is heated quickly, large crystals form. If the solution is heated slowly, small crystals form.

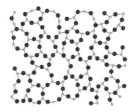

Before being heated, molecules in a mixture of copper sulfate and water are randomly and evenly distributed.

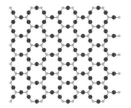

When water is heated and has evaporated, the copper sulfate molecules are concentrated enough to connect and build crystals.

Simple Distillation

Distillation is a process that uses heat, evaporation, and condensation to distill (collect) a liquid from a solution. The solution is heated, and the liquid with the lower boiling point will evaporate, leaving behind the solute with the higher boiling point. The evaporated gas is cooled and condensed back into a liquid, and then collected.

Key Facts

✓ Simple distillation separates one liquid from a solution.

✓ Simple distillation only works if the liquid has a lower boiling point than the solid dissolved within it.

✓ Simple distillation leaves you with a pure substance.

Separating water from ink
Mixtures such as water and ink can be separated by distillation. The mixture is heated to pure water's boiling point (212°F/100°C).

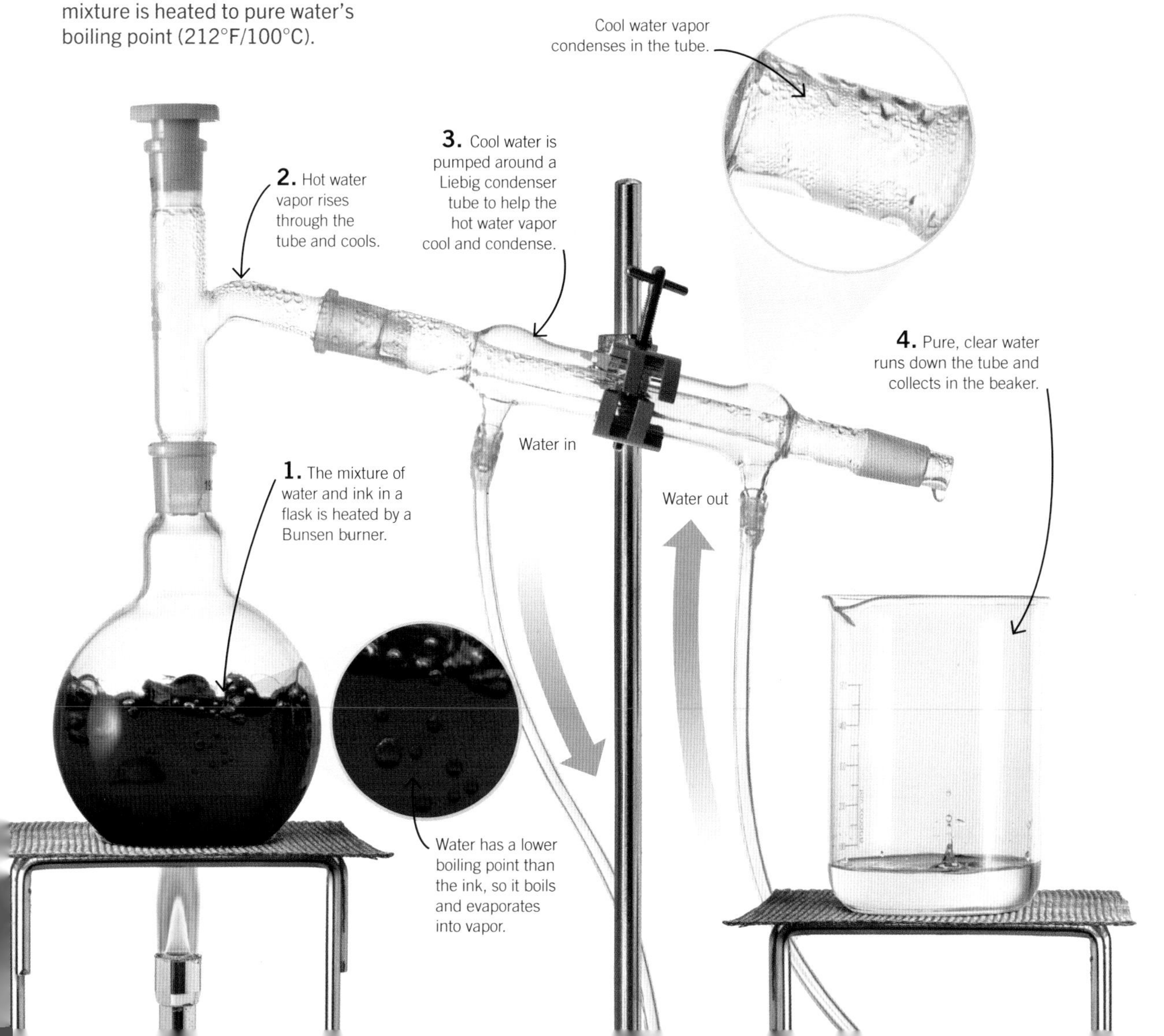

Cool water vapor condenses in the tube.

2. Hot water vapor rises through the tube and cools.

3. Cool water is pumped around a Liebig condenser tube to help the hot water vapor cool and condense.

4. Pure, clear water runs down the tube and collects in the beaker.

Water in

Water out

1. The mixture of water and ink in a flask is heated by a Bunsen burner.

Water has a lower boiling point than the ink, so it boils and evaporates into vapor.

Fractional Distillation
In the Laboratory

Fractional distillation separates mixtures made of many liquids. In the laboratory, the solution is heated more than once to different temperatures because each liquid has a different boiling point. An additional piece of equipment, a fractionating column, helps separate each liquid.

Key Facts

✓ Fractional distillation separates multiple liquids from a solution.

✓ Fractional distillation works because the liquids in the solution have different boiling points.

Distilling crude oil
Crude oil is usually separated in industry (see pages 204–05), however it can also be done in the laboratory. Steps 1–6 are repeated for each liquid that is distilled.

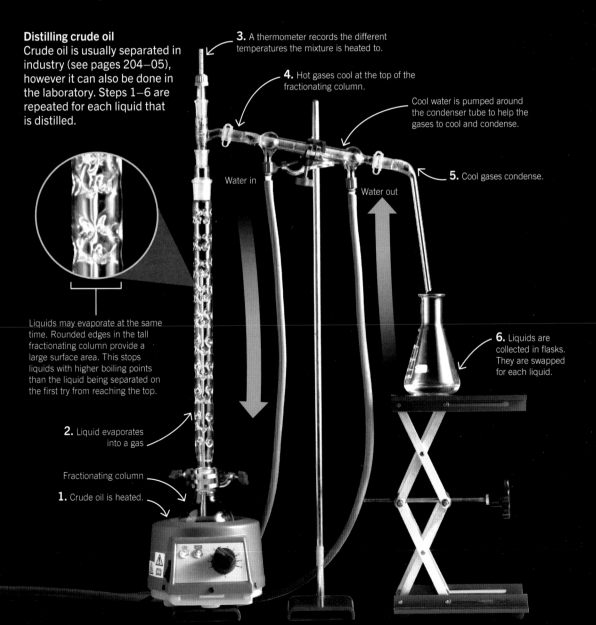

3. A thermometer records the different temperatures the mixture is heated to.

4. Hot gases cool at the top of the fractionating column.

Cool water is pumped around the condenser tube to help the gases to cool and condense.

Water in

Water out

5. Cool gases condense.

Liquids may evaporate at the same time. Rounded edges in the tall fractionating column provide a large surface area. This stops liquids with higher boiling points than the liquid being separated on the first try from reaching the top.

6. Liquids are collected in flasks. They are swapped for each liquid.

2. Liquid evaporates into a gas

Fractionating column

1. Crude oil is heated.

Elements

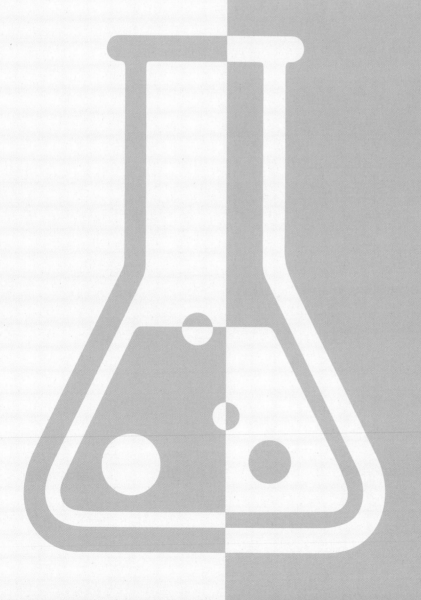

The Periodic Table

The periodic table lists all known 118 elements. Scientists organize elements in the periodic table according to their atomic number and by the similar properties they have as groups.

Key Facts

✓ The periodic table lists all known elements, in order of increasing atomic number.

✓ Horizontal rows are called periods.

✓ Vertical columns are called groups.

✓ Trends (or patterns) relating to a property can be seen as you go down or up a group.

Groups and Periods

Groups run from left to right.

Periods run from top to bottom.

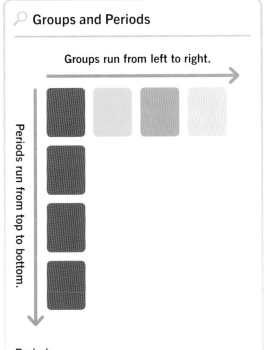

Periods
Elements in the same period (row) have the same number of electron shells (see page 28) in their atoms (see page 26). For example, elements in period one have one electron shell, while those in period six have six electron shells.

Groups
Members of a group (column) have the same number of electrons in their outermost shells. For example, Group 1 elements have one electron in their outer shell, while Group 7 elements have seven outer electrons.

Periodic table's colors
The colors used on this periodic table highlight elemental groups.

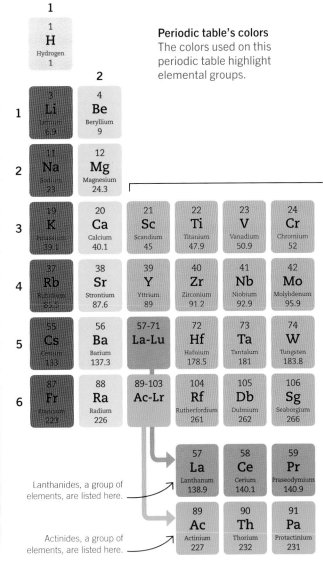

Lanthanides, a group of elements, are listed here.

Actinides, a group of elements, are listed here.

🔍 Reading the Table

Each element has a unique one or two letter symbol. These always start with a capital letter. These symbols are used in formulas (see page 34) and equations (see page 36), and are recognized in all languages. The atomic number is the number of protons in each of the element's atoms. The relative atomic mass is the average mass of an element's atoms, including all of its isotopes (see page 31).

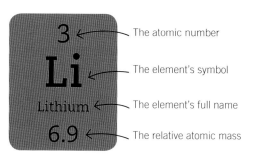

3 ← The atomic number

Li ← The element's symbol

Lithium ← The element's full name

6.9 ← The relative atomic mass

Transition metals do not have a group but they do have similar properties, and they can be found positioned between groups 2 and 3.

						0					
											2 **He** Helium 4
				3	**4**	**5**	**6**	**7**			
				5 **B** Boron 10.8	6 **C** Carbon 12	7 **N** Nitrogen 14	8 **O** Oxygen 16	9 **F** Fluorine 19	10 **Ne** Neon 20.2		
				13 **Al** Aluminum 267	14 **Si** Silicon 28.1	15 **P** Phosphorus 31	16 **S** Sulfur 32.1	17 **Cl** Chlorine 35.5	18 **Ar** Argon 40		

25 **Mn** Manganese 54.9	26 **Fe** Iron 55.9	27 **Co** Cobalt 58.9	28 **Ni** Nickel 58.7	29 **Cu** Copper 63.6	30 **Zn** Zinc 65.4	31 **Ga** Gallium 69.7	32 **Ge** Germanium 72.6	33 **As** Arsenic 74.9	34 **Se** Selenium 79	35 **Br** Bromine 79.9	36 **Kr** Krypton 83.8
43 **Tc** Technetium 96	44 **Ru** Ruthenium 101.1	45 **Rh** Rhodium 102.9	46 **Pd** Palladium 106.4	47 **Ag** Silver 107.9	48 **Cd** Cadmium 112.4	49 **In** Indium 114.8	50 **Sn** Tin 118.7	51 **Sb** Antimony 121.8	52 **Te** Tellurium 127.6	53 **I** Iodine 126.9	54 **Xe** Xenon 131.3
75 **Re** Rhenium 186.2	76 **Os** Osmium 190.2	77 **Ir** Iridium 192.2	78 **Pt** Platinum 195.1	79 **Au** Gold 197	80 **Hg** Mercury 200.6	81 **Tl** Thallium 204.4	82 **Pb** Lead 207.2	83 **Bi** Bismuth 209	84 **Po** Polonium 209	85 **At** Astatine 210	86 **Rn** Radon 222
107 **Bh** Bohrium 264	108 **Hs** Hassium 277	109 **Mt** Meitnerium 268	110 **Ds** Darmstadtium 281	111 **Rg** Roentgenium 272	112 **Cn** Copernicium 285	113 **Nh** Nihonium 284	114 **Fl** Flerovium 289	115 **Mc** Moscovium 288	116 **Lv** Livermorium 293	117 **Ts** Tennessine 294	118 **Og** Oganesson 294

60 **Nd** Neodymium 144.2	61 **Pm** Promethium 145	62 **Sm** Samarium 150.7	63 **Eu** Europium 152	64 **Gd** Gadolinium 157.3	65 **Tb** Terbium 158.9	66 **Dy** Dysprosium 162.5	67 **Ho** Holmium 164.9	68 **Er** Erbium 167.3	69 **Tm** Thulium 168.9	70 **Yb** Ytterbium 173	71 **Lu** Lutetium 175
92 **U** Uranium 238	93 **Np** Neptunium 237	94 **Pu** Plutonium 244	95 **Am** Americium 243	96 **Cm** Curium 247	97 **Bk** Berkelium 247	98 **Cf** Californium 251	99 **Es** Einsteinium 252	100 **Fm** Fermium 257	101 **Md** Mendelevium 258	102 **No** Nobelium 259	103 **Lr** Lawrencium 262

History of the Periodic Table

At the end of the 19th century, scientists studying the properties of elements found patterns when they listed them in order of increasing atomic mass. John Newlands ordered elements by atomic mass, and every eighth element has similar properties. However, in 1869, Russian chemist Dmitri Mendeleev improved his method.

Key Facts

✓ In the 1800s, scientists were looking for patterns within the properties of the known elements.

✓ Mendeleev created the first periodic table, similar to the one in use today, in 1869.

✓ Mendeleev left gaps in this table that predicted the existence of elements that were discovered later.

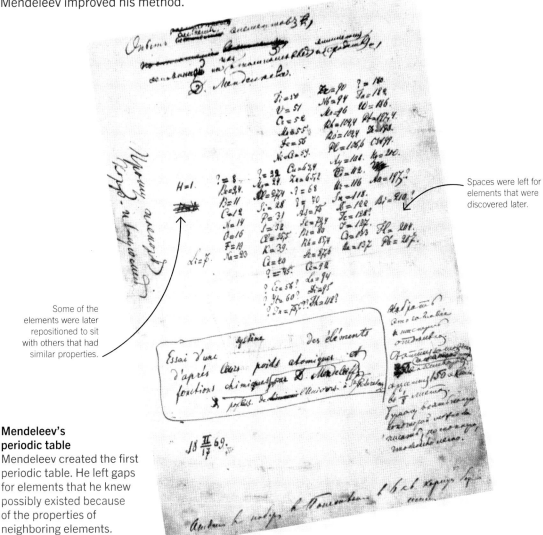

Spaces were left for elements that were discovered later.

Some of the elements were later repositioned to sit with others that had similar properties.

Mendeleev's periodic table
Mendeleev created the first periodic table. He left gaps for elements that he knew possibly existed because of the properties of neighboring elements.

Hydrogen

Hydrogen is the first element in the periodic table, and the most common element in the Universe. Hydrogen usually exists as a gas, and has the smallest and simplest atoms of any element.

Atomic structure

Hydrogen is usually diatomic (two atoms), each containing one proton and one electron. They share their electrons and bond together to form one hydrogen molecule.

Key Facts

✓ Hydrogen is a nonmetal.

✓ Hydrogen is a gas at room temperature.

✓ Hydrogen is the lightest element in the Universe.

✓ Hydrogen is highly reactive and its combustion forms water.

✓ Hydrogen is usually diatomic.

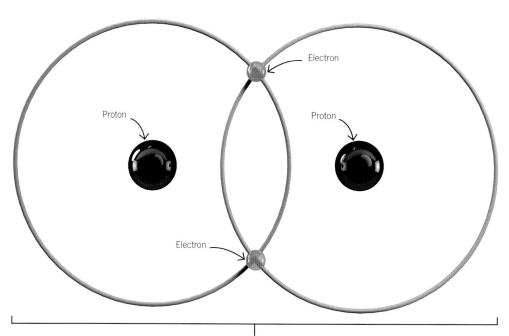

Electron

Proton

Proton

Electron

One hydrogen molecule

⚙ Lightest Element

As a gas, hydrogen is the lightest element because it has the smallest atoms, and so also has the smallest molecules. This is why hydrogen-filled balloons float upward in the air.

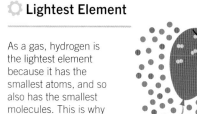

Hydrogen molecule

Air molecules

⚙ Water Molecules

When hydrogen burns, two hydrogen atoms (H) form covalent bonds with one oxygen atom (O) in the air. This reaction forms one molecule of water (H_2O).

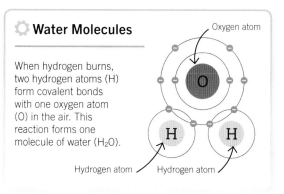

Oxygen atom

O

H   H

Hydrogen atom   Hydrogen atom

Metals

Over three-quarters of elements (see page 30) are classified as metals. They share many properties that are very useful. Iron, aluminum, copper, and zinc are the four most commonly used metals in alloys (see page 89). The properties of nonmetals are not as consistent as those of metals.

Most metals are shiny and able to withstand pressure.

Key Facts

✓ Most elements are metals.

✓ Most metals are solids at room temperature.

✓ Most metals are strong and shiny.

✓ Metals are malleable and ductile.

✓ Metals are good conductors of electricity.

✓ Metals are good conductors of heat.

✓ Most metals have high melting and boiling points.

✓ A few metals are magnetic.

Shiny and strong
Metals can resist forces without bending or breaking. They are often shiny when their surfaces have been polished.

Conduct electricity
Metals can conduct electricity because electrons are able to move freely between their atoms. Metals such as copper are used in electrical wiring.

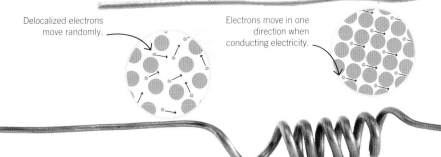

Delocalized electrons move randomly.

Electrons move in one direction when conducting electricity.

Conduct heat
Metals are good conductors of heat because their atoms are tightly packed together. Heat energy causes atoms inside metals to vibrate, causing them to bump into each other, spreading heat through the metal.

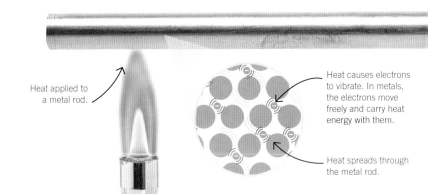

Heat applied to a metal rod.

Heat causes electrons to vibrate. In metals, the electrons move freely and carry heat energy with them.

Heat spreads through the metal rod.

Malleable

Metals are malleable—they can be hammered into different shapes. They are also ductile, and can be stretched out into a wire.

Ions are held together by the opposite charge of their delocalized electrons.

Ions can slide over one another while still being held by electrons.

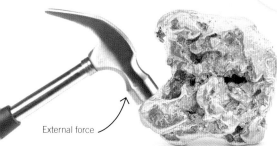

External force

Lump of gold

Flattened gold

Magnetic

Magnets are objects that produce a magnetic field, which attract the metals iron, cobalt, nickel, manganese, and gadolinium. Only these metals can be attracted by a magnet, or made into magnets. Most other metals are not magnetic.

Iron filings are attracted to magnets.

High melting points

Metals are made of positive ions and negative electrons. The attraction between the two is very strong. Only very high temperatures can break this attraction, and this is why many metals have high melting points.

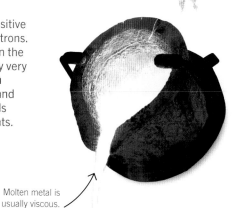

Molten metal is usually viscous.

🔍 Nonmetals

Nonmetals generally have a range of properties, many of which are almost the opposite of metals. Nonmetals can be dull instead of shiny, brittle, and easily broken instead of malleable or ductile, poor conductors of heat and electricity, and have low melting and boiling points. Not all nonmetals have these properties and there are a few exceptions. Groups and their properties are covered in more detail in the following pages.

Group 1
Physical Properties

Group 1 elements (except hydrogen, see page 57) are also called the alkali metals. These elements have such low melting points that they can be cut with a knife. They also have such a low density that they float on water.

(except hydrogen, see page 57)

Key Facts

✓ Group 1 metals are very reactive.

✓ Group 1 metals are shiny and soft.

✓ Group 1 metals are good conductors of heat and electricity.

✓ Group 1 metals have very low melting and boiling points.

✓ Group 1 metals are not dense.

Physical properties of Group 1
These metals are not found pure in nature. They must be refined in a laboratory into their pure forms, and held within glass cases so they don't react with air.

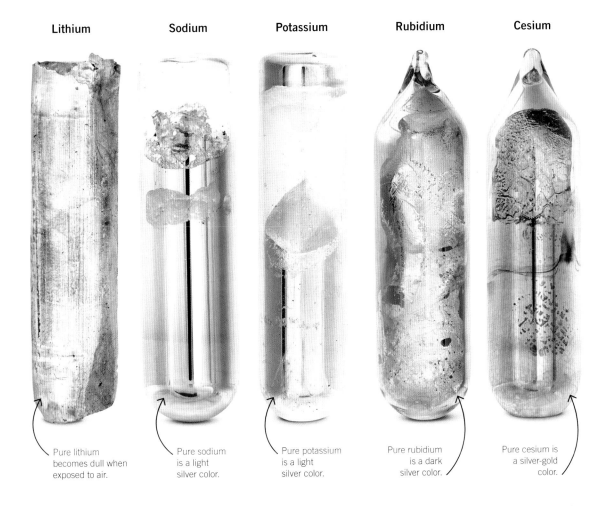

| Lithium | Sodium | Potassium | Rubidium | Cesium |

Pure lithium becomes dull when exposed to air.

Pure sodium is a light silver color.

Pure potassium is a light silver color.

Pure rubidium is a dark silver color.

Pure cesium is a silver-gold color.

Group 1
Chemical Properties

Group 1 metals are dangerous because they react easily and violently in water and acid. They also react with air to form compounds called metal oxides. They react with water to form alkaline compounds called metal hydroxides, giving this group the name alkali metals.

Bright reaction
Potassium reacts vigorously with water to create potassium hydroxide (a type of metal hydroxide).

Key Facts

✓ Group 1 elements are very reactive.

✓ Group 1 elements have one electron in their outer shell.

✓ Group 1 elements react with nonmetals to form ionic compounds.

Property Trends

Group 1 elements become more reactive as you go down the group. At the bottom of the group, electrons are far away from the nucleus. The electrostatic attraction (the attraction between the negative electrons and positive nucleus) is weak. The weaker this attraction is, the easier it is for electrons to be lost during a reaction—this is why metals at the bottom of Group 1 are more reactive.

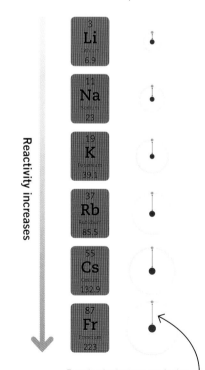

Reactivity increases

3
Li
Lithium
6.9

11
Na
Sodium
23

19
K
Potassium
39.1

37
Rb
Rubidium
85.5

55
Cs
Cesium
132.9

87
Fr
Francium
223

Francium's electrons are further away from its nucleus, so it is more reactive than lithium.

Potassium burns with a purple hue.

Hydrogen gas is released.

Group 2

Group 2 elements have metallic properties (see pages 56–57). They are also called the alkaline earth metals. They are reactive, but not as reactive as Group 1 elements.

Physical properties of Group 2
Pure samples of Group 2 elements are shiny and solids at room temperature.

Key Facts

✓ Group 2 elements are metals.

✓ Group 2 elements are reactive.

✓ Group 2 elements have two electrons in their outer shells.

✓ Group 2 elements typically react with nonmetals to form ionic compounds.

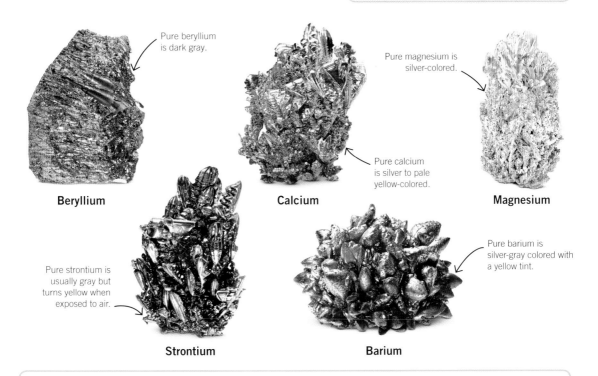

Pure beryllium is dark gray.

Pure magnesium is silver-colored.

Pure calcium is silver to pale yellow-colored.

Beryllium

Calcium

Magnesium

Pure strontium is usually gray but turns yellow when exposed to air.

Pure barium is silver-gray colored with a yellow tint.

Strontium

Barium

☼ Radium and Decay

Radium, the last element in Group 2 on the periodic table, has the largest atoms of its group. Their nuclei may undergo radioactive decay (break up) and give out an alpha particle (two protons and two neutrons). They may also lose an electron, giving out a beta particle.

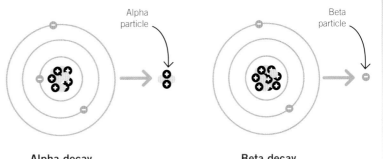

Alpha particle

Beta particle

Alpha decay

Beta decay

Group 3

Most of the elements in Group 3 are metals. They are less reactive than Group 1 and 2 elements. Most Group 3 metals react with oxygen and water, forming ionic metal oxides and hydroxides.

Physical properties of Group 3
Most of the elements in Group 3 are shiny metals, except boron, which is a dull nonmetal.

Pure boron is dark compared to other elements in its group.

Pure aluminum is silver-colored.

Gallium melts slightly above room temperature.

Boron   **Aluminum**   **Gallium**

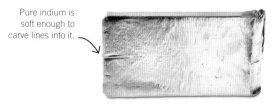

Pure indium is soft enough to carve lines into it.

Pure thallium is kept in glass vials to prevent it reacting with air.

Indium   **Thallium**

🔍 Artificial Element

Nihonium, at the bottom of Group 3, is an artificial element that can be formed when scientists collide zinc and bismuth atoms together. Nuclear fusion (see page 253) occurs, and the larger atom that forms is the element nihonium. Moscovium (see page 68) can also break down into nihonium.

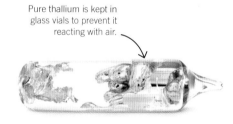

— 113
+ 113
● 183

Nihonium atom

Transition Metals

The transition metals are a large group of elements found in the center of the periodic table. They have the typical properties of metals, and their atoms can form many ions (see page 73). Many transition metals are used as catalysts (see page 184) to speed up production in the chemical industry.

(see page 73)
(see page 184)

Key Facts

✓ Transition metals can be found in the center of the periodic table.

✓ They have a range of uses and properties (most of them metallic).

✓ Most have more than one ion.

✓ Their ionic compounds are usually colorful.

✓ Some are good catalysts.

Colorful solutions
Transition metals form many colorful ionic compounds that dissolve in water. They are kept in tall flasks with markings that clearly indicate the volume of each solution.

Chromium (C^{3+}) is a pale green color.

Titanium solutions are usually colorless unless with certain anions.

🔍 Varying Colors

Transition metals can create different colored solutions, depending on how many electrons their atoms have lost during a reaction. For example, vanadium solutions may appear in three different colors. Light interacts with the varying amount of electrons in different ways, producing different colors in the solutions.

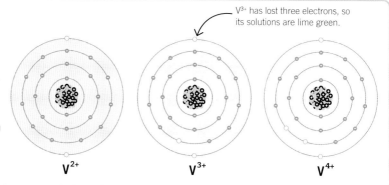

V^{3+} has lost three electrons, so its solutions are lime green.

V^{2+} V^{3+} V^{4+}

Tight stoppers are fitted onto the flask so air does not react with the solution.

This nickel ion is a pale turquoise color.

Copper ions in a water solution are usually a pale sky blue color.

Lanthanides

Lanthanides are a group of elements with the atomic numbers 57–71 in the periodic table. They have similar properties to transition metals. Lanthanides tarnish (lose their shine) easily in air, and they are sometimes stored in argon or under oil to prevent this.

Physical properties of lanthanides
Lanthanides are found mixed with other elements in Earth's crust, and must be extracted and purified into pure samples.

Key Facts

✓ Lanthanides are elements with the atomic numbers 57–71 on the periodic table.

✓ They are commonly found in Earth's crust, in compounds with other elements.

✓ Lanthanides are reactive and form ionic compounds with nonmetals.

✓ Lanthanides have large atoms.

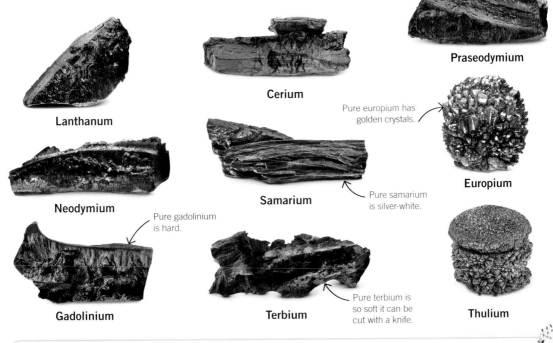

Praseodymium

Cerium

Lanthanum

Pure europium has golden crystals.

Neodymium

Samarium

Europium

Pure samarium is silver-white.

Pure gadolinium is hard.

Gadolinium

Terbium

Pure terbium is so soft it can be cut with a knife.

Thulium

⚙ Common Uses

Lanthanides are used to manufacture certain objects because they have useful properties. For example, lanthanum used in bulbs reduces the amount of yellow light emitted, and some TV screens have small amounts of cerium, which emits color.

Fluorescent bulb

TV

This metal is made of samarium-cobalt alloys.

Guitar

Actinides

Actinides are the group of elements with the atomic numbers 89–103 in the periodic table. They have similar properties to lanthanides, but they are more reactive. Actinide atoms are very large and are radioactive (see page 60). Most of the elements in this group are artificial.

(see page 60)

Key Facts

✓ Many actinides are artificial.
✓ Actinides are more reactive than lanthanides and react easily with air.
✓ Actinides have large atoms.
✓ Actinide atoms are radioactive.

Physical properties of actinides
Pure samples of actinides are very rare because they are radioactive. Actinides are usually found in trace amounts inside certain minerals.

**Autunite
(mineral containing
traces of actinium)**

**Monazite
(mineral containing
thorium)**

**Torbernite
(mineral containing
traces of protactinium)**

Californium, an artificial actinide, are contained in pellets in the laboratory.

Pure uranium is shiny and gray.

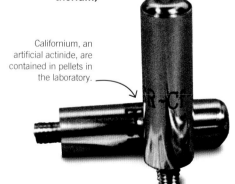

Californium

Uranium

Carbon

Carbon is a nonmetal element that is important because it can combine with many other elements to form millions of natural and artificial compounds, including carbon dioxide gas, plastics, and fuels.

Carbon atom
One carbon atom normally contains six protons, six neutrons, and six electrons.

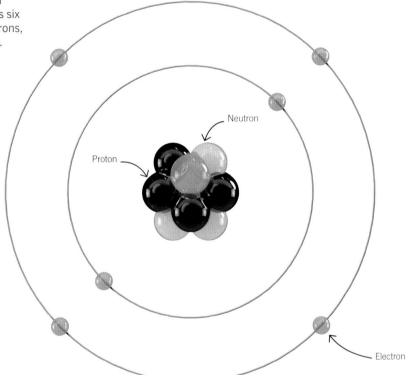

Neutron

Proton

Electron

🔍 Carbon-Based Life

Carbon is one of four main elements (including hydrogen, oxygen, and nitrogen) that make up all living things. Carbon atoms form complex molecules essential for life, such as DNA, proteins, carbohydrates (see pages 224–26), and fats.

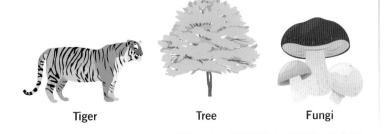

Tiger   **Tree**   **Fungi**

Group 4

Group 4 elements have quite different properties from each other. Carbon (see page 66) is a solid nonmetal, silicon and germanium are semimetals, and the remaining three are metals.

(see page 66)

Key Facts

✓ Group 4 elements includes metals and nonmetals.

✓ Group 4 elements have four electrons in their outermost shell.

✓ Group 4 elements react with hydrogen to form hydrides.

Physical properties of Group 4
Group 4 elements in their pure forms are all solids at room temperature and shiny.

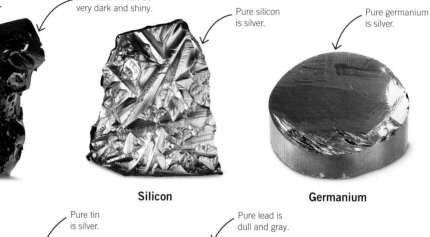

Pure carbon can be very dark and shiny.

Pure silicon is silver.

Pure germanium is silver.

Carbon

Silicon

Germanium

Pure tin is silver.

Tin

Pure lead is dull and gray.

Lead

⚙ Conductors of electricity

Pure silicon and germanium are semiconductors. If a small amount of another element, such as gallium (their atoms have 3 outer electrons), is added to either silicon or germanium, their spare electrons allow electricity to be conducted. Silicon wafer chips used in computers are made of these alloys.

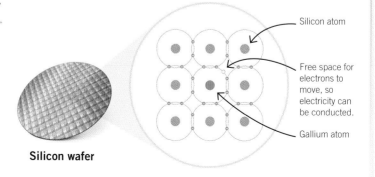

Silicon wafer

Silicon atom

Free space for electrons to move, so electricity can be conducted.

Gallium atom

Group 5

Group 5 elements vary in their appearance and properties. They are also called the nitrogen group, after the first element in the group. They range from nitrogen, a relatively unreactive colorless gas, to bismuth, a shiny, solid metal.

Physical properties of Group 5
Aside from nitrogen, all of the elements in Group 5 are solids at room temperature.

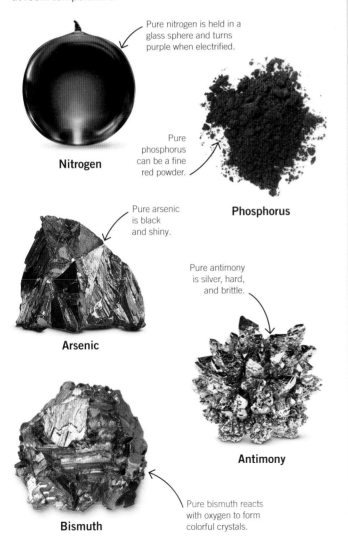

Pure nitrogen is held in a glass sphere and turns purple when electrified.

Nitrogen

Pure phosphorus can be a fine red powder.

Phosphorus

Pure arsenic is black and shiny.

Arsenic

Pure antimony is silver, hard, and brittle.

Antimony

Pure bismuth reacts with oxygen to form colorful crystals.

Bismuth

Property Trends

As we go down Group 5, the size of each element's atoms increases. The elements also become more metallic closer to the bottom of the group. Melting points, boiling points, and densities generally increase down the group.

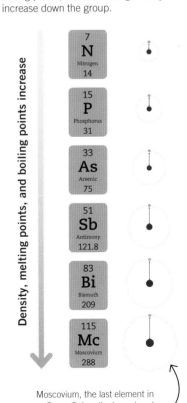

Density, melting points, and boiling points increase

| 7 |
| N |
| Nitrogen |
| 14 |

| 15 |
| P |
| Phosphorus |
| 31 |

| 33 |
| As |
| Arsenic |
| 75 |

| 51 |
| Sb |
| Antimony |
| 121.8 |

| 83 |
| Bi |
| Bismuth |
| 209 |

| 115 |
| Mc |
| Moscovium |
| 288 |

Moscovium, the last element in Group 5, has the largest and most dense atoms.

Group 6

Group 6 elements include the nonmetals oxygen and sulfur, the semimetals (properties of both metals and nonmetals) selenium, tellurium, and the metal polonium, and the artificial element livermorium. This group is also called the oxygen group. Both nonmetals react with metals to form ionic compounds.

Key Facts

✓ Group 6 contains semimetals and nonmetals.

✓ Group 6 elements are highly reactive.

✓ Group 6 elements contain six electrons in their outermost shells.

Physical properties of Group 6
Most of the elements in Group 6 are solids at room temperature, except oxygen, which is a gas. Polonium and livermorium exist as tiny trace amounts and are not pictured here.

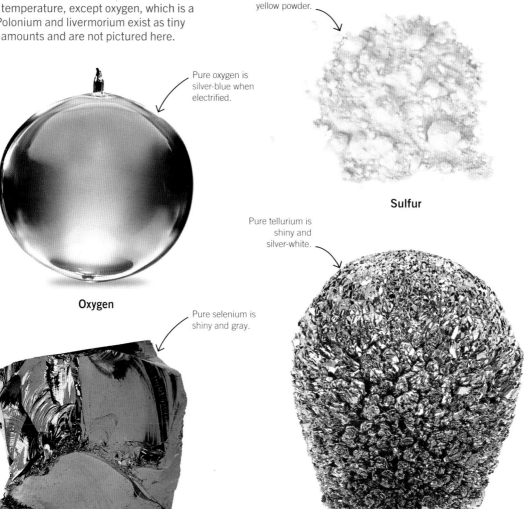

Pure sulfur is a fine yellow powder.

Sulfur

Pure oxygen is silver-blue when electrified.

Oxygen

Pure tellurium is shiny and silver-white.

Pure selenium is shiny and gray.

Selenium

Tellurium

Group 7

Group 7 elements are highly reactive nonmetals. They are also called the halogens (meaning "salt-forming," because they react with metals to make salts, see pages 141–42). These elements have many properties, and some are used in common household products, such as in disinfectants and bleaches.

see pages 141–42

Key Facts

✓ Group 7 elements are nonmetals.

✓ Group 7 elements react with metals to form ionic compounds.

✓ Group 7 elements are diatomic (consist of two atoms).

✓ Group 7 elements have seven electrons in their outermost shell.

Physical properties of Group 7
Most Group 7 elements are found as gases. As you go down the group, they also get darker.

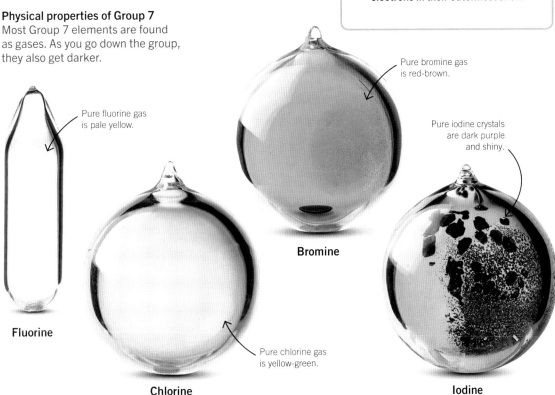

Pure fluorine gas is pale yellow.

Pure bromine gas is red-brown.

Pure iodine crystals are dark purple and shiny.

Pure chlorine gas is yellow-green.

Fluorine

Bromine

Chlorine

Iodine

🔍 Property trends

Group 7 elements have seven electrons in their outer shell. Their outer shell can take one more electron when it reacts with the atoms of other elements. Group 7 elements become less reactive as you go down the group. This is because their electrostatic attraction (see page 59) becomes weaker.

see page 59

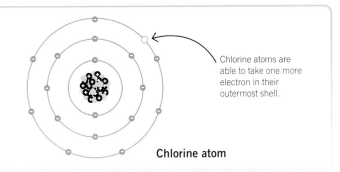

Chlorine atoms are able to take one more electron in their outermost shell.

Chlorine atom

Group 0

Group 0 elements are colorless, odorless gases with very low boiling points. They are also called the noble gases or Group 8. The atoms of Group 0 elements have full outer shells, so they can't lose or gain electrons and are therefore unreactive. They are usually found as single atoms.

Physical properties of Group 0
Group 0 elements are gases at room temperature. They are only visible when electrified within clear glass spheres.

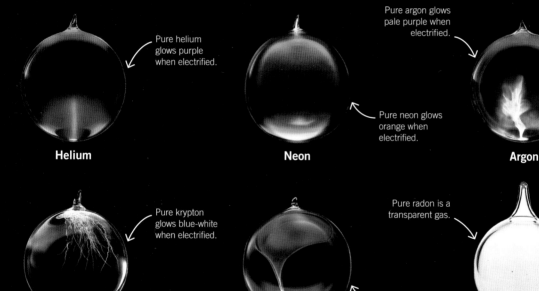

Pure helium glows purple when electrified.

Helium

Pure neon glows orange when electrified.

Neon

Pure argon glows pale purple when electrified.

Argon

Pure krypton glows blue-white when electrified.

Krypton

Pure xenon glows blue when electrified.

Xenon

Pure radon is a transparent gas.

Radon

🔍 Unreactive elements

Most Group 0 elements are very unreactive because their atoms cannot take on any extra electrons. For example, the outer shells in argon atoms have eight electrons, and so are full.

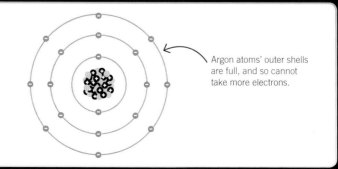

Argon atoms' outer shells are full, and so cannot take more electrons.

Structure and Bonding

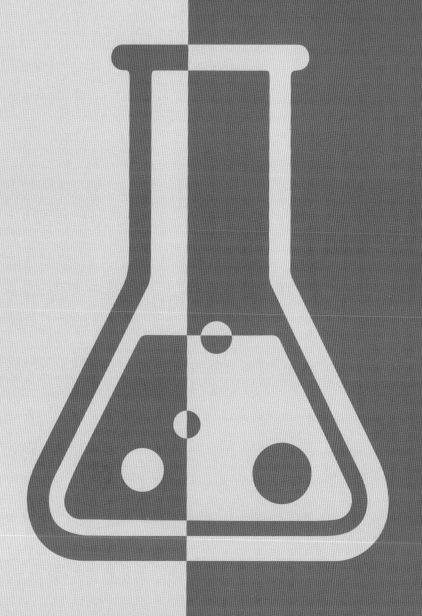

Ions

Ions are atoms, or groups of atoms, that have gained or lost at least one electron. Electrons have a negative charge, so if an atom gains electrons it becomes negatively charged (an anion). If an atom loses electrons, it becomes positively charged (a cation). The charge corresponds to the number of electrons gained or lost.

Loss
Some atoms lose electrons to achieve a full outer shell.

A lithium atom loses its single outer electron to form a positive lithium ion.

One electron lost

Ions are drawn inside a square bracket with the charge of the ion written on the top right.

Lithium atom

Lithium ion

Having lost its single outer electron, the lithium ion's new outer shell is full.

Gain
Some atoms gain electrons to achieve a full outer shell.

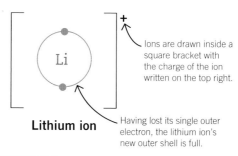

A fluorine atom needs to gain an electron in its outer shell to form a negative fluoride ion.

The electron gained completes the outermost shell.

One electron gained

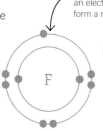

Fluorine atom

Fluoride ion

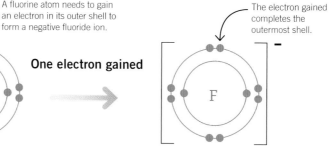

⚙ **Transfer of Electrons**

Metal atoms can only lose electrons to form positive ions (cations). Nonmetal atoms can either gain or lose electrons, but negatively charged ions (anions) are more common.

Element	Type	Atom	Ion	Number of electrons gained or lost
Potassium	Metal	K	K^+ (potassium)	One lost
Calcium	Metal	Ca	Ca^{2+} (calcium)	Two lost
Hydrogen	Nonmetal	H	H^- (hydride)	One gained
Oxygen	Nonmetal	O	O^{2-} (oxide)	Two gained

Ionic Bonding

When metals and nonmetals react with each other they form ionic bonds—electrostatic attractions between positive and negative charges. Metal atoms always lose negatively charged electrons to form positively charged ions, while nonmetal atoms gain those same electrons to form negative ions. The resulting ions always have a stable, full outer shell of electrons.

Key Facts

✓ Ionic bonds form between metals and nonmetals.

✓ During chemical reactions, atoms gain or lose electrons to achieve a full outer shell, which is more stable.

✓ Metals always lose electrons to form positive ions.

✓ When ionic bonds form, nonmetals gain electrons to form negative ions.

Forming an ionic bond

Only atoms of the noble gases in Group 0 (see page 71) of the periodic table have full outer shells of electrons. Other atoms achieve this by gaining or losing electrons to form ions.

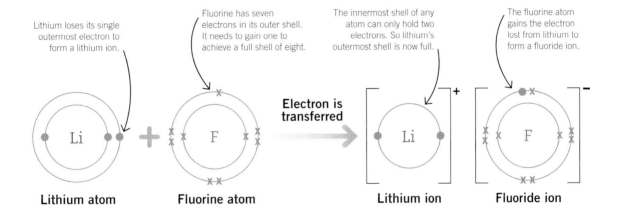

Lithium loses its single outermost electron to form a lithium ion.

Fluorine has seven electrons in its outer shell. It needs to gain one to achieve a full shell of eight.

The innermost shell of any atom can only hold two electrons. So lithium's outermost shell is now full.

The fluorine atom gains the electron lost from lithium to form a fluoride ion.

Electron is transferred

Lithium atom   Fluorine atom   Lithium ion   Fluoride ion

⚙ Why Ions Are Formed

Atoms lose or gain electrons to achieve a full outer shell. As a result, the electronic configuration of the ion is always the same as the configuration of the nearest noble gas.

Element	Type	Atom	Electronic configuration of atom	Ion formed	Electronic configuration of ion
Sodium	Metal	Na	2, 8, 1	Na^+	2, 8
Magnesium	Metal	Mg	2, 8, 2	Mg^{2+}	2, 8
Oxygen	Nonmetal	O	2, 6	O^{2-}	2, 8
Chlorine	Nonmetal	Cl	2, 8, 7	Cl^-	2, 8, 8

Ions and the Periodic Table

Atoms have an equal number of protons and electrons, which means they have no overall charge. An ion is an atom (or group of atoms) that has gained or lost at least one electron. Metals tend to lose electrons, forming positively charged ions (cations). Nonmetals tend to gain electrons, forming negatively charged ions (anions).

Key Facts

✓ Metals in Groups 1, 2, and 3 lose electrons to form positive ions (cations).

✓ Nonmetals in Groups 5, 6, and 7 gain electrons to form negative ions (anions).

✓ Hydrogen is unusual because it can form both positive and negative ions.

✓ Elements in the same group form ions with the same charges.

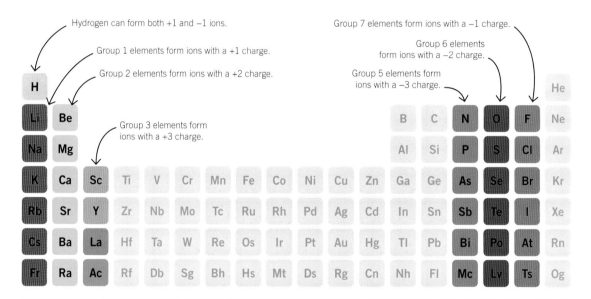

Hydrogen can form both +1 and −1 ions.

Group 1 elements form ions with a +1 charge.

Group 2 elements form ions with a +2 charge.

Group 3 elements form ions with a +3 charge.

Group 7 elements form ions with a −1 charge.

Group 6 elements form ions with a −2 charge.

Group 5 elements form ions with a −3 charge.

⚙ Predicting Charge

The periodic table allows us to predict the charge of an ion by looking at its group number. Elements in the same group (ignoring the transition elements) have the same number of electrons in their outermost shell, which means they form ions with the same charges.

Element	Group	Type	Atom	Ion	Ions formed
Sodium	1	Metal	Na	Na^+	Loses one electron to form a sodium ion
Magnesium	2	Metal	Mg	Mg^{2+}	Loses two electrons to form a magnesium ion
Oxygen	6	Non-metal	O	O^{2-}	Gains two electrons to form an oxide ion
Chlorine	7	Non-metal	Cl	Cl^-	Gains one electron to form a chloride ion

Dot and Cross Diagrams

Chemical reactions are all about moving electrons. Dot and cross diagrams help us to visualize where electrons start from and where they end up. Dot and cross diagrams without circles around the atoms are often called Lewis structures, after the US scientist who first suggested the idea.

Sodium fluoride

When sodium reacts with fluorine, an electron is transferred from the sodium atom to the fluorine atom, forming a positive sodium ion (Na⁺) and a negative fluoride ion (F⁻). This makes the compound sodium fluoride (NaF).

The sodium electrons are drawn as dots.

The fluorine electrons are drawn as crosses.

This electron in the fluoride ion originally came from the sodium atom.

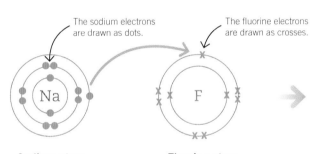

Sodium atom · Fluorine atom

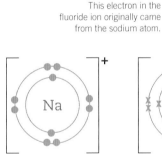

Sodium fluoride

Magnesium oxide

Magnesium forms 2+ ions, and oxygen forms 2− ions. This time, we only need one magnesium ion and one oxide ion to form neutral magnesium oxide (MgO).

Magnesium loses its two outer electrons and becomes an Mg²⁺ ion.

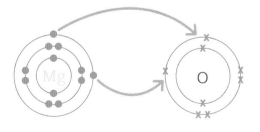

Magnesium atom · Oxygen atom

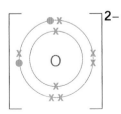

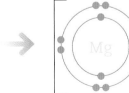

Magnesium oxide

Sodium oxide

Sodium forms 1+ ions while oxygen forms 2− ions. In order to balance these charges and form a neutral ionic substance, sodium oxide (Na_2O), two sodium atoms must combine with one oxygen atom.

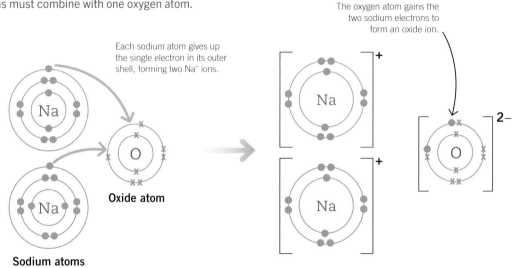

Each sodium atom gives up the single electron in its outer shell, forming two Na^+ ions.

The oxygen atom gains the two sodium electrons to form an oxide ion.

Oxide atom

Sodium atoms

Sodium oxide

Magnesium fluoride

Magnesium fluoride (MgF_2) is made up of Mg^{2+} ions and F^- ions. Two F^- ions are needed to balance the 2+ charge on a single magnesium ion.

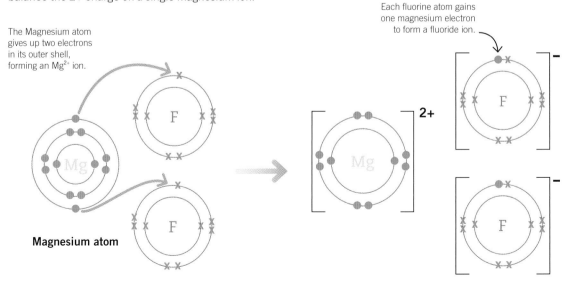

The Magnesium atom gives up two electrons in its outer shell, forming an Mg^{2+} ion.

Each fluorine atom gains one magnesium electron to form a fluoride ion.

Magnesium atom

Fluorine atoms

Magnesium fluoride

Ionic Structures

When metals and nonmetals react with each other, they form ionic compounds. Unlike simple compounds such as water and carbon dioxide, these aren't made up of individual molecules, but instead are repeating, three-dimensional structures of positive and negative ions. This type of arrangement is called a giant ionic lattice.

Key Facts

✓ Ionic compounds are made up of alternating positive and negative ions.

✓ The ions are held together by strong electrostatic attractions between positive and negative charges.

✓ This arrangement is called a giant ionic lattice.

Sodium chloride

While the "spacefill" diagram below shows just a few ions, a single crystal of sodium chloride actually contains around six hundred quadrillion sodium and chloride ions.

The repeating pattern of sodium and chloride ions forms a giant ionic lattice structure.

Each positively charged sodium ion is surrounded by negatively charged chloride ions.

Each negatively charged chloride ion is surrounded by positively charged sodium ions.

Sodium ions are smaller than chloride ions.

Table salt, also known as sodium chloride (NaCl), is made up of sodium ions (Na$^+$) and chloride ions (Cl$^-$) in a repeating pattern.

🔍 Ball-and-Stick Models

"Ball-and-stick" models are also used to represent ionic structures, and can make it easier to visualize how the ions are arranged. However, the relative sizes of the ions may not be as clear, and in reality the space between the ions does not exist.

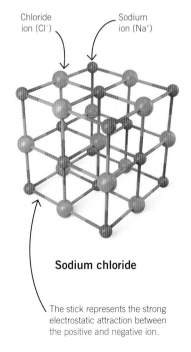

Chloride ion (Cl$^-$)

Sodium ion (Na$^+$)

Sodium chloride

The stick represents the strong electrostatic attraction between the positive and negative ion.

Ionic Properties

Ionic compounds have particular properties due to their ionic lattice structure (see page 78). They are crystalline when solid and generally have high melting and boiling points, although there are some exceptions. Ionic compounds can conduct electricity when molten or dissolved in water, but they do not conduct electricity when solid.

Key Facts

✓ There are strong electrostatic attractions between the ions in ionic compounds.

✓ Ionic solids tend to have high melting points because it takes a lot of energy to overcome the attractions between ions.

✓ Solid ionic compounds do not conduct electricity.

✓ When molten or dissolved in water, ionic compounds do conduct electricity.

Crystals

Sodium ions and chloride ions are arranged in a regular, repeating pattern in sodium chloride crystals.

Sodium ions (Na^+)

Chloride ions (Cl^-)

There are strong electrostatic attractions between the positive and negative ions.

Sodium chloride is a solid at room temperature.

⚙ Melting and Dissolving

In ionic solids, the ions cannot move. When ionic compounds melt or dissolve, the ions break down and are able to move and carry an electrical charge. Some ionic compounds dissolve easily in water, but not all of them.

The ions are not able to move so they cannot conduct electricity.

The ions are able to move so they can conduct electricity.

Solid

Liquid

Covalent Bonding

A covalent bond forms when two atoms share a pair of electrons between them. By sharing in this way, each atom acquires a full outer shell of electrons, making it more stable. Covalent bonds vary in strength, but generally require a lot of energy to break, and so are considered strong.

Nonmetal atoms

Covalent bonds can form between nonmetal atoms, which may be the same, such as in the element chlorine (Cl_2), or different, such as in the compounds water (H_2O) or carbon dioxide (CO_2).

Key Facts

✓ Covalent bonds form when two atoms share a pair of electrons.

✓ Atoms share electrons in order to acquire a full outer shell.

✓ Only electrons in the outermost shell are shared.

✓ Covalent bonds form between nonmetal atoms.

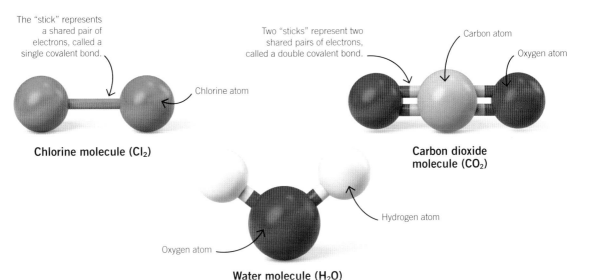

The "stick" represents a shared pair of electrons, called a single covalent bond.

Chlorine atom

Chlorine molecule (Cl_2)

Two "sticks" represent two shared pairs of electrons, called a double covalent bond.

Carbon atom

Oxygen atom

Carbon dioxide molecule (CO_2)

Hydrogen atom

Oxygen atom

Water molecule (H_2O)

🔍 How Covalent Bonding Works

The most stable electronic configuration (see page 29) for an atom is to have a full outer shell of electrons. By sharing electrons, each atom effectively gains one or more electrons to "fill" its outer shell and achieve the same stable electronic configuration as its nearest noble gas (see page 71).

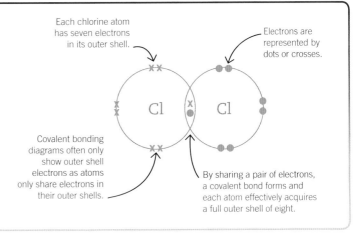

Each chlorine atom has seven electrons in its outer shell.

Electrons are represented by dots or crosses.

Covalent bonding diagrams often only show outer shell electrons as atoms only share electrons in their outer shells.

By sharing a pair of electrons, a covalent bond forms and each atom effectively acquires a full outer shell of eight.

Representing Covalent Bonds

In molecules, covalent bonds form between atoms when they share electrons with each other. A single bond is formed when two atoms share one pair of electrons, a double bond is two shared pairs, and so on. There are different ways to represent these covalent bonds.

3D structures
Sometimes called "ball-and-stick" models, these show atoms and the angles of bonds in a molecule. They are helpful for visualizing shapes, but can be confusing when we consider larger molecules.

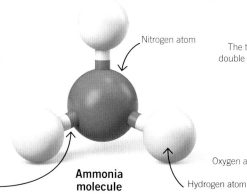

Nitrogen atom

The two "sticks" represent a double covalent bond between the oxygen atoms.

The "stick" represents a single covalent bond between a nitrogen atom and a hydrogen atom.

Ammonia molecule

Oxygen atom

Hydrogen atom

Oxygen molecule

Dot and cross diagrams
These show how the electrons are arranged and which atom the electrons came from. Unlike other types of diagram, they also show electrons that are not involved in bonding, which can be useful for figuring out why molecules have certain shapes.

A Lewis structure is a dot and cross diagram without circles around the atoms.

The oxygen atoms share two pairs of electrons, forming a double covalent bond.

H x • N x H
x x

Ammonia molecule

The nitrogen electrons are represented by crosses and the hydrogen electrons by dots.

Oxygen molecule

Structural formulas
These show how all the atoms are connected in two dimensions, and whether bonds are double, single, or triple. They make it easy to see how atoms are connected at a glance.

Chemical symbols are used to identify atoms.

A single covalent bond (one pair of shared electrons) is shown as a single straight line between two atoms.

Two lines represent a double bond between the oxygen atoms.

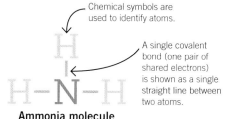

H—N—H

Ammonia molecule

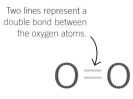

O=O

Oxygen molecule

Simple Molecules

A molecule is made up of two or more atoms joined by one or more covalent bonds. Simple molecules, such as oxygen and water, are all around us. The atoms in a molecule may be of the same element or different elements. But molecules of the same substance always contain the same number and type of atoms.

Key Facts

✓ A molecule is two or more atoms bonded together.

✓ Molecular bonds are covalent.

✓ Molecules of the same substance always contain the same number and type of atoms. For example, water molecules always contain two hydrogen atoms and one oxygen atom.

Hydrogen
Hydrogen atoms each have one electron in their outer shell and need a total of two electrons to achieve a full outer shell.

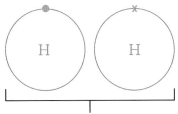

The atoms are joined by a single covalent bond and each has a share in two electrons.

Two hydrogen atoms

One hydrogen molecule

Carbon dioxide
Carbon dioxide is a simple molecule with the formula CO_2. Carbon and oxygen are bigger atoms than hydrogen— they need eight electrons to achieve a full outer shell.

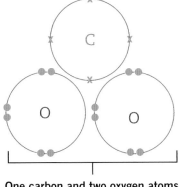

The atoms are joined by double covalent bonds and each has a share in eight electrons overall.

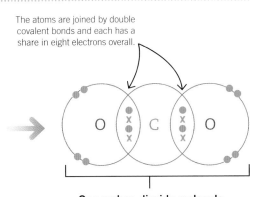

One carbon and two oxygen atoms

One carbon dioxide molecule

Water
Water (H_2O) contains hydrogen and oxygen. Each hydrogen atom only needs two electrons to have a full outer shell, while an oxygen atom needs eight in total.

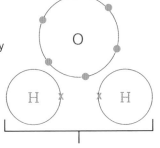

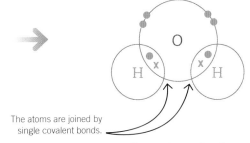

The atoms are joined by single covalent bonds.

One oxygen and two hydrogen atoms

One water molecule

Properties of Simple Molecules

The atoms in molecules such as water (H_2O) and chlorine (Cl_2) are held together by covalent bonds. Between individual molecules, there are weak forces of attraction called intermolecular forces. It takes relatively little energy to disrupt these forces, so simple molecules tend to have low melting and boiling points.

Chlorine
Chlorine (Cl_2) is a simple molecular substance with weak intermolecular forces between individual Cl_2 molecules. It's a gas at room temperature and pressure with a boiling point of −29.2°F (−34°C).

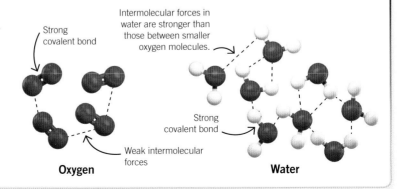

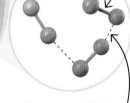

Chlorine atoms in molecules are held together by a shared pair of electrons (or a covalent bond).

Chlorine is a yellow–green gas at room temperature and pressure.

There are weak forces of attraction, known as intermolecular forces, between individual chlorine molecules.

Intermolecular Forces

When simple molecular substances melt or boil, only the intermolecular forces between molecules are broken, not the covalent bonds. Larger molecules have stronger intermolecular forces, and higher melting and boiling points, but the types of atoms make a difference as well.

Strong covalent bond

Intermolecular forces in water are stronger than those between smaller oxygen molecules.

Strong covalent bond

Weak intermolecular forces

Oxygen

Water

Polymers

Polymers are very big molecules—sometimes called macromolecules—that form when lots of monomers (smaller molecules) join together in long chains. Polymers have useful properties, and in particular they can be very strong. They occur naturally and can also be made artificially. For more on polymers, see pages 213, 214, 222, 260 and 261.

Key Facts

✓ Polymers are formed from many smaller molecules called monomers.

✓ Monomers join together to produce long polymer chains of repeating units.

✓ The monomers can be different or can be all the same type of molecule.

✓ Most polymers are held together with covalent bonds.

The outer layer of this hair shaft has overlapping scales of keratin.

Human hair

There are many different polymers in our bodies. This is a strand of human hair that has been magnified under a microscope. Hair is made of keratin—a natural polymer that's also found in our nails.

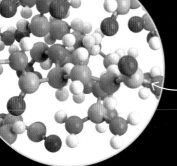

The atoms in the keratin polymer are joined by covalent bonds.

⚙ How Polymers Form

Both natural and artificial polymers, such as plastics, are made from lots of smaller molecules called monomers. Some polymers are made from one type of monomer, but proteins (see page 225) such as keratin form from different types of monomers (amino acids).

Monomer

Smaller molecules (monomers) join end to end to form long polymer chains.

Polymerization

Polymer

Covalent Network Solids

Covalent network solids are made up of many atoms arranged in a repeating pattern, called a lattice. All the atoms are connected by covalent bonds to form very strong substances. For more on the properties of covalent network solids, see page 86.

Key Facts

✓ Covalent network solids are made up of many atoms joined by covalent bonds and arranged in a repeating, 3D pattern called a lattice.

✓ They have high melting points and tend to be hard.

✓ Most covalent network solids have no charged particles that are free to move, so do not conduct electricity.

Silicon dioxide
The silicon and oxygen atoms in silicon dioxide, also known as silica, are joined by covalent bonds and arranged in a giant repeating lattice.

Covalent bonds link all of the atoms together.

Each silicon atom bonds covalently to four oxygen atoms.

Oxygen–silicon bonds are very strong and cannot be easily broken.

Silicon atom

Oxygen atom

Silicon dioxide (SiO$_2$)

🔍 Silicon Dioxide

It takes a lot of energy to break the bonds in covalent network solids, so silicon dioxide has a very high melting point. Silicon dioxide does not easily conduct electricity as it does not have any delocalized electrons that are free to move around.

The mineral form of silicon dioxide is called quartz. Quartz is the main mineral component in sand.

Allotropes of Carbon

Key Facts

Allotropes are forms of an element that are in the same physical state but with different arrangements of atoms. Diamond, graphite, and graphene are three allotropes of carbon. They are all solids at room temperature and are covalent network solids (see page 85), but have different properties because of the differences in their structures.

- ✓ Allotropes are forms of an element in the same physical state but with different arrangements of atoms.
- ✓ Diamond, graphite, and graphene are three allotropes of carbon.
- ✓ Diamond, graphite, and graphene have different properties because of differences in their structures.

Diamond
Each carbon atom in diamond is covalently bonded to four others. Diamond is very hard and it does not conduct electricity, although it is a good conductor of heat.

Diamond is the hardest naturally occurring substance.

It takes a lot of energy to break all the covalent bonds in diamond, so it has a very high melting point.

Graphite
Each carbon atom in graphite is covalently bonded to three others, leaving one free electron. These free electrons become delocalized, giving graphite particular properties, including high electrical conductivity.

The carbon atoms in graphite form layers of hexagons.

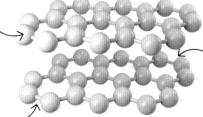

Layers can slide over each other as the attraction between them is weak.

The covalent bonds cannot be broken easily, so graphite has a high melting point.

Graphene
Graphene is essentially a single layer of graphite. It is extremely strong, very lightweight, and can be used to enhance the strength of other materials. It is better at conducting electricity than many other materials.

Graphene is almost transparent and very light.

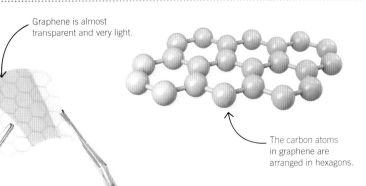

The carbon atoms in graphene are arranged in hexagons.

Fullerenes

Fullerenes are another allotrope of carbon (see page 86). They are large molecules of pure carbon, shaped like balls or tubes. The first fullerene to be discovered, buckminsterfullerene (C_{60}), was discovered in 1985 and was named after the American architect R. Buckminster Fuller, who was famous for building dome structures.

Buckminsterfullerene

Buckminsterfullerene is the most common naturally occurring fullerene and small amounts of it are found in soot. Its molecules are also known as "buckyballs" because of their spherical shape.

Each carbon atom is bonded to three others.

The carbon atoms are connected by covalent bonds.

Buckminsterfullerene is a hollow sphere.

60 carbon atoms are arranged in 12 pentagons and 20 hexagons, like a ball.

🔍 Nanotubes

Nanotube structures have a diameter of just a few billionths of a meter, but are thought to be the strongest and stiffest materials yet discovered. They are used in electronics, solar cells, and in composite materials, such as sport equipment, because of their lightness and strength.

Carbon nanotubes are like a sheet of graphene (see page 86) rolled into a tube.

Nanotubes are just a few billionths of a meter across, but they can be many centimeters long.

Metallic Bonding

In a piece of metal, the outer shell electrons of all the ions are delocalized around positive metal ions in a fixed lattice. The free electrons allow metals to conduct electricity. The electrostatic attractions between all the electrons and the metal ions result in most metals having high melting points.

How metallic bonding works

In metals, the electrons are free to move around the positive metal ions. This means metals have "mobile charge carriers"—the electrons—so they all conduct electricity, although some are better conductors than others.

Key Facts

✓ Metals have giant structures, with particles arranged in a lattice pattern.

✓ The outer shell electrons are delocalized (free to move around).

✓ This results in positive metal ions surrounded by a "sea" of negatively charged electrons.

✓ As the electrons are free to move, metals are good electrical conductors.

The delocalized electrons are free to move around the lattice structure, which allows metals to conduct electricity.

The ions are arranged in layers to form a giant lattice structure.

The particles of gold are held together by forces of electrostatic attraction between the metal ions and the delocalized electrons. This is called metallic bonding.

Positive metal ions

🔍 Gold

Gold has a high melting point because a lot of energy is needed to overcome all the electrostatic attractions between the ions and the negatively charged electrons within its structure.

Gold is a solid at room temperature—its structure consists of closely packed metal ions.

Pure Metals and Alloys

An alloy is a combination of two or more metals, or a combination of metals with nonmetallic elements. Alloys have different properties from the elements used to make them and, in particular, are sometimes harder than any of the pure metals used to make them. Some everyday alloys include steel, bronze, brass, and amalgam (used in dentistry)—for more examples, see page 262.

for more examples, see page 262.

Iron alloy
Iron (Fe) is a silvery-gray metal that reacts readily with oxygen and water to form rust (see page 264). Steel is an alloy of iron with a very small amount of carbon, and is harder and stronger than pure iron.

The alloy steel is much harder than pure iron and is often used in construction.

Pure metals are often softer than alloys.

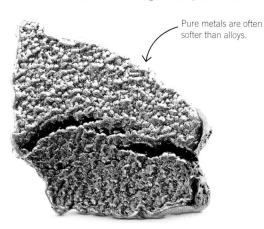

Iron

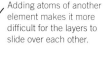

Steel

⚙ Alloy Hardness

Alloys are made by combining two or more pure elements. Atoms of different elements have different sizes, making it more difficult for the layers to move over each other, and as a result alloys are harder than pure metals.

The atoms can be forced to slide over each other, by actions such as hammering.

Adding atoms of another element makes it more difficult for the layers to slide over each other.

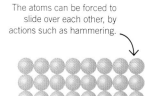

Pure metal

Alloy

States of Matter

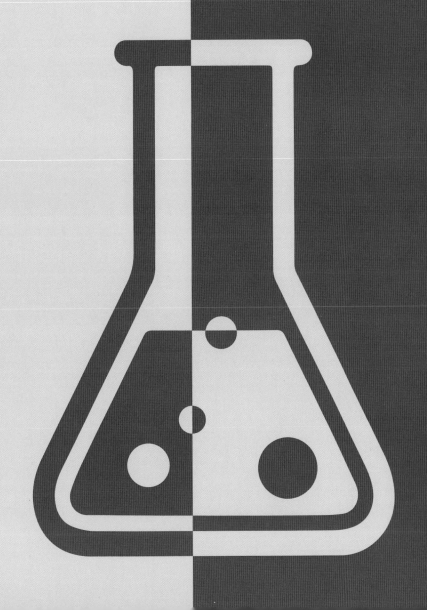

Solids

Solids are one of the three key states of matter. Unlike liquids and gases, solids keep their shape and do not flow to the sides of a container. The particles in a solid can't easily move past one another, but at any temperature above −459.4°F (−273°C)—absolute zero—they do constantly vibrate in place.

Key Facts

✓ The particles in solids are held in fixed positions by forces of attraction.

✓ The particles vibrate in their fixed positions.

✓ Because particles cannot move from their positions, solids have a fixed shape and do not flow.

Ice cube
Ice is the solid form of water (H$_2$O). The water molecules are in fixed positions and cannot move over each other, unless the ice melts and becomes liquid water.

Ice is rigid and does not flow until the temperature increases and it begins to melt.

The particles are arranged in a repeating pattern.

The particles in a solid are packed closely together and do not have space to move around.

⚙ Properties of Solids

Having particles in fixed positions gives solids a set of properties that distinguish them from liquids and gases. They have a fixed shape, tend to be dense, and do not flow to fill a container they're placed in. They also cannot be compressed.

Volume and shape
Solids have fixed shapes with defined edges. Their volume changes only slightly with temperature.

Density and compressibility
Since the particles are close together, most solids have a high density, and can't easily be compressed.

Flow
Forces of attraction stop particles in a solid moving over each other; solids do not flow.

Liquids

When a substance is in its liquid form, its particles have gained enough energy to move past each other. As a result, liquids flow to the edges of their container and form a nearly flat surface. However, although the shape of a liquid changes to fit the shape of its container, the total volume remains the same.

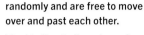

Key Facts

✓ Particles in a liquid are arranged randomly and are free to move over and past each other.

✓ Liquids flow to the edges of a container and form a flat surface.

✓ The volume of liquids changes only slightly with temperature.

✓ The particles are very close together, so liquids are not easily compressed.

Water
The word "water" is usually used to describe the liquid state of the compound H_2O.

Water is a colorless liquid at room temperature.

The particles are packed tightly but are randomly arranged and can move over each other.

⚙ Properties of Liquids

When a substance is in the liquid state, it means its particles have gained enough energy (usually in the form of heat) to overcome some of the forces of attraction holding them together in a solid. The particles can now move over each other, giving liquids particular properties.

Volume and shape
Liquids flow to the edges of a container, but while their shape may change, the total volume stays the same.

Density and compressibility
Liquids have a high density, so can't be easily compressed as their particles are close together.

Flow
The particles in a liquid are free to move over each other, so liquids flow and can pass through narrow spaces.

Gases

Substances exist as gases when their particles gain enough energy to overcome the forces of attraction keeping them together. Gases are less dense than solids and liquids, and so are easy to compress. Gases have no fixed shape, and their volume is very sensitive to temperature and pressure.

Key Facts

✓ Particles in a gas are very far apart.

✓ Gases have a low density—there are few particles in a large volume.

✓ The particles are constantly moving—they move in straight lines until they collide with another particle.

✓ Gases do not have a fixed shape.

Iodine forms a purple gas when it's heated.

Gases spread quickly in all directions.

The particles in a gas are typically far apart.

Iodine

Iodine sublimes (changes straight from a solid to a gas) when heated. This is because the attractions between particles are quite weak, and it doesn't take much energy to overcome them.

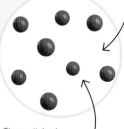

The particles have space to move randomly.

⚙ Properties of Gases

When a substance is in its gaseous state, it means its particles have gained enough energy to overcome the forces of attraction between them. The particles move freely, giving gases particular properties.

Volume and shape
Gases have no fixed volume and take the shape of the container they are in.

Density and compressibility
Gases have a low density and can be easily compressed as their particles are far apart.

Flow
Gas particles are completely free to move and can pass through very small gaps.

Diffusion in Liquids

The particles in a liquid, such as water, are constantly moving. If another substance is added, its particles bump into the water particles, causing the new particles to move around and mix with the water. This process is called diffusion and it happens spontaneously, without any need for stirring.

Key Facts

✓ Particles in liquids move randomly.

✓ Diffusion is the process where the particles of one substance mix with another.

✓ The random movement of particles allows the two substances to eventually mix evenly without shaking or stirring.

✓ Particles in liquids keep moving, even after they have completely mixed.

Dissolving purple dye in water

When brightly colored dye is added to water, the particles diffuse and the mixture gradually becomes an even purple.

At first, the colored dye is concentrated in one place.

The color spreads through the liquid by diffusion.

Eventually, the water and the dye are thoroughly mixed together.

⚙ How Diffusion in Liquids Works

When the particles of a substance are placed in water, they gradually move from areas of high concentration to low concentration to become evenly spread.

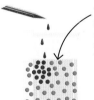

The water and dye molecules move around each other as they start to mix.

Before diffusion

The particles of dye diffuse among particles of water, and eventually both substances are evenly mixed.

After diffusion

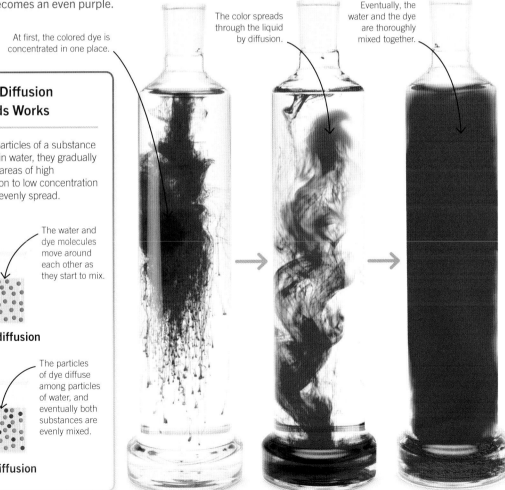

Diffusion in Gases

In gases, particles move very quickly in all directions. When two gases are allowed to mix, the particles of both substances spread out in all directions, moving from an area of high concentration to one of low concentration. This diffusion of gases happens spontaneously, as does diffusion in liquids (see page 94) and solids.

Bromine

Bromine (Br_2) forms an orange–brown gas under atmospheric pressure. Here, we see bromine gas diffusing into a container of air.

Key Facts

✓ Gas particles move very fast, bumping into each other.

✓ When two different gases meet, their particles spread out, mixing with each other.

✓ As they spread out, they end up moving from areas of high concentration to areas of low concentration.

⚙ How Diffusion in Gases Works

Gas particles move randomly. When mixed, they gradually move from areas of high concentration to areas of low concentration to become evenly spread.

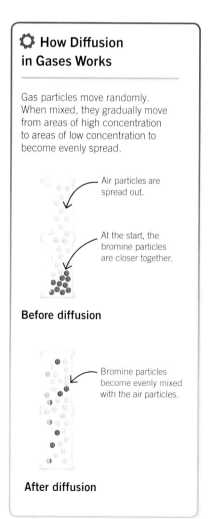

Air particles are spread out.

At the start, the bromine particles are closer together.

Before diffusion

Bromine particles become evenly mixed with the air particles.

After diffusion

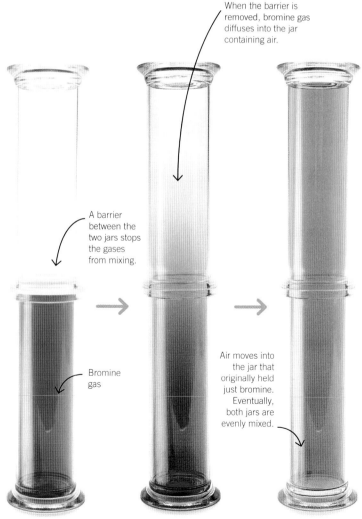

When the barrier is removed, bromine gas diffuses into the jar containing air.

A barrier between the two jars stops the gases from mixing.

Bromine gas

Air moves into the jar that originally held just bromine. Eventually, both jars are evenly mixed.

Changes of State

Changes of state—between solid, liquid, and gas—are physical changes, meaning no chemical changes are taking place. These changes are related to temperature (and pressure) and are reversible. A pure substance, containing only one element or compound, is a solid below its melting point, a liquid at temperatures between its melting and boiling point, and a gas above its boiling point.

States of matter

Water exists in three states—ice (solid), water (liquid), and steam (gas). Ice melts to form liquid water, and water boils to form steam. Under certain conditions, it can also sublime (go straight from solid to gas).

Liquids form when gases condense.

Liquid

Gas is formed when a liquid reaches its boiling point.

Melting

Freezing

Boiling

Condensing

Solids form when liquids freeze.

Blue arrows represent cooling.

Sublimation

Deposition

Red arrows represent warming.

Solid

Gas

⚙ How Particles are Arranged

A simple model can be used to represent how the particles in solids, liquids, and gases are arranged. These diagrams have limitations—for example, drawn to scale, gas particles would be much further apart than shown here.

In a liquid, particles are still touching, but now they've acquired enough energy to move over each other.

In a gas, there are very large gaps between particles, so the particles are completely free to move.

In a solid, the particles are tightly packed and cannot move past each other, but they do vibrate in position.

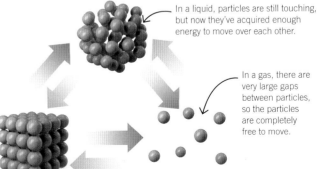

Heating and Cooling Curves

Heating and cooling curves give information about energy changes that happen when a substance changes state. A substance is heated or cooled and time and temperature are recorded to obtain information for the graph. The curves show us that temperature does not change significantly during changes of state, indicating that energy is absorbed (or released) by the substance.

Key Facts

✓ Heating and cooling curves show what happens to the temperature of a substance when it is heated or cooled over a period of time.

✓ A substance absorbs heat energy from its surroundings when it melts or boils, and energy is transferred to the surroundings when it freezes or condenses.

✓ The temperature of a substance remains the same during changes of state.

Heating curve

A heating curve experiment is carried out by gradually warming a substance and measuring the temperature change over time. These graphs have a characteristic "stepped" shape.

The temperature increases over time as the substance is warmed.

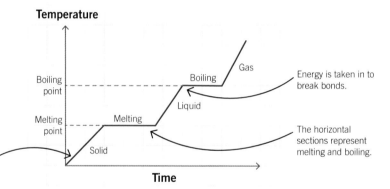

Energy is taken in to break bonds.

The horizontal sections represent melting and boiling.

Cooling curve

A cooling curve experiment is carried out by cooling a substance and measuring the temperature change over time. Its shape is similar to a heating curve, but reversed.

The horizontal sections represent condensing and freezing.

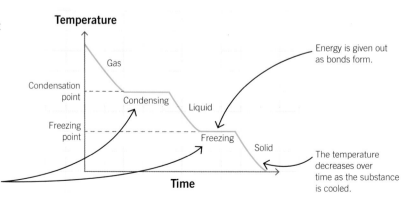

Energy is given out as bonds form.

The temperature decreases over time as the substance is cooled.

State Symbols and Predicting States

State symbols are added to equations to provide extra information about what's happening. There are four—(s), (l), (g), and (aq), representing solid, liquid, gas, and aqueous (dissolved in water) respectively. We can figure out the state of a substance at a given temperature if we know its melting and boiling points.

Key Facts

✓ State symbols show the physical state of each substance in a chemical reaction.

✓ (s), (l), (g), and (aq) represent solid, liquid, gas, and aqueous (dissolved in water) respectively.

✓ The state of a substance at a given temperature can be predicted if its melting and boiling points are known.

States and equations

Here, sodium and water react to form hydrogen gas and an aqueous solution of sodium hydroxide. The physical state of each substance is shown in the balanced chemical equation below.

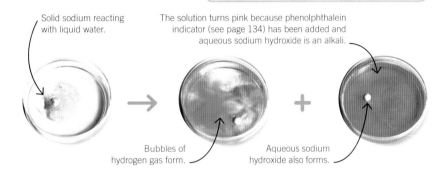

Solid sodium reacting with liquid water.

The solution turns pink because phenolphthalein indicator (see page 134) has been added and aqueous sodium hydroxide is an alkali.

Bubbles of hydrogen gas form.

Aqueous sodium hydroxide also forms.

sodium	+	water	$\longrightarrow$	hydrogen	+	sodium hydroxide
$2Na_{(s)}$	+	$2H_2O_{(l)}$	$\longrightarrow$	$H_{2(g)}$	+	$2NaOH_{(aq)}$

⚙ Predicting States

Below melting point, substances are solids. Between melting and boiling points, substances are liquids. Above melting point, substances are gases.

Element	Melting point	Boiling point
Oxygen	−362.2°F (−219°C)	−297.4°F (−183°C)
Gallium	86°F (30°C)	4,044°F (2,229°C)
Bromine	19.4°F (−7°C)	138.02°F (58.9°C)

Question

Which of the substances in the table would be a liquid at room temperature? Assume room temperature is 68°F (20°C).

Figuring it out

1. Oxygen boils at −297.4°C (−183°C), so is a gas at all temperatures above that.
2. Gallium does not melt (become liquid) until 86°F (30°C), so will be solid at 68°F (20°C).
3. Bromine melts at 19.4°F (−7°C) and does not boil until 138.02°F (58.9°C).

Answer

Bromine is the only substance that would be a liquid at room temperature.

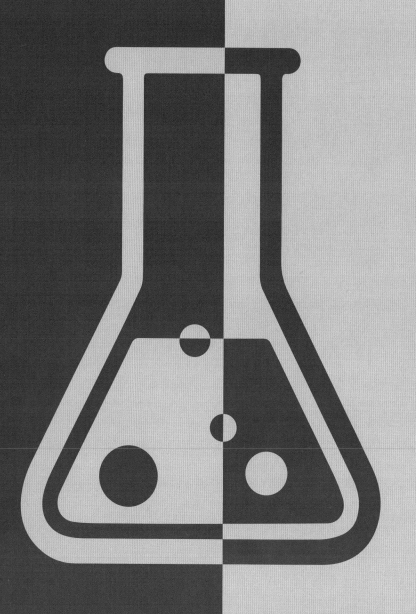

Nanoscience and Smart Materials

Nanoparticles

Nanoparticles are tiny particles made up of a few hundred atoms. A nanometer (nm) is one billionth of a meter (1×10^{-9} m) in length, and nanoparticles are between 1 nm and 100 nm in diameter. Nanoparticles cannot be seen with the naked eye, or even an optical microscope—an electron microscope is needed to observe them.

Key Facts

✓ The size of a nanoparticle is between 1 nm and 100 nm.

✓ One nanometer is equal to one billionth of a meter.

✓ Nanoparticles can be only seen under electron microscopes.

Tiny particles
Nanoparticles are found in nature, but can also be made in the laboratory. These images show computer-generated illustrations of nanoparticle spheres.

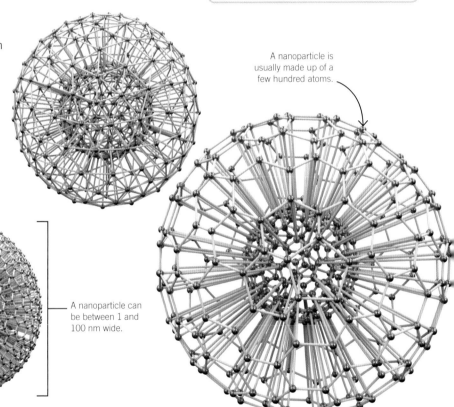

A nanoparticle is usually made up of a few hundred atoms.

A nanoparticle can be between 1 and 100 nm wide.

🔍 How Big Are Nanoparticles?

Nanoparticles are between 1 and 100 nm in diameter. The table shows the size of nanoparticles compared to other objects. More than 1,000 nanoparticles would fit across the width of a single human hair, and about 1 million nanoparticles would fit across the head of a pin.

Particle	Diameter
Atom	0.1 nm
Small molecule	0.5 nm
Nanoparticle	1–100 nm
Red blood cell	7,000 nm
Human hair	100,000 nm

Properties of Nanoparticles

Nanoparticles have very different properties compared to the same substance "in bulk" (powders, lumps, and sheets). In a bulk material, only a small proportion of its atoms are on the surface. A nanoparticle is much smaller, so many more of its atoms are on the surface. As a result, materials containing nanoparticles can be much more reactive.

Key Facts

✓ A nanoparticulate material may have very different properties compared to the same material in bulk.

✓ Nanoparticles have a very high surface area to volume ratio, making them more likely to get involved in chemical reactions.

Surface area to volume ratio
Nanoparticles have an extremely large surface area for their volume. This is because as a particle reduces in size, its surface area increases in comparison to its volume. Figure this out by comparing the surface area to volume ratios of two cube-shaped nanoparticles of different sizes.

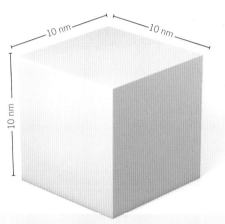

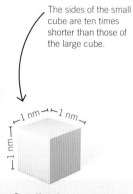

The sides of the small cube are ten times shorter than those of the large cube.

Figuring it out	Large cube	Small cube
Calculate the surface area	The surface area of each side is 10 nm × 10 nm = 100 nm^2 The cube has 6 sides, so the surface area of the cube is 100 nm^2 × 6 = 600 nm^2	The surface area of each side is 1 nm × 1 nm = 1 nm^2 The cube has 6 sides, so the surface area of the cube is 1 nm^2 × 6 = 6 nm^2
Calculate the volume	10 nm × 10 nm × 10 nm = 1000 nm^3	1 nm × 1 nm × 1 nm = 1 nm^3
Calculate the surface area to volume ratio.	$\text{Ratio} = \dfrac{\text{surface area}}{\text{volume}}$ $= \dfrac{600 \text{ nm}^2}{1000 \text{ nm}^3} = 0.6 : 1$	$\text{Ratio} = \dfrac{\text{surface area}}{\text{volume}}$ $= \dfrac{6 \text{ nm}^2}{1 \text{ nm}^3} = 6 : 1$

The surface area to volume ratio of the small cube is ten times bigger than that of the large cube.

Uses and Risks of Nanoparticles

Because nanoparticles have an extremely large surface area to volume ratio, materials made up of nanoparticles are needed in smaller quantities to make an effective catalyst (see page 184). Useful materials that may be too expensive to use in bulk can be used in nanoparticles. However, not all the effects of nanoparticles are known, and scientists are concerned about their safety.

(see page 184)

Key Facts

✓ Nanoparticles have many useful properties because of their tiny size and large surface area to volume ratio.

✓ Nanoparticles can be breathed in, or even absorbed through skin.

✓ Some nanoparticles could be harmful to our health and the environment.

Nanomedicine
Nanoparticles are so tiny that they can be absorbed by the body and cross cell membranes. This means they can be used to deliver drugs to specific cells—nanovaccines have been developed to fight some cancers.

The vaccine-loaded immune cells are injected back into the blood stream to search out and destroy cancerous cells.

Porous silicon discs loaded with nanovaccine are mixed with cells of the immune system.

🔍 How Nanoparticles Are Used

Nanoparticles have some very important practical uses, including in medicine and electronics. However, as they appear more in everyday products, scientists have become concerned about the impact they could have on the environment and our bodies.

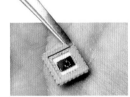

Tiny electronics
Graphene is just one atom thick, super-strong, and a brilliant conductor of electricity. Nanoparticles can be used to make microchips for tiny electronic devices.

Sunscreen
Sunscreens containing nanoparticles of titanium oxide and zinc oxide are more effective at protecting against harmful UV rays than traditional sunscreens.

Synthetic skin
Nanoparticles of gold have enabled scientists to create touch-sensitive synthetic skin, capable of picking up heat, cold, and moisture.

Thermochromic and Photochromic Pigments

Smart materials react to their surroundings and have properties that allow them to return to their original form. Thermochromic pigments change color with temperature, while photochromic pigments change color when exposed to light.

Key Facts

✓ A pigment is a substance that gives something else a particular color.

✓ Thermochromic pigments change color with temperature.

✓ Photochromic pigments change color when exposed to light.

Changing colors
Thermochromic film changes color at different temperatures. It starts out black at room temperature, changes color when heated above about 80.6°F (27°C), and reverts to black as it cools.

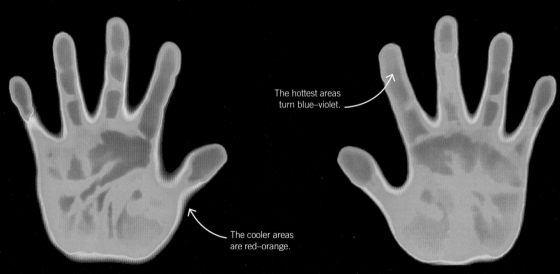

The hottest areas turn blue–violet.

The cooler areas are red–orange.

⚙ How Photochromic Pigments Work

Photochromic materials change color when they're exposed to light. Typically, they're made from compounds that change their form as they absorb light. One common use is to make lenses for sunglasses that turn dark when exposed to bright light.

The lenses darken and act as sunglasses when exposed to light.

Sunglasses in sunlight

In shade, the lenses return to their original color.

Sunglasses in shade

Shape Memory Materials

Shape memory (or "smart memory") materials can be manipulated into different shapes and return to their original shape when warmed or when pressure is released. They can be used to make surgical stitches, car bumpers, and glasses.

Smart alloys
Nitinol is an example of a shape memory alloy (a mixture of metals). It's made from nickel and titanium, and is often used to make glasses.

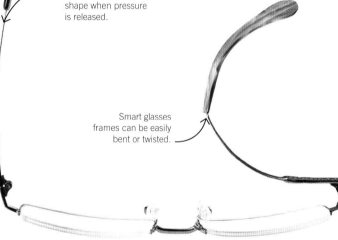

Nitinol glasses spring back to their original shape when pressure is released.

Smart glasses frames can be easily bent or twisted.

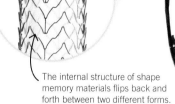

The internal structure of shape memory materials flips back and forth between two different forms.

⚙ Shape Memory Polymers

Shape memory polymers, like shape memory alloys, can also return to their original shape when heated, and are used to make many things, including sports equipment such as mouth guards.

Shape memory material in its original shape.

At cool temperatures, the material can be bent and shaped.

When warmed, the particles gain just enough energy to move and the material "remembers" its original shape.

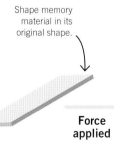

Force applied

Heat applied

Hydrogels

Hydrogels are smart materials that can absorb huge amounts of water. They have lots of uses, such as in diapers, sanitary products, contact lenses, artificial snow, and watering plants. Their ability to absorb water is reversible—they can release the water and then absorb it again.

Key Facts

✓ Hydrogels can absorb up to 1,000 times their own weight in water.

✓ They release absorbed water when the surroundings are dry.

✓ Hydrogels are used in diapers and provide slow-release moisture for plants.

Hydrogel granules
Colorful hydrogel granules can be used in place of soil for indoor houseplants. They release water to the plant's roots gradually.

Plants can be kept hydrated using hydrogels.

The multicolored beads can absorb up to 1,000 times their own weight in water.

🔍 How Hydrogels Work

Hydrogel granules can absorb a large amount of water and later release it. They're added to the soil where water is scarce. Special hydrogels are also used to release pesticides (substance that kills pests) over a long period.

1. When water is available, hydrogel granules in the soil absorb it and swell up.

2. When water is in short supply, hydrogel granules release water slowly and keep the soil moist.

Quantitative Chemistry

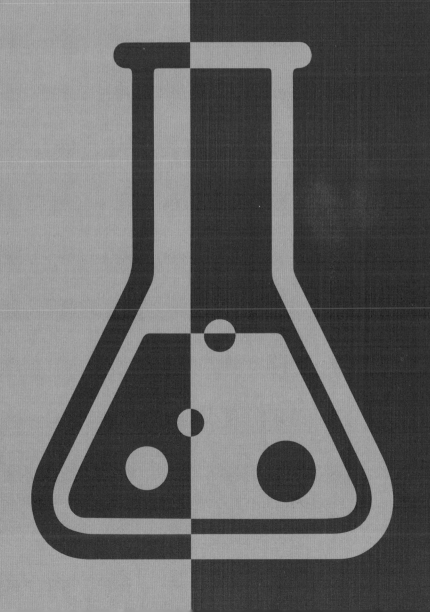

Relative Formula Mass

The relative atomic mass (A_r) of each element is often shown in the periodic table—it is the bigger number next to the chemical symbol. You calculate the relative formula mass (M_r) of a substance by adding together the A_r values for all the atoms in the substance's formula.

Key Facts

✓ Molecules and compounds can be described by their relative formula mass (M_r).

✓ The M_r of a substance is the total A_r for all the atoms in its formula.

✓ Percentage mass is calculated using A_r and M_r values.

Copper sulfate

Copper sulfate exists as blue crystals or blue powder. Its chemical formula is $CuSO_4$.

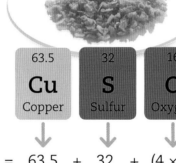

One copper atom

$CuSO_4$

One sulfur atom

Four oxygen atoms

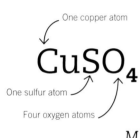

The relative atomic mass of oxygen is 16.

63.5	32	16
Cu	**S**	**O**
Copper	Sulfur	Oxygen

The relative formula mass of copper sulfate is 159.5.

$$M_r = 63.5 + 32 + (4 \times 16) = 159.5$$

Calculating Percentage Mass

You can calculate the percentage mass of an element in a compound if you know three things: the element's relative atomic mass, the compound's formula, and the compound's relative formula mass.

$$\text{Percentage mass of an element} = \frac{\text{(atoms of the element)} \times (A_r \text{ of the element})}{M_r \text{ of the compound}} \times 100$$

Question

Calculate the percentage of oxygen in copper sulfate using the equation above.

Figuring it out

$$\text{Percentage mass of oxygen} = \frac{(4 \times 16)}{159.5} \times 100 = \frac{64}{159.5} \times 100 = 40.1\%$$

Answer

The percentage of oxygen in copper sulfate is 40.1%.

Using the Percentage Mass Formula

The percentage mass of an element in a compound is a measure of the mass of its atoms.

Key Facts

✓ The total mass of a compound is due to the atoms it contains.

✓ The atoms of different elements have different masses.

✓ The percentage mass of an element in a compound takes into account the number and mass of its atoms.

Question

A gardener has a fertilizer that is a mixture of 75% ammonium nitrate and 25% potassium sulfate. Calculate the mass of fertilizer that is needed to supply 10.5 g of nitrogen.

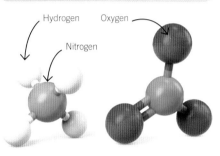

Hydrogen   Oxygen

Nitrogen

Ammonium nitrate

Figuring it out

1. Calculate the relative formula mass (M_r) of ammonium nitrate.
The formula of ammonium nitrate is NH_4NO_3.
Relative atomic masses (A_r): H = 1, N = 14, O = 16.
Relative formula mass (M_r): $14 + (4 \times 1) + 14 + (3 \times 16) = 80$

2. Calculate the percentage by mass of nitrogen in ammonium nitrate.

$$\text{percentage mass of an element} = \frac{\text{(number of atoms of the element in formula)} \times (A_r \text{ of the element})}{M_r \text{ of the compound}} \times 100$$

$$\text{percentage mass of nitrogen in ammonium nitrate} = \frac{2 \times 14}{80} \times 100 = \frac{28}{80} \times 100 = 35\%$$

3. Calculate the mass of ammonium nitrate needed.

$$\text{mass of compound needed} = \frac{\text{required mass of the element}}{\text{percentage by mass}} \times 100$$

We want to supply 10.5 g of nitrogen, so mass of ammonium nitrate needed = $\frac{10.5}{35} \times 100 = 30\,g$

4. Calculate the mass of fertilizer needed.
The fertilzer is 75% ammonium nitrate and we need 30 g of ammonium nitrate, so:

$$\text{mass of fertilizer needed} = \frac{\text{mass of ammonium nitrate needed}}{\text{percentage of ammonium nitrate in the mixture}} \times 100$$

$$\text{mass of fertilizer needed} = \frac{30}{75} \times 100 = 40\,g$$

Answer

The mass of fertilizer needed is 40 g.

Moles

It is useful in chemistry to know the number of particles in a substance. This is the amount of substance. It is measured in moles (mol). One mole of particles contains the Avogadro number of particles. It is important to say what the particles are (atoms, molecules, ions, or electrons).

Key Facts

✓ The amount of a substance is the number of particles it contains.

✓ The unit for amount of substance is the mole.

✓ Its symbol is "mol."

✓ The mass of 1 mol of a substance is its relative atomic mass (A_r) or relative formula mass (M_r) in grams.

The Avogadro number
The number of particles in one mole of a substance is known as the Avogadro number. It is equal to 6.02×10^{23}. The particles can be atoms, molecules, ions, or electrons.

$$6.02 \times 10^{23}$$
$$\downarrow$$
$$602\ 000\ 000\ 000\ 000\ 000\ 000\ 000\ 000$$

Moles of atoms
The relative atomic mass (A_r) of each element is often shown in the periodic table. The mass of 1 mol of atoms of an element is equal to its A_r in grams.

Element	Symbol	Relative atomic mass (A_r)	Mass of 1 mol (g)
Iron	Fe	56	56g

Moles of molecules and compounds
The relative formula mass (M_r) of a substance is the total A_r of the atoms it contains. The mass of 1 mol of a molecule or compound is equal to its M_r in grams.

Compound	Formula	Relative formula mass (M_r)	Mass of 1 mol (g)
Water	H_2O	1+1+16 = 18	18g

One mole of a selection of substances
From left to right: table sugar, nickel(II) chloride, copper(II) sulfate, potassium manganate(VII), copper shavings, and iron filings.

Mole Calculations

The amount of a substance is measured in moles (mol), and is related to its mass and its relative mass. If you know two of these three values, you can calculate the unknown one. When doing mole calculations, use A_r for atoms and M_r for molecules and compounds.

Key Facts

✓ Moles, mass, and relative mass are all related.

✓ Number of moles = mass ÷ relative mass.

✓ This equation can be rearranged to find mass or relative formula mass.

📑 Calculating the Number of Moles

You can calculate the amount of a substance in moles if you know the mass of the substance and its relative mass.

Question
Calculate the number of moles of water molecules in 9.0 g of water (H_2O).
Relative atomic masses (A_r): H = 1, O = 16
Relative formula mass (M_r) of H_2O = (2 × 1) + 16 = 18

$$\text{number of moles} = \frac{\text{mass}}{\text{relative mass}}$$

Figuring it out
$$\text{number of moles} = \frac{9.0}{18} = 0.5 \text{ mol}$$

Answer
There are 0.5 moles of water molecules in 9.0 g of water.

📑 Calculating the Mass

You can calculate the mass of a substance if you know the amount in moles and its relative mass.

Question
Calculate the mass of 2.0 mol of water molecules (H_2O).

$$\text{mass} = \text{moles} \times \text{relative mass}$$

Figuring it out
mass = 2.0 × 18 = 36 g

Answer
The mass of 2.0 mol of water molecules is 36 g.

📑 Calculating the Relative Mass

You can calculate the A_r or M_r of a substance if you know its mass and number of moles.

Question
16 g of sulfur dioxide contains 0.25 mol of sulfur dioxide molecules (SO_2). Calculate the relative formula mass of sulfur dioxide.

$$\text{relative mass} = \frac{\text{mass}}{\text{number of moles}}$$

Figuring it out
$$\text{relative formula mass} = \frac{16}{0.25} = 64$$

Answer
The relative formula mass of sulfur dioxide is 64.

Conservation of Mass

The law of conservation of mass states that the total mass of reactants and products does not change during a reaction, because no atoms are created or destroyed. This is why the numbers of atoms of each element is the same on both sides of a balanced chemical equation.

Key Facts

✓ Mass is conserved in chemical reactions.

✓ The total mass of reactants and products stays the same.

✓ No atoms are created or destroyed during a chemical reaction.

Making precipitates

Silver nitrate solution reacts with potassium dichromate solution to produce potassium nitrate and silver dichromate.

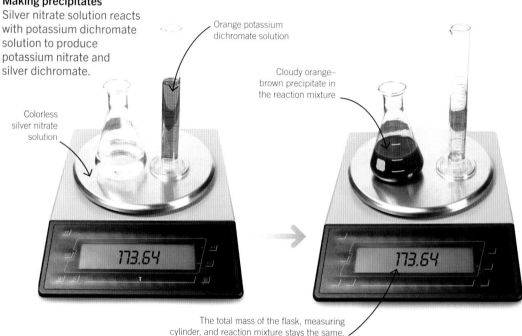

Orange potassium dichromate solution

Cloudy orange–brown precipitate in the reaction mixture

Colorless silver nitrate solution

The total mass of the flask, measuring cylinder, and reaction mixture stays the same.

The Law of Conservation of Mass

This equation shows how magnesium reacts with chlorine when it is heated to form magnesium chloride. No atoms are created or destroyed in this reaction. They just separate and join together in different ways.

magnesium Mg	chlorine Cl_2	magnesium chloride $MgCl_2$

There is one magnesium atom at the start of the reaction.	There are two chlorine atoms at the start of the reaction.	The number of atoms is the same at the start and end of the reaction.

Changing Mass

The recorded mass may change in some chemical reactions, but the law of conservation of mass (see page 111) still applies. When reactions happen in open containers, gases can enter or leave. The mass of the remaining reaction mixture may decrease if a gas escapes, or increase if a gas enters.

📌 **Key Facts**

✓ Substances can leave or enter open containers.

✓ The mass decreases if a product in the gas state escapes.

✓ The mass increases if a reactant in the gas state enters.

Losing mass to air
Some reactions produce a gas or gases. They may escape from the reaction mixture, making the remaining mass go down.

The magnesium reacts with dilute hydrochloric acid, producing magnesium chloride solution and hydrogen gas.

The hydrogen escapes from the open beaker, reducing the mass of the remaining reaction mixture.

Magnesium ribbon in an open beaker

⚙️ **Gaining Mass from Air**

When magnesium is heated in air, it reacts with oxygen to form magnesium oxide. Oxygen is gained by the magnesium but lost from the air. The total mass stays the same, even though the solid increases in mass.

metal + oxygen ⟶ metal oxide

magnesium	+	oxygen	⟶	magnesium oxide
$2Mg_{(s)}$	+	$O_{2(g)}$	⟶	$2MgO_{(s)}$

Moles and Equations

📌 **Key Facts**

The amount of a substance is measured in moles (mol). A balanced equation shows you the relative amounts of reactants and products in a reaction. The ratio of the amounts of two substances is called a mole ratio. This can be used to calculate the amount of one substance from the known amount of another substance in the reaction.

✓ Numbers before formulas show the relative numbers of moles of each substance.

✓ Subscripts after chemical symbols tell you the number of atoms of an element in a compound.

✓ The ratio of moles of reactants and products stays the same.

Balancing numbers tell you the relative amounts of each substance in the reaction.

Subscripts show if there is more than one atom of an element in a unit of the substance.

$$CH_4 \quad + \quad 2O_2 \quad \longrightarrow \quad CO_2 \quad + \quad 2H_2O$$

| 1 mol of methane | 2 mol of oxygen | | 1 mol of carbon dioxide | 2 mol of water |

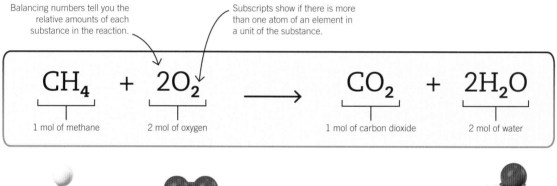

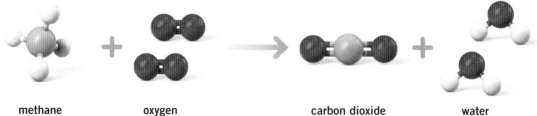

methane   oxygen   carbon dioxide   water

📑 **Molar Ratios**

Question

Nitrogen reacts with hydrogen to form ammonia: $N_2 + 3H_2 \longrightarrow 2NH_3$
Using this balanced equation, calculate the amount of ammonia formed from 6 mol of hydrogen.

Figuring it out

Divide the moles of hydrogen by the 3 in $3H_2$, then multiply by the 2 in $2NH_3$.

Amount of $NH_3 = \dfrac{6 \text{ mol}}{3} \times 2 = 4 \text{ mol}$

Answer

4 mol of ammonia is formed from 6 mol of hydrogen.

Balancing Equations Using Masses

You can balance an equation if you know the masses of all the substances in that reaction as well as their relative masses (A_r or M_r). You can then calculate the number of moles of each substance (see page 110).

Key Facts

✓ A balanced equation shows the formula of each substance in a reaction, in the correct amounts so no reactants are left over.

✓ You can balance an equation if you know the formulas of all the reactants and products.

Using Reacting Masses: An Example

Question

Two students carried out an experiment. They heated a piece of magnesium in a crucible so that it reacted with oxygen to form magnesium oxide. Use the results to determine the balanced chemical equation for the reaction.

Mass of crucible (g)	30.00
Mass of crucible + magnesium (g)	30.48
Mass of crucible + magnesium oxide (g)	30.80

Figuring it out

1. Calculate the mass of each substance.

Mass of magnesium = 30.48 − 30.00 = 0.48 g
Mass of magnesium oxide = 30.80 − 30.00 = 0.80 g
Mass of oxygen = 30.80 − 30.48 = 0.32 g

2. Calculate the relative formula mass (see page 107) of each substance.

A_r of Mg = 24 M_r of O_2 = (2 × 16) = 32 M_r of MgO = 24 + 16 = 40

3. Calculate the number of moles of each substance using this equation:

$$\text{number of moles} = \frac{\text{mass of substance}}{\text{relative formula mass of substance}}$$

Mg: $\dfrac{0.48}{24}$ = 0.02 mol O_2: $\dfrac{0.32}{32}$ = 0.01 mol   MgO: $\dfrac{0.80}{40}$ = 0.02 mol

4. Simplify the ratios by dividing all the numbers by the smallest number (in this example 0.01). If some numbers are not whole, multiply them all by the same amount so they are all whole numbers.

Mg: $\dfrac{0.02}{0.01}$ = 2 O_2: $\dfrac{0.01}{0.01}$ = 1   MgO: $\dfrac{0.02}{0.01}$ = 2

Answer

The balanced chemical equation for the reaction is $2Mg + O_2 \rightarrow 2MgO$

Limiting Reactants

A chemical reaction carries on until one of the reactants is completely used up. This reactant is called the limiting reactant. The other reactants in the reaction are described as being in excess. As the amount of the limiting reactant increases, the amount of product formed increases.

Key Facts

✓ Reactions stop when the limiting reactant runs out.

✓ The other reactants are in excess.

✓ The amount of product formed is directly proportional to the amount of the limiting reactant.

A color change reaction
Iodine dissolves in water to form a brown solution.
Zinc reacts with the iodine to form colorless zinc iodide.

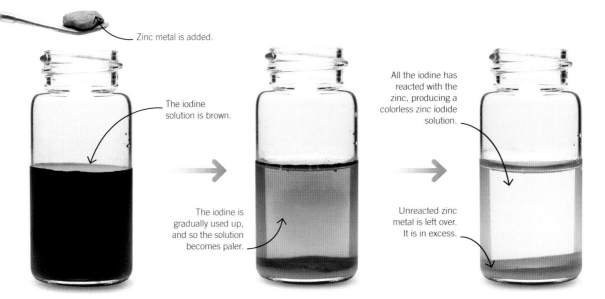

Zinc metal is added.

The iodine solution is brown.

The iodine is gradually used up, and so the solution becomes paler.

All the iodine has reacted with the zinc, producing a colorless zinc iodide solution.

Unreacted zinc metal is left over. It is in excess.

⚙ Maximum Product Calculations

If you know the mass of a product formed by a given mass of a limiting reactant, you can predict the mass formed by a different mass.

Question
0.2 g of hydrogen is produced when 2.4 g of magnesium ribbon reacts completely with excess dilute hydrochloric acid. Calculate the mass of hydrogen produced when 6.0 g of magnesium reacts completely instead.

Figuring it out

$$\frac{\text{mass of Mg in second reaction}}{\text{mass of Mg in first reaction}} = \frac{6.0}{2.4} = 2.5$$

So 2.5 times more magnesium was used in the second reaction.
Mass of hydrogen in second reaction = $2.5 \times 0.2 = 0.5$ g

Answer
So 0.5 g of hydrogen is produced when 6.0 g of magnesium reacts completely with excess dilute hydrochloric acid.

Calculating Masses in Reactions

The mass of the limiting reactant (see page 115) determines the masses of the products that can be formed in a reaction. You can calculate the maximum mass of a product using the relative formula masses of the limiting reactant and product, the balanced chemical equation, and the mass of limiting reactant.

Key Facts

✓ The amount of limiting reactant is calculated from its mass and its M_r.

✓ The maximum amount of product is calculated from the amount of limiting reactant and mole ratio.

✓ The maximum mass of product is calculated from its amount and its M_r.

Question

Iron reacts with chlorine to form iron chloride:
$2Fe + 3Cl_2 \longrightarrow 2FeCl_3$
Iron + chlorine $\longrightarrow$ iron chloride

What is the maximum mass of iron chloride that can be produced when 2.24 g of iron reacts with excess chlorine?

Figuring it out

1. Calculate the relative formula mass (see page 107) of iron chloride.

Relative atomic masses (A_r): Fe = 56, Cl = 35.5
Relative formula mass (M_r) of $FeCl_3$ = 56 + (3 × 35.5) = 162.5

2. Calculate the amount in moles of the limiting reactant from its mass and relative formula mass. Iron is the limiting reactant because we know chlorine is in excess.

$$\text{number of moles} = \frac{\text{mass}}{\text{relative mass}} = \frac{2.24}{56} = 0.04 \text{ mol}$$

3. Calculate the amount in moles of the product formed. Use the mole ratio from the balanced chemical equation.

Mole ratio is $2Fe : 2FeCl_3$ which simplifies to 1 : 1
So 0.04 mol of Fe forms 0.04 mol of $FeCl_3$

4. Calculate the mass of product formed. Use your answer to step 3 and the M_r from step 1.

$$\text{mass = moles × relative mass} = 0.04 × 162.5 = 6.5 \text{g}$$

Answer

The maximum mass of iron chloride that can be produced is 6.5 g.

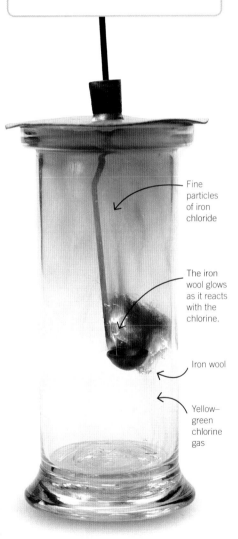

Fine particles of iron chloride

The iron wool glows as it reacts with the chlorine.

Iron wool

Yellow–green chlorine gas

Iron reacting with chlorine

The Volume of Gas

The volume of any substance in the gas state depends on how many molecules of gas there are, its temperature, and its pressure. The volume does not depend on the type of gas. One mole of any gas occupies 24 dm³ at room temperature (20 °C) and pressure (101 kPa).

Key Facts

✓ Volume of gas and moles are related by the molar gas volume.

✓ The molar gas volume is 24 dm³ at room temperature and pressure.

 Molar Gas Volume

Room temperature (20°C) and atmospheric pressure is called RTP. One mole of any gas occupies 24 dm³ (24,000 cm³) at RTP. You can calculate the volume of a gas at RTP if you know its amount in moles.

Question
Calculate the volume occupied by 0.25 mol of carbon dioxide at RTP.

> **volume of gas at RTP (dm³) = amount of gas (mol) × 24**

Figuring it out
Volume = 0.25 mol × 24 = 6.0 dm³

Answer
At RTP, the volume occupied by 0.25 mol of carbon dioxide is 6.0 dm³.

 Amount of Gas

You can calculate the amount of any gas in moles if you know its volume. Remember that the molar gas volume is 24 dm³ or 24,000 cm³.

Question
Calculate the amount of oxygen that occupies 3.0 dm³ at RTP.

$$\text{amount of gas (mol)} = \frac{\text{volume of gas at RTP (dm}^3)}{\text{molar volume}}$$

Figuring it out
amount of gas (mol) = $\frac{3}{24}$ = 0.125 mol

Answer
At RTP, 0.125 mol of oxygen occupies 3.0 dm³.

 Volume of Gas from Its Mass

You can calculate the volume occupied by a known mass of a gas if you know its relative formula mass (M_r). For a reminder about the equation used here, see page 110.

Question
Calculate the volume occupied by 1.5 g of hydrogen at RTP. (M_r of H_2 = 2.0)

> **mass (g) = amount (mol) × M_r**

Figuring it out
1. Calculate the amount of gas in moles.
1.5 g = amount (mol) × 2.0
number of moles (hydrogen) = $\frac{1.5}{2}$ = 0.75 mol

2. Calculate the volume of gas using the equation at the top of this page.
volume (dm³) = 0.75 mol × 24 = 18 dm³

Answer
At RTP, the volume occupied by 1.5 g of hydrogen is 18 dm³.

Empirical Formulas

The empirical formula of a compound is the simplest whole-number ratio of the atoms of each element found in the compound. Since ionic compounds have giant structures, they're always described with empirical formulas. Compounds with covalent bonding are usually given a molecular formula, but it's possible to figure out an empirical formula for them, too.

Key Facts

✓ The empirical formula of a compound is the simplest whole-number ratio of atoms of each element in the compound.

✓ The formulas of ionic compounds are always empirical formulas.

✓ The charges of the ions in the empirical formulas of an ionic compound add up to zero.

The oxygen ions have a 2– charge.

The lithium ions have a 1+ charge.

Lithium oxide
Lithium oxide is an ionic compound with a giant ionic structure. Its empirical formula is Li_2O, because two lithium ions are needed to balance the charge of the oxide ion.

⚙ **Calculating an Empirical Formula**

The idea of empirical formula is also applied to covalent compounds.

Oxygen atom

Phosphorus atom

Question
What is the empirical formula of phosphorus pentoxide, which has the molecular formula of P_4O_{10}?

Figuring it out
1. Find the highest common factor: the highest common factor of 4 and 10 is 2.
2. Divide the molecular formula by the highest common factor.

$$P = \frac{4}{2} = 2 \quad O = \frac{10}{2} = 5$$

Answer
The empirical formula is P_2O_5.

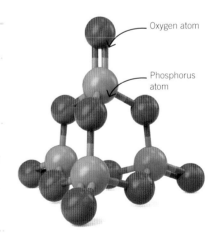

Phosphorus pentoxide

A Reacting Masses Experiment

You can calculate the empirical formula of a metal oxide by carrying out the experiment below. You need to know the mass of the metal before it reacts with oxygen, and the mass of the metal oxide formed. Magnesium is a reactive metal that is suitable for this type of experiment.

The empirical formula of magnesium oxide
To calculate the empirical formula of magnesium oxide (see page 120), you need to know the mass of magnesium, and the mass of magnesium oxide it forms.

Key Facts

✓ An empirical formula is the smallest whole-number ratio of atoms in a compound.

✓ An empirical formula can be determined using experimental results.

✓ You need to find the masses of reactants and products in your experiment.

✓ Measure each mass carefully.

✓ Wear eye protection and gloves during the experiment.

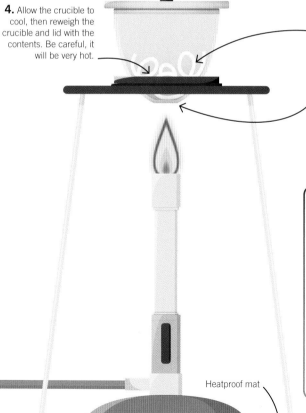

1. Record the mass of the crucible and its lid.

2. Loosely coil a clean piece of magnesium and put it in the crucible. Record the mass of the crucible, lid, and magnesium together.

3. Heat the crucible, lifting the lid from time to time to let air in. Continue heating for about 10 minutes until the magnesium turns white and then turn the Bunsen burner off.

4. Allow the crucible to cool, then reweigh the crucible and lid with the contents. Be careful, it will be very hot.

Heatproof mat

📑 Recording Your Results

You need to record your results so that you can calculate the empirical formula (see page 120). Here are two calculations you need:

1. mass of magnesium
= (mass at step 2) − (mass at step 1)

2. mass of oxygen
= (mass at step 4) − (mass at step 2)

Calculating the Reacting Mass

You can use the information gathered in the reacting masses experiment outlined on page 119 to determine the empirical formula of the compound magnesium oxide.

 Key Facts

✓ Set out your work in columns to make it easier to follow.

✓ Figuring out the mass of each element and divide by its relative atomic mass.

✓ Find the simplest whole-number ratio.

Question

The table shows the results collected in the experiment on page 119. Determine the empirical formula of magnesium oxide using these results. Relative atomic masses (M_r): Mg = 24, O = 16

Mass of crucible (g)	30.00
Mass of crucible + magnesium (g)	30.48
Mass of crucible + magnesium oxide (g)	30.80

Figuring it out

Before figuring out the empirical formula, calculate the mass of each element in magnesium oxide (see page 119).

Mass of magnesium (Mg) = 30.48 − 30.00 = 0.48 g

Mass of oxygen (O) = 30.80 − 30.48 = 0.32 g

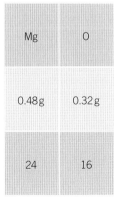

Magnesium   Oxygen

Magnesium oxide

1. Write the symbols of the elements in columns.

Mg	O

2. Write the mass of each element.

0.48 g	0.32 g

3. Write the relative atomic mass of each element.

24	16

4. Divide Step 2 numbers by Step 3 numbers.

$$\frac{0.48}{24} = 0.02 \qquad \frac{0.32}{16} = 0.02$$

5. Divide Step 4 numbers by their smallest number.

$$\frac{0.02}{0.02} = 1 \qquad \frac{0.02}{0.02} = 1$$

6. If needed, simplify the ratio, then write the formula.

$Mg_1O_1 = MgO$

Answer

The empirical formula of magnesium oxide is MgO.

Water of Crystallization

Some salts contain water molecules. These molecules are in the salt's crystal lattice, but are only loosely held there – the water can be removed by heating. A salt containing water of crystallization is described as "hydrated". A salt without any water of crystallization is described as "anhydrous".

Key Facts

✓ Salt crystals may contain water of crystallization.

✓ The water can be removed from a hydrated salt by heating.

✓ A salt without water of crystallization is an anhydrous salt.

Dehydration of hydrated copper sulfate
Hydrated copper sulfate is blue. You can remove its water of crystallization by heating, forming white anhydrous copper sulfate.

Water is released.

1. Record the mass of an evaporating basin.

2. Add some hydrated copper sulfate and record the mass of the basin and hydrated copper sulfate together.

5. Let the basin cool then reweigh it with its contents.

3. Heat the evaporating basin. Take care to avoid any hot solid spitting out.

4. Continue heating to remove the water until the copper sulfate turns white. Turn the Bunsen burner off.

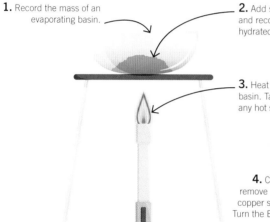

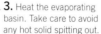

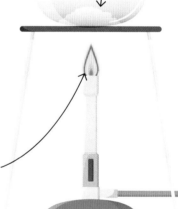

⚙ Hydrated and Anhydrous Copper Sulfate

Anhydrous copper sulfate is $CuSO_4$. The general formula for hydrated copper sulfate is $CuSO_4 \cdot x H_2O$ where × is a whole number. The dot (·) separates the two parts of the formula. In the hydrated form, water of crystallization (H_2O) is held within the structure by very weak bonds.

Water molecule (H_2O)

The hydration bonds break when heated and the water evaporates, leaving behind anhydrous copper (II) sulfate.

Sulfate ion (SO_4^{2-})

Copper ion (Cu^{2+})

Water molecules (H_2O)

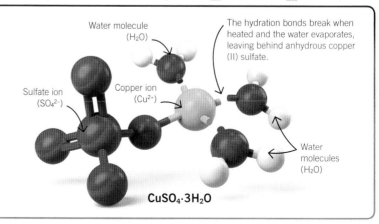

$CuSO_4 \cdot 3H_2O$

Calculating Water of Crystallization

You can use the masses collected in the experiment outlined on page 121 to determine the amount of water of crystallization (water in the crystal lattice) involved. If you know the mass of hydrated salt and anhydrous salt, you can figure out the mass of water lost.

Key Facts

✓ Set up your work in columns.

✓ Figure out the mass of each compound and divide by its relative formula mass.

✓ Find the simplest whole-number ratio to get the value of x.

Question

Determine the value of x in $CuSO_4 \cdot xH_2O$ using the results in this table. Give the formula of the hydrated copper sulfate.
Relative formula masses (M_r):
$CuSO_4 = 159.6$, $H_2O = 18$

Mass of basin (g)	30.25
Mass of basin + hydrated copper sulfate (g)	45.22
Mass of basin + anhydrous copper sulfate (g)	39.82

Figuring it out

Before figuring out the value of x, calculate the mass of anhydrous copper sulfate and the mass of water lost.

Mass of anhydrous copper sulfate
$= 39.82 - 30.25 = 9.57\,g$
Mass of water
$= 45.22 - 39.82 = 5.40\,g$

Sulfur ion (SO_4^{2-})

Copper ion (Cu^{2+})

Anhydrous copper sulfate

1. Write the formulas of the compounds in columns.

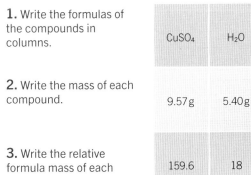

$CuSO_4$	H_2O
9.57 g	5.40 g
159.6	18

2. Write the mass of each compound.

3. Write the relative formula mass of each compound.

4. Divide Step 2 numbers by Step 3 numbers.

$$\frac{9.57}{159.6} = 0.06 \qquad \frac{5.40}{18} = 0.3$$

5. Divide Step 4 numbers by their smallest number.

$$\frac{0.06}{0.06} = 1 \qquad \frac{0.3}{0.06} = 5$$

6. If needed, simplify the ratio, then write the value of x.

$1:5$ so $x = 5$

Answer

$x = 5$ so the formula of the hydrated copper sulfate is: $CuSO_4.5H_2O$

Concentration

A solute can dissolve in a solvent to form a solution. The greater the mass or the amount of dissolved solute in a given volume, the greater the concentration. Concentrations in terms of mass are measured in g/dm³. Concentrations in terms of amount of substance are measured in mol/dm³.

Key Facts

✓ A solute dissolves in a solvent to form a solution.

✓ The concentration of a solution is a measure of how "crowded" the solute particles are.

✓ Concentration is measured in g/dm³ or mol/dm³.

Converting cm³ to dm³

Volumes used in concentration calculations are in cubic decimeters (dm³). Convert from cm³ to dm³ first in a concentration calculation.

$1\,dm^3 = 1{,}000\,cm^3$

> **Divide by 1,000 to convert from cm³ to dm³**

> **Multiply by 1,000 to convert from dm³ to cm³**

For example, $125\,cm^3 = \dfrac{125}{1{,}000} = 0.125\,dm^3$

Calculating concentration

To calculate a concentration, you need to know the mass or amount of solute, and volume of solution.

$$\text{concentration (g/dm}^3) = \frac{\text{mass of solute (g)}}{\text{volume of solution (dm}^3)}$$

$$\text{concentration (mol/dm}^3) = \frac{\text{amount of solute (mol)}}{\text{volume of solution (dm}^3)}$$

An Example

Question

10 g of sodium hydroxide is dissolved in water to make 250 cm³ of solution. Calculate the concentration of this solution.

Figuring it out

1. Convert the volume to dm³.

Volume of solution = $\dfrac{250}{1{,}000} = 0.25\,dm^3$

2. Substitute values into the concentration equation above.

Concentration = $\dfrac{10\,g}{0.25\,dm^3} = 40\,g/dm^3$

Answer

The concentration of the solution formed is 40 g/dm³.

Titration Calculations

Titration is a technique that is used to find unknown concentrations (see page 136). You carry out an experiment to find the volumes of acid and alkali that exactly neutralize each other. If you know the concentration of one substance, you can figure out the concentration of the other.

 Key Facts

✓ Titrations involve finding out the volumes of acid and alkali that neutralize each other.

✓ You can use the results to calculate an unknown concentration.

✓ You need to know both volumes, and the known concentration.

Titrations

In a titration, the concentration of one solution is known and the other is unknown. If you know the volumes that react together, you can calculate the unknown concentration.

$$\text{concentration (mol/dm}^3) = \frac{\text{amount of solute (mol)}}{\text{volume of solution (dm}^3)}$$

 An Example

Question

15 cm³ of 2.0 mol/dm³ hydrochloric acid neutralizes 25 cm³ of a sodium hydroxide solution:
HCl + NaOH ⟶ NaCl + H₂O. Calculate the concentration of the sodium hydroxide solution.

Figuring it out

1. Convert the volumes into dm³.

$15 \text{cm}^3 = \dfrac{15}{1,000} = 0.015 \text{dm}^3$

$25 \text{cm}^3 = \dfrac{25}{1,000} = 0.025 \text{dm}^3$

2. Substitute the values for hydrochloric acid into the concentration equation (because you know its concentration).

$2.0 \text{ mol/dm}^3 = \dfrac{\text{amount of HCl}}{0.015 \text{dm}^3}$

3. Rearrange the equation above, then solve.
amount of HCl = 2.0 × 0.015 = 0.03 mol

4. Figure out the amount of sodium hydroxide using the mole ratio in the balanced chemical equation. 1 mol of HCl reacts with 1 mol of NaOH, so 0.30 mol of HCl reacts with 0.30 mol of NaOH.

$$\text{concentration of NaOH} = \frac{0.03 \text{ mol}}{0.025 \text{ (dm}^3)} = 1.2 \text{ mol/dm}^3$$

Answer

The concentration of the sodium hydroxide solution is 1.2 mol/dm³.

Atom Economy

One of the ways to evaluate a chemical process is to calculate its atom economy. This is a measure of its efficiency in converting reactants into a desired product. In many chemical processes, the desired product is not the only one—other products called by-products may be produced, too.

Key Facts

✓ Reactions often make more than one product. Some will be useful, but others will be waste.

✓ Atom economy is a measure of how efficiently reactants form a product.

✓ The higher the atom economy, the less waste there is.

Equation
The atom economy of a reaction gives the percentage of atoms in the reactants that become atoms in the desired product. You can calculate it using this equation.

$$\text{percentage atom economy} = \frac{\text{total } M_r \text{ of the desired product}}{\text{total } M_r \text{ of all reactants}} \times 100$$

Calculating Atom Economy

Question
Most hydrogen is manufactured by reacting methane with steam. Calculate the atom economy of this process.

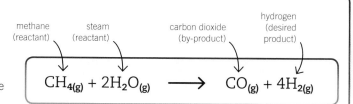

methane (reactant)   steam (reactant)   carbon dioxide (by-product)   hydrogen (desired product)

$$CH_{4(g)} + 2H_2O_{(g)} \longrightarrow CO_{(g)} + 4H_{2(g)}$$

Figuring it out
1. Calculate the relative formula masses (M_r) of the reactants and the desired product (if not given to you). See page 107 for a reminder of how to do this. Carbon dioxide (CO_2) is a waste product so isn't included here.

M_r of $CH_4 = 12 + (4 \times 1) = 16$
M_r of $H_2O = (2 \times 1) + 16 = 18$
M_r of $H_2 = 2 \times 1 = 2$

2. Calculate the total relative formula mass of the desired product.

M_r of $4H_2 = 4 \times (2 \times 1) = 8$

3. Calculate the total relative formula masses of the reactants.

M_r of $CH_4 + M_r$ of $2H_2O$
$= 16 + (2 \times 18) = 52$

4. Put your answers to steps 2 and 3 into the equation above to calculate the percentage atom economy.

$\%$ atom economy $= \dfrac{8}{52} \times 100 = 15.4\%$

Answer
The atom economy of this process is 15.4%.

The Advantages of Atom Economy

Processes with high atom economies are more efficient than those with low atom economies (see page 125). They reduce the use of raw materials and limit harm to the environment. They are important for sustainable development (see page 263), ensuring we meet our needs without preventing people in the future from meeting their needs.

Key Facts

✓ Processes with high atom economies reduce waste and the use of raw materials.

✓ High atom economy is important for sustainable development and profitability.

✓ The atom economy of a reaction can be increased by finding a use for waste products.

Resources

Reactions with a low atom economy can waste resources, which makes those resources unsustainable. One way to make hydrogen involves reacting coal with steam. This process has a low atom economy, just 8.3%, so it wastes a lot of coal.

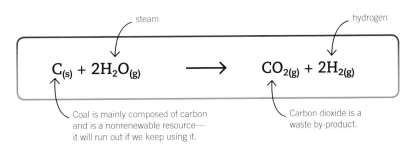

steam

hydrogen

$$C_{(s)} + 2H_2O_{(g)} \longrightarrow CO_{2(g)} + 2H_{2(g)}$$

Coal is mainly composed of carbon and is a nonrenewable resource— it will run out if we keep using it.

Carbon dioxide is a waste by-product.

Profits

If you are making a lot of waste, or the waste is hazardous, a chemical process may not be profitable. Carbon disulfide is a useful industrial solvent. It is made by reacting methane with sulfur. The atom economy for this reaction is 52.8%, so just under half the mass of the products is waste.

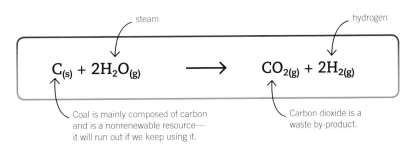

sulfur

carbon disulfide

$$CH_{4(g)} + 4S_{(g)} \longrightarrow CS_{2(g)} + 2H_2S_{(g)}$$

Methane is expensive.

Hydrogen sulfide is a very poisonous and corrosive gas. It is expensive to remove and dispose of responsibly.

By-products

The atom economy of a process can be increased by finding a use for the waste products, rather than throwing them away. Ethanol is a useful biofuel. The atom economy for making it is 51.1%.

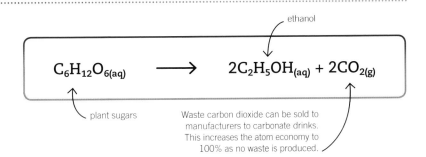

ethanol

$$C_6H_{12}O_{6(aq)} \longrightarrow 2C_2H_5OH_{(aq)} + 2CO_{2(g)}$$

plant sugars

Waste carbon dioxide can be sold to manufacturers to carbonate drinks. This increases the atom economy to 100% as no waste is produced.

Percentage Yield

In chemical reactions, no atoms are made or destroyed, so the total mass stays the same. The theoretical yield of a product is the maximum mass it is possible to make from a given mass of reactants. However, you may not get the mass that you expect. The percentage yield of a reaction is the mass of product actually made, compared to the maximum theoretical mass of products.

 Key Facts

✓ The actual yield is the mass actually made in a reaction.

✓ The theoretical yield is the maximum possible mass that can be made.

✓ The percentage yield varies from 0% (no product made) to 100% (maximum mass of product made).

Theoretical yield

You may be given the theoretical yield to use in a percentage yield calculation. It is possible to calculate the theoretical yield if you know the mass of the limiting reactant. For a reminder about limiting reactants, see page 115. For a reminder about calculating masses in reactions, see page 116.

Red–brown pieces of copper form in the reaction when copper oxide powder and carbon are heated.

$$\text{percentage yield} = \frac{\text{mass of product actually made}}{\text{maximum theoretical mass of product}} \times 100$$

 An Example

Question

When heated, copper oxide reacts with carbon. Copper and carbon dioxide are produced in the reaction. In an experiment, the actual yield of copper was 0.90 g but the theoretical yield of copper was 1.2 g. Calculate the percentage yield of copper in the experiment.

Figuring it out

The percentage yield can vary from 100% (no product has been lost) to 0% (no product has been made or collected).

$$\text{percentage yield} = \frac{0.9\,g}{1.2\,g} \times 100 = 75\%$$

Answer

The percentage yield is 75%.

100% Yield

Actual yields are less than theoretical yields. The mass of product made is usually less than expected for two main reasons. Some of the product can revert to the original reactants in reversible reactions (see page 191), and unwanted side reactions form by-products. Also, some of the product is lost during separation and purification.

(see page 191)

Key Facts

✓ Actual yields are always less than 100%.

✓ Reversible reactions do not go to completion, so yields will be less than 100%.

✓ Side reactions result in unwanted by-products.

✓ Some product gets lost during separation from the reaction mixture.

Reversible reactions

Reversible reactions do not go to completion. Some reactants will be left, so the yield is less than 100%. For example, nitrogen reacts with hydrogen to form ammonia, and ammonia breaks down to form nitrogen and hydrogen.

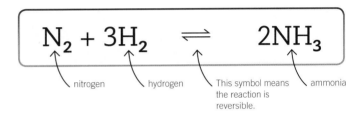

$$N_2 + 3H_2 \rightleftharpoons 2NH_3$$

nitrogen   hydrogen   This symbol means the reaction is reversible.   ammonia

Side reactions

Reactants may react in an unexpected way, forming unintentional products. For example, magnesium burns in air, reacting with oxygen to make magnesium oxide. It also reacts with nitrogen in the air to make magnesium nitride as it burns.

This is the intended reaction:

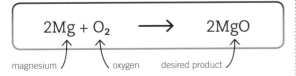

$$2Mg + O_2 \longrightarrow 2MgO$$

magnesium   oxygen   desired product

This side reaction happens at the same time:

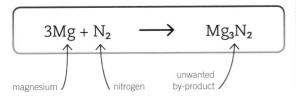

$$3Mg + N_2 \longrightarrow Mg_3N_2$$

magnesium   nitrogen   unwanted by-product

Product loss

When a liquid is filtered to remove a solid, some liquid or solid always gets lost.

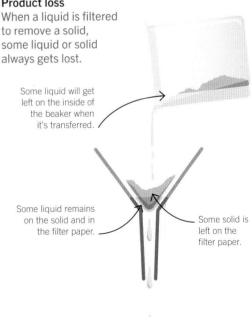

Some liquid will get left on the inside of the beaker when it's transferred.

Some liquid remains on the solid and in the filter paper.

Some solid is left on the filter paper.

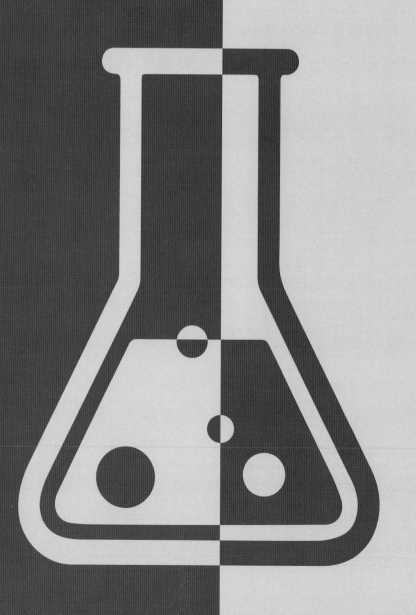

The Chemistry of Acids

The pH Scale

The pH scale is a way of measuring how acidic or alkaline a substance is. On this scale pH 7 is neutral —neither alkaline, nor acid. Values below 7 are acidic, while values of 8 to 14 are alkaline. The pH of a solution can be measured using a pH indicator (see below and page 134)—these change color at different pH levels.

Universal indicator
The approximate pH can be determined by adding a few drops of universal indicator to a sampled solution and comparing the color against a color chart. The range of colors for universal indicator is shown below.

Key Facts

✓ The pH scale is a measure of how acidic or alkaline substances are, and most substances fall within the range of 0 to 14.

✓ Acidic substances have lower pHs.

✓ Alkaline substances have higher pHs.

✓ A substance with a pH of 7 is neutral—neither acidic nor alkaline.

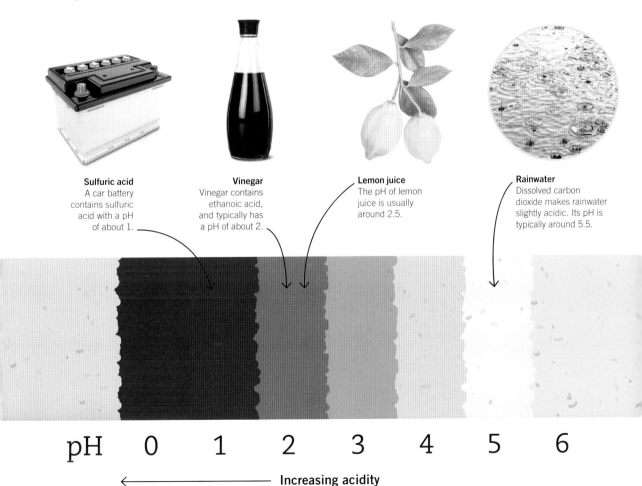

Sulfuric acid
A car battery contains sulfuric acid with a pH of about 1.

Vinegar
Vinegar contains ethanoic acid, and typically has a pH of about 2.

Lemon juice
The pH of lemon juice is usually around 2.5.

Rainwater
Dissolved carbon dioxide makes rainwater slightly acidic. Its pH is typically around 5.5.

pH   0   1   2   3   4   5   6

← —————————————— **Increasing acidity**

⚙ A Digital pH Meter

The pH of a substance can be measured electronically using an electronic probe that detects the number of hydrogen ions (H^+) in a solution. The more hydrogen ions there are, the more acidic the solution is, and the lower the pH.

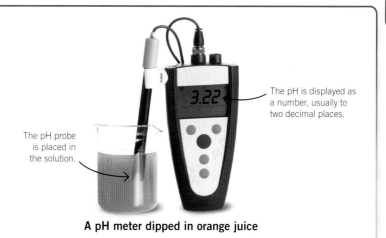

The pH probe is placed in the solution.

The pH is displayed as a number, usually to two decimal places.

A pH meter dipped in orange juice

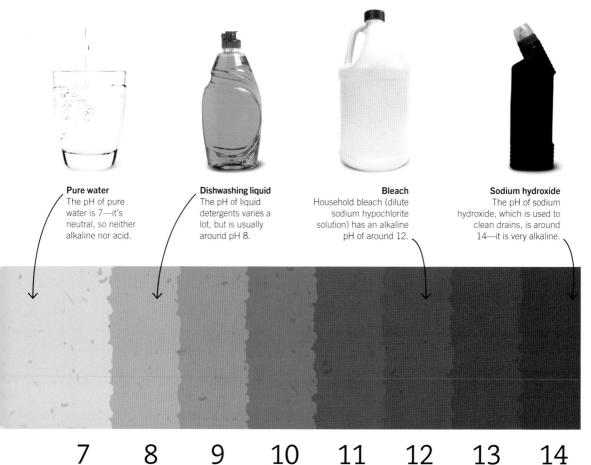

Pure water
The pH of pure water is 7—it's neutral, so neither alkaline nor acid.

Dishwashing liquid
The pH of liquid detergents varies a lot, but is usually around pH 8.

Bleach
Household bleach (dilute sodium hypochlorite solution) has an alkaline pH of around 12.

Sodium hydroxide
The pH of sodium hydroxide, which is used to clean drains, is around 14—it is very alkaline.

7   8   9   10   11   12   13   14

Neutral   **Increasing alkalinity** ⟶

Acids

Acids are substances that release hydrogen ions (H⁺) when added to water. A solution is described as acidic if it has a pH of less than 7. Strong acids can be corrosive while weak acids, such as citric acid (lemon juice) and ethanoic acid (vinegar), are common in foods.

Forming acids

Ethanoyl chloride reacts instantly when added to water to produce hydrogen chloride and ethanoic acid. Some of the hydrogen chloride escapes from the beaker as gas, and some dissolves in the water to form hydrochloric acid.

Ethanoyl chloride (CH₃COCl) is added to a beaker of cold water.

A glass rod dipped in ammonia is used to test for hydrogen chloride gas.

Ammonia reacts with hydrogen chloride gas to form ammonium chloride, which produces visible fumes.

Ethanoic acid and hydrochloric acid form in the beaker.

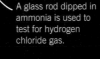

Key Facts

✓ When dissolved in water, acids release hydrogen ions (H⁺).

✓ A solution is acidic if has a pH of less than 7.

✓ Acids are commonly found in foods and give them a sour taste.

How Acids Work

Acids ionize (break apart) in water to produce positive hydrogen ions (H⁺) and negative ions—for example, when the covalent compound hydrogen chloride (HCl) gas is dissolved in water.

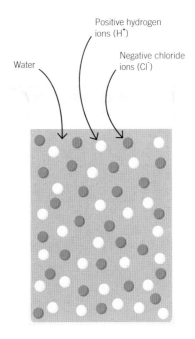

Positive hydrogen ions (H⁺)

Negative chloride ions (Cl⁻)

Water

Hydrogen chloride gas dissolved in water

Bases

A base is any substance that can neutralize an acid. A soluble base—which releases hydroxide ions (OH⁻) when added to water—is called an alkali. Bases have a pH greater than 7. Common household bases include sodium bicarbonate, often used in baking and soaps.

Potassium reacts with water to form an alkaline solution of potassium hydroxide.

Phenolphthalein indicator turns pink in the presence of alkalis (see page 134).

Forming an alkali
When a Group 1 metal, such as potassium, is added to water, it reacts to form hydrogen gas and an alkali metal hydroxide. This is why Group 1 metals are also known as the alkali metals.

Alkalis and bases
All alkalis are bases, but many bases are insoluble (they do not dissolve in water), so these are not alkalis.

Bases

Alkalis (soluble bases)

How Alkalis Work

Alkalis ionize (break apart) in water to release negative hydroxide ions (OH⁻) and positive ions—for example, when potassium hydroxide is added to water.

Negative hydroxide ions (OH⁻)

Positive potassium ions (K⁺)

Water

Potassium hydroxide in water

Indicators

Indicators are substances that change color in acidic or alkaline conditions. There are many types of indicator that produce vastly different colors, with specific colors appearing at certain pH values. Universal indicator (see page 130) is a mixture of several different indicators, and can be used to measure the approximate pH of a solution.

Key Facts

✓ Indicators are substances that change color when mixed with acids and alkalis.

✓ Different colors appear at different, specific pH values.

✓ Universal indicator is a mixture of several different indicators.

Litmus
Litmus is an indicator made from lichen. It changes from red (acid) to purple (neutral) to blue (alkaline). Blue litmus paper is used to indicate the presence of acid, while red litmus paper is used to check for alkalis.

When red litmus paper is dipped in an alkali, it turns blue.

When blue litmus paper is dipped in acid, it turns red.

Phenolphthalein
Phenolphthalein is colorless in acidic solutions but turns bright pink in the presence of an alkali solution. The color change is sharp and easy to see, and it's a popular choice in titrations (see page 136) with strong alkalis, such as sodium hydroxide.

The solution turns bright pink when the pH is above 8.

Phenolphthalein indicator is colorless below pH 8.

Methyl orange
Methyl orange turns from red (acidic) to orange to yellow (more alkaline). It changes color over a range of pH values, so methyl orange is used in titrations where phenolphthalein will not work.

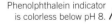

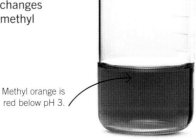

The solution turns yellow above about pH 4.5.

Methyl orange is red below pH 3.

Neutralization

Neutralization is a chemical reaction between an acid and a base. If the quantities of acid and base are just right, the resulting solution will be neutral with a pH of 7. When acids and bases react with each other, the products are always a salt and water. The salt formed depends on the acid and base used.

Key Facts

✓ Neutralization is a reaction between an acid and a base.

✓ Hydrogen ions (H⁺) from the acid combine with hydroxide ions (OH⁻) from the base to form water (H₂O) and a salt.

✓ The salt produced depends on the acid and base used.

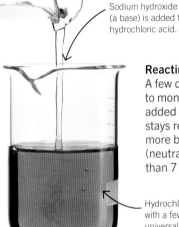

Sodium hydroxide (a base) is added to hydrochloric acid.

Reacting hydrochloric acid and sodium hydroxide
A few drops of universal indicator have been used to monitor the reaction when sodium hydroxide is added to hydrochloric acid. At first, the solution stays red as the pH is below 7 (acidic). But as more base is added, the solution turns green (neutral), and then blue as the pH is now more than 7 (alkaline).

Hydrochloric acid with a few drops of universal indicator.

The solution turns blue after the acid becomes alkaline.

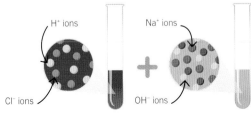

acid	+	base	$\longrightarrow$	salt	+	water

hydrochloric acid HCl	+	sodium hydroxide NaOH	$\longrightarrow$	sodium chloride NaCl	+	water H₂O

⚙ How Neutralization Works

Acidic solutions contain hydrogen ions, while alkaline solutions contain hydroxide ions. These react together to form salt and water.

H⁺ ions

Cl⁻ ions

Hydrochloric acid

Na⁺ ions

OH⁻ ions

Sodium hydroxide

The OH⁻ ions combine with the H⁺ ions to form water (H₂O).

The Na⁺ ions combine with Cl⁻ ions to form sodium chloride (NaCl).

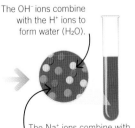

Titrations

Titration is a technique that is used to find the concentration of an unknown solution (an acid or alkali) by reacting it with a solution of known concentration. A few drops of indicator are added so the amount of solution needed to cause a color change can be recorded. For more on titration calculations, see page 124.

Burette
A burette is a piece of laboratory glassware used to measure very small volumes. Most burettes are marked from 0 cm³ (at the top) to 50 cm³ (at the bottom). In this example, the burette is filled with acid.

Key Facts

✓ Titration is a chemical technique used to find the concentration of an unknown solution.

✓ The concentration of acids or alkalis can be calculated by carrying out titrations.

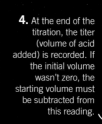

4. At the end of the titration, the titer (volume of acid added) is recorded. If the initial volume wasn't zero, the starting volume must be subtracted from this reading.

Calculating the Mean Titer

Question
Determine the mean titer from the results given in the table below using two concordant (close together) results. For accuracy, titrations are repeated at least twice.

Start volume (cm³)	0.00	12.00	23.20	5.50
Final volume (cm³)	12.00	23.20	34.35	17.00
Titer (cm³)	12.00	11.20	11.15	11.50

Figuring it out
1. The closest results are 11.20 cm³ and 11.15 cm³
2. The mean of closest results (to two decimal points)

$$\frac{11.20 + 11.15}{2} = 11.18 \, cm^3$$

Answer
Mean titer = 11.18 cm³

2. The tap on the burette is turned, allowing acid to be added drop by drop.

3. Acid is added until the indicator changes color, showing the solution has been neutralized.

1. An accurate volume of alkali is added to the flask, along with a few drops of indicator.

Strong and Weak Acids

In chemistry, the words "strong" and "weak" have specific meanings. In water, acids ionize (break up) into hydrogen ions (H^+) and anions (negative ions). All of the molecules in strong acids ionize in water, while only a small number of the molecules in weak acids ionize in water.

Key Facts

✓ Strong acids completely ionize in water—all their molecules break into ions in water.

✓ Weak acids barely ionize at all in water—only a small number of their molecules break into ions in water.

✓ Strong acids have a lower pH than weak acids of the same concentration as they have more H^+ ions.

Comparing strong and weak acids

These flasks contain solutions of a strong acid and a weak acid that have the same concentration—the same amount of acid molecules compared to the amount of water. Universal indicator has been added to show the pHs.

This red color shows the pH of this solution is about 2.

This orange-yellow color indicates that the pH is about 4.

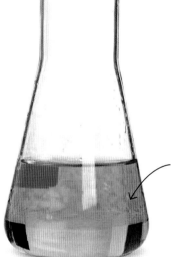

Strong acid　　　　　**Weak acid**

⚙ Ionization in Acids

In strong acids, the molecules ionize completely into H^+ ions and anions (negative ions). In weak acids, only some of the molecules ionize, so fewer H^+ ions are released into the solution.

All of the acid molecules ionize (break up) into H^+ ions and negatively charged ions.

H^+ ion

Negatively charged ion

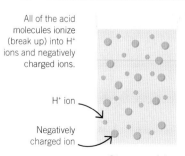
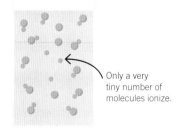

Only a very tiny number of molecules ionize.

Strong acid　　　　　**Weak acid**

Dilute and Concentrated Acids

A dilute acid solution has a low ratio of acid molecules to water, while a concentrated solution has a higher ratio of acid to water. Remember that "strong" and "weak" relate to the level of ionization of acids in water (see page 137), and "dilute" and "concentrated" relate to the amount of acid dissolved in the solution.

Key Facts

✓ A dilute acid has a low ratio of acid molecules to water.

✓ A concentrated acid has a higher ratio of acid to water.

✓ "Strong" and "weak" refer to how ionized an acid is in water, and "dilute" and "concentrated" refer to the amount of acid a solution contains.

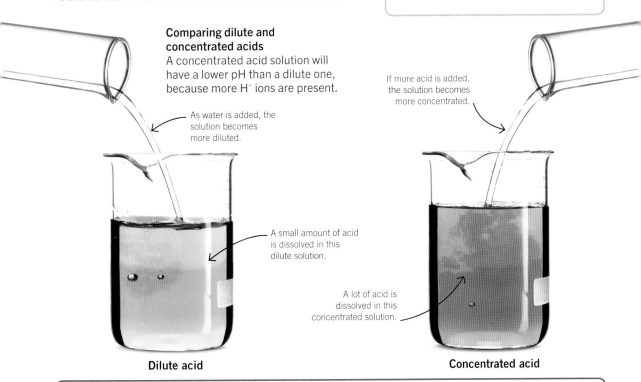

Comparing dilute and concentrated acids
A concentrated acid solution will have a lower pH than a dilute one, because more H⁺ ions are present.

As water is added, the solution becomes more diluted.

If more acid is added, the solution becomes more concentrated.

A small amount of acid is dissolved in this dilute solution.

A lot of acid is dissolved in this concentrated solution.

Dilute acid

Concentrated acid

🔍 How Concentration Works

It is possible to have both a concentrated and dilute solution of a weak acid. Likewise, concentrated and dilute solutions of strong acids are possible. The hazardousness of an acid depends on both its concentration and strength.

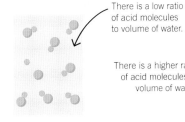

There is a low ratio of acid molecules to volume of water.

There is a higher ratio of acid molecules to volume of water.

Dilute solution of a weak acid

Concentrated solution of a weak acid

Reactions with Bases

Acids react with bases to produce a salt and water. There are several different kinds of base, including metal hydroxides, metal oxides, and metal carbonates. In each case, the salt produced forms from the metal ion in the base and the negative ion in the acid.

Key Facts

✓ Metal oxides and metal hydroxides react with acids to form a salt and water.

✓ These are neutralization reactions.

✓ We can predict the salt that will form from the acid and the metal ion present in the base.

Acids and metal oxides

| acid | + | metal oxide | ⟶ | salt | + water |

| hydrochloric acid | + | sodium oxide | ⟶ | sodium chloride | + | water |
| $2HCl$ | + | Na_2O | ⟶ | $2NaCl$ | + | H_2O |

| sulfuric acid | + | copper(II) oxide | ⟶ | copper(II) sulfate | + | water |
| H_2SO_4 | + | CuO | ⟶ | $CuSO_4$ | + | H_2O |

Acids and metal hydroxides

| acid | + metal hydroxide | ⟶ | salt | + water |

| hydrochloric acid | + | sodium hydroxide | ⟶ | sodium chloride | + | water |
| HCl | + | $NaOH$ | ⟶ | $NaCl$ | + | H_2O |

| sulfuric acid | + | calcium hydroxide | ⟶ | calcium sulfate | + | water |
| H_2SO_4 | + | $Ca(OH)_2$ | ⟶ | $CaSO_4$ | + | $2H_2O$ |

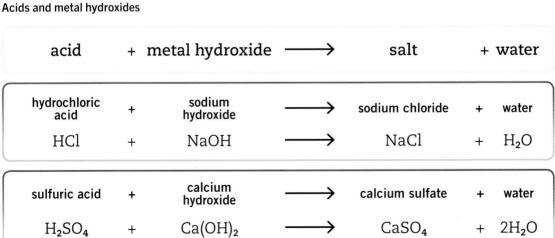

Reactions with Metal Carbonates

Acids react with metal carbonates to form a salt, water, and carbon dioxide. This reaction between acids and metal carbonates is a neutralization reaction (see page 135).

(see page 135)

Key Facts

✓ Acids react with metal carbonates to form a salt, water, and carbon dioxide.

✓ This is a neutralization reaction.

✓ You can predict the salt that will form from the acid and the metal ion present in the carbonate.

Limestone and hydrochloric acid
Limestone is mostly calcium carbonate ($CaCO_3$), which reacts with hydrochloric acid to form carbon dioxide, water, and calcium chloride salt.

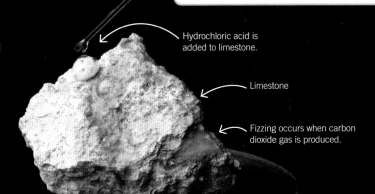

Hydrochloric acid is added to limestone.

Limestone

Fizzing occurs when carbon dioxide gas is produced.

⚙ Common Reactions

Metal carbonates react with acid to form a salt, water, and carbon dioxide. We can figure out which salt forms by looking at the acid and the metal ion in the metal carbonate. Some common examples are listed below:

| acid + metal carbonate | ⟶ | salt + water + carbon dioxide |

hydrochloric acid	+	sodium carbonate	⟶	sodium chloride	+	water	+	carbon dioxide
$2HCl$	+	Na_2CO_3	⟶	$2NaCl$	+	H_2O	+	CO_2

sulfuric acid	+	calcium carbonate	⟶	calcium sulfate	+	water	+	carbon dioxide
H_2SO_4	+	$CaCO_3$	⟶	$CaSO_4$	+	H_2O	+	CO_2

Making Insoluble Salts

An insoluble salt may form when two solutions containing soluble salts are mixed. In such cases, the insoluble salt (also known as the precipitate) can be separated by filtration. A pure sample of the salt then remains after the sample dries.

Making lead iodide
Lead iodide is a bright yellow compound that is insoluble in cold water. It can be made by mixing solutions of lead nitrate and potassium iodide, both of which are colorless and soluble.

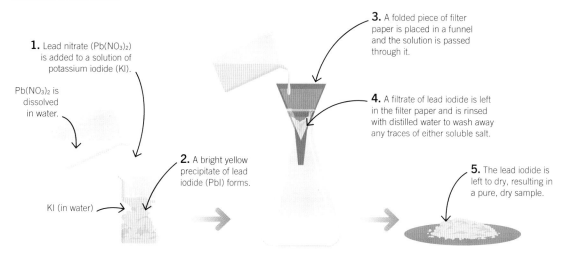

1. Lead nitrate ($Pb(NO_3)_2$) is added to a solution of potassium iodide (KI).

$Pb(NO_3)_2$ is dissolved in water.

KI (in water)

2. A bright yellow precipitate of lead iodide (PbI) forms.

3. A folded piece of filter paper is placed in a funnel and the solution is passed through it.

4. A filtrate of lead iodide is left in the filter paper and is rinsed with distilled water to wash away any traces of either soluble salt.

5. The lead iodide is left to dry, resulting in a pure, dry sample.

🔍 Reacting Potassium Iodide and Lead Nitrate

Potassium iodide and lead nitrate are both soluble. When their solutions are mixed, the reaction between them produces insoluble lead iodide and soluble potassium nitrate.

Lead iodide is solid and does not dissolve.

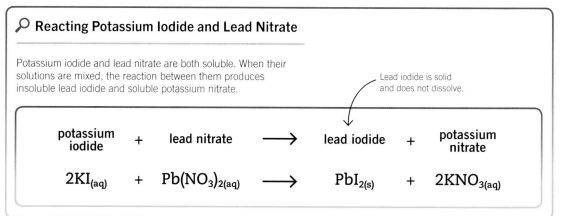

potassium iodide	+	lead nitrate	$\longrightarrow$	lead iodide	+	potassium nitrate
$2KI_{(aq)}$	+	$Pb(NO_3)_{2(aq)}$	$\longrightarrow$	$PbI_{2(s)}$	+	$2KNO_{3(aq)}$

Making Soluble Salts

An acid reacts with a base to form a salt and water, but unless you have precise quantities, the final product will contain traces of one of the reactants. You can get around this by using a more insoluble base than you need and filtering off the excess.

Making pure copper sulfate
Copper(II) sulfate is a soluble, bright blue salt. In this experiment it's prepared by reacting an excess of insoluble copper(II) oxide with a solution of sulfuric acid.

Key Facts

✓ To make a pure sample of a soluble salt, you can either use precise quantities of acid and alkali so they react completely, or an excess of an insoluble base.

✓ When using an insoluble base, the excess solid is filtered off to leave a pure solution of the soluble salt.

✓ Once the water has evaporated, pure salt crystals are left.

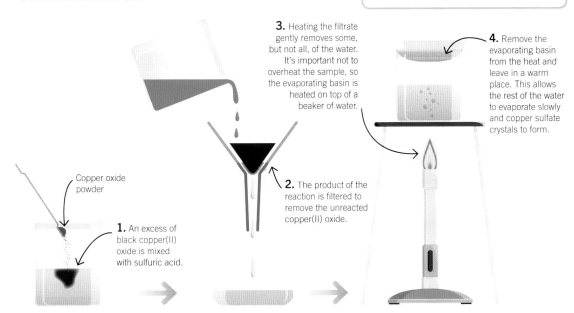

3. Heating the filtrate gently removes some, but not all, of the water. It's important not to overheat the sample, so the evaporating basin is heated on top of a beaker of water.

4. Remove the evaporating basin from the heat and leave in a warm place. This allows the rest of the water to evaporate slowly and copper sulfate crystals to form.

Copper oxide powder

2. The product of the reaction is filtered to remove the unreacted copper(II) oxide.

1. An excess of black copper(II) oxide is mixed with sulfuric acid.

Making a Salt from Copper(II) Oxide and Sulfuric Acid

The reaction between copper(II) oxide and sulfuric acid produces a soluble salt: copper(II) sulfate. An excess of copper(II) oxide is used to make sure all the acid reacts. Here's the equation for the above reaction.

copper(II) oxide	+	sulfuric acid	$\longrightarrow$	copper(II) sulfate	+	water
$CuO_{(s)}$	+	$H_2SO_{4(aq)}$	$\longrightarrow$	$CuSO_{4(aq)}$	+	$H_2O_{(l)}$

Metals and Their Reactivity

The Reactivity Series

A reactivity series is a list of elements (most of them are metals) in order of their reactivity, from most reactive at the top to least reactive at the bottom. Reactivity can mean how readily the element reacts with other substances, but in this list it describes how easily the element loses electrons.

List of elements
These elements are commonly listed in a reactivity series. A reactivity series can include all or just some of these elements.

Key Facts

✓ Some elements are more likely to chemically react than others.

✓ A reactivity series lists elements in order of how readily they lose electrons when they react.

✓ Elements that lose electrons easily are found at the top of reactivity series. Those that don't are at the bottom.

✓ These lists are usually made up of metals, but some nonmetals may be included.

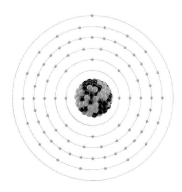

Potassium
Potassium is very reactive because its atoms easily lose their outermost electrons during reactions.

Gold
Gold isn't very reactive because its atoms don't easily lose their outermost electrons during reactions.

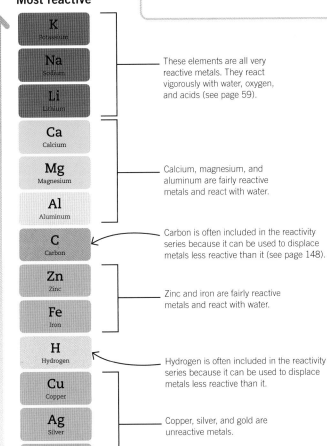

Most reactive

K
Potassium

Na
Sodium

Li
Lithium

These elements are all very reactive metals. They react vigorously with water, oxygen, and acids (see page 59).

Ca
Calcium

Mg
Magnesium

Al
Aluminum

Calcium, magnesium, and aluminum are fairly reactive metals and react with water.

C
Carbon

Carbon is often included in the reactivity series because it can be used to displace metals less reactive than it (see page 148).

Zn
Zinc

Fe
Iron

Zinc and iron are fairly reactive metals and react with water.

H
Hydrogen

Hydrogen is often included in the reactivity series because it can be used to displace metals less reactive than it.

Cu
Copper

Ag
Silver

Au
Gold

Copper, silver, and gold are unreactive metals.

Least reactive

Reactions with Acids

Some metals react vigorously with acids. Metals that react spontaneously with acids at room temperature are found at the top of the reactivity series (see opposite page). When metals react with acids, their atoms lose electrons. The most common products of this reaction are a solution of a metal salt and hydrogen gas.

Metals reacting with hydrochloric acid
Magnesium, zinc, iron, and lead all have different levels of reactivity. When placed in hydrochloric acid, magnesium reacts vigorously, but the lead barely reacts at all.

Only a few hydrogen gas bubbles are produced when an iron screw is placed in hydrochloric acid.

Lots of hydrogen gas bubbles are produced when magnesium reacts with hydrochloric acid.

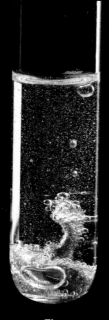

Magnesium　　　　**Zinc**　　　　**Iron**　　　　**Lead**

Equation
A reaction between a metal and an acid produces a salt and hydrogen gas.

$$\text{metal} + \text{acid} \longrightarrow \text{metal salt} + \text{hydrogen}$$

Reactions with Water

Most metals react slowly with water, if they react at all. However, Group 1 and Group 2 metals are exceptions. When placed in water at room temperature, they react vigorously, leaving behind a metal hydroxide (alkaline solution) and producing hydrogen gas. Some metals even react with water vapor (see opposite page).

Key Facts

✓ Group 1 and Group 2 metals are so reactive that they react spontaneously with water.

✓ When dropped in water, the metals fizz and dissolve.

✓ Group 1 and Group 2 metals react with water to produce a metal hydroxide and hydrogen gas.

Metals react with water
Potassium, sodium, and lithium (Group 1 metals) and calcium (a Group 2 metal) react vigorously with water.

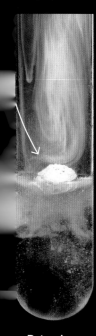

A lump of potassium fizzes loudly and even jumps.

Bubbles of hydrogen gas.

Lithium reacts with water to produce large bubbles of hydrogen gas.

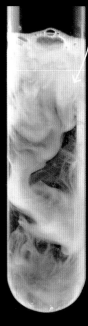

Calcium hydroxide forms as a cloudy precipitate in the solution.

Potassium **Sodium** **Lithium** **Calcium**

Equation
A reaction between a metal and water produces a metal hydroxide (alkaline solution) and hydrogen gas.

metal + water $\longrightarrow$ metal hydroxide + hydrogen

Reactions with Steam

Some metals will react with steam (water as a gas), also known as water vapor, at high temperatures. In these cases, the products are a metal oxide and hydrogen gas.

Key Facts

✓ Some metals won't react with liquid water, but will react with steam at high temperatures.

✓ In these cases, the products are a metal oxide and hydrogen.

Magnesium oxidized
A ribbon of magnesium burns in steam to produce magnesium oxide and hydrogen gas.

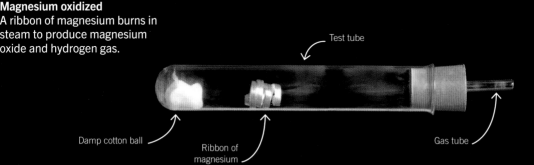

Test tube

Damp cotton ball

Ribbon of magnesium

Gas tube

1. The damp cotton ball is gently heated by a Bunsen burner flame to produce steam.

2. The ribbon of magnesium starts to react with steam and burn.

3. This produces hydrogen gas, which is burned off at the end of the test tube (see page 231).

4. Magnesium starts to react more vigorously, producing clouds of magnesium oxide.

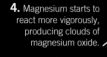

5. The flame at the end of the test tube grows as more hydrogen gas is released.

metal + water ⟶ metal oxide + hydrogen

Extracting Metals with Carbon

Metals that are less reactive than carbon (see page 144) can be extracted from their ores by using carbon. Copper and iron can both be produced in this way, although the sample is not very pure.

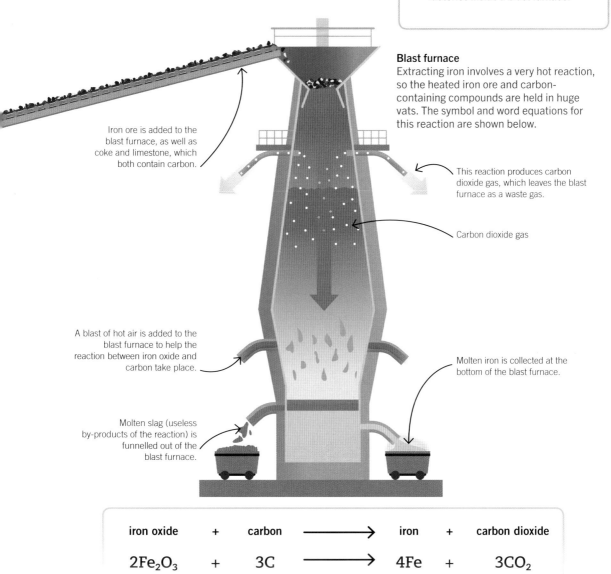

Blast furnace
Extracting iron involves a very hot reaction, so the heated iron ore and carbon-containing compounds are held in huge vats. The symbol and word equations for this reaction are shown below.

Iron ore is added to the blast furnace, as well as coke and limestone, which both contain carbon.

This reaction produces carbon dioxide gas, which leaves the blast furnace as a waste gas.

Carbon dioxide gas

A blast of hot air is added to the blast furnace to help the reaction between iron oxide and carbon take place.

Molten iron is collected at the bottom of the blast furnace.

Molten slag (useless by-products of the reaction) is funnelled out of the blast furnace.

iron oxide	+	carbon	$\longrightarrow$	iron	+	carbon dioxide
$2Fe_2O_3$	+	$3C$	$\longrightarrow$	$4Fe$	+	$3CO_2$

Redox Reactions

The word redox is derived from the words "reduction" and "oxidation." In redox reactions, electrons are transferred from one substance to another. One substance is reduced (gains electrons) while the other is oxidized (loses electrons). A thermite reaction (a reaction that involves heating metals) is an example of a redox reaction.

Thermite reaction
Powdered aluminum metal reacts with iron(III) oxide to form aluminum oxide and iron metal. In this case, the iron is reduced, while the aluminum is oxidized.

The aluminum sparks brightly during the reaction.

The metal tray contains the explosive reaction.

Thermite reaction formula equation

aluminum	+	iron oxide	$\longrightarrow$	aluminum oxide	+	iron
$2Al$	+	Fe_2O_3	$\longrightarrow$	Al_2O_3	+	$2Fe$

Group 7 Displacement Reactions

In a displacement reaction, a more reactive element displaces a less reactive element from its compound. Group 7 elements react in this way. Their reactivity decreases down the group (see page 70), so a higher element can displace those below it.

(see page 70)

Key Facts

✓ In a displacement reaction, a more reactive element displaces a less reactive element from its compound.

✓ The reactivity of Group 7 elements decreases down the group.

✓ Chlorine, for example, can displace both bromine and iodine from their compounds.

Chlorine displacement
Chlorine is more reactive than both bromine and iodine, so it'll displace both of them from their compounds with potassium.

Chlorine water added

Chlorine displaces bromine and the solution turns yellow.

Potassium bromide solution

Displacement of bromine

Chlorine water added

Chlorine displaces iodine and the solution turns brown.

Potassium iodide solution

Displacement of iodine

Bromine displacement
Bromine is more reactive than iodine, but less reactive than chlorine—so it'll only displace iodine from its compounds with potassium.

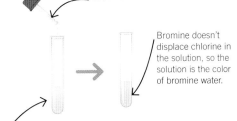

Bromine water added

Bromine doesn't displace chlorine in the solution, so the solution is the color of bromine water.

Potassium chloride solution

No displacement

Bromine water added

Bromine displaces iodine and the solution turns brown.

Potassium iodide solution

Displacement of iodine

Iodine displacement
Iodine is less reactive than chlorine or bromine, so won't displace either of them from their compounds with potassium.

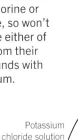 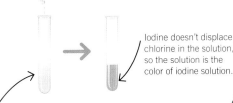 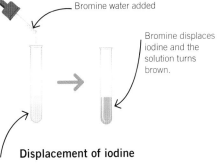

Iodine solution added

Iodine doesn't displace chlorine in the solution, so the solution is the color of iodine solution.

Potassium chloride solution

No displacement

Iodine solution added

Iodine doesn't displace bromine in the solution, so the solution is the color of iodine solution.

Potassium bromide solution

No displacement

Ionic Equations

Equations use symbols and formulas to show the changes that happen to substances during chemical reactions (see page 36). Ionic equations show us the number of ions (see page 73) involved, and their respective charges. The number of atoms (see page 37) and the charges must be balanced in an ionic equation.

Key Facts

✓ Ionic equations show the ions and their charges involved in an ionic chemical reaction.

✓ The ion's charge is shown as either a plus ($^+$) or minus ($^-$) symbol next to the elemental formula.

✓ The charges in an ionic equation must be balanced.

Ionic formula equation

Bromine forms when chlorine is added to potassium bromide solution (KBr). The formula equation for this is shown below, with the potassium bromide molecules split into ions. The overall charge on each side of the equation is neutral.

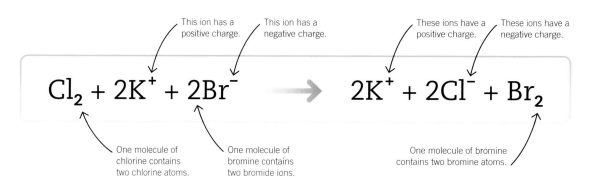

This ion has a positive charge.

This ion has a negative charge.

These ions have a positive charge.

These ions have a negative charge.

$$Cl_2 + 2K^+ + 2Br^- \longrightarrow 2K^+ + 2Cl^- + Br_2$$

One molecule of chlorine contains two chlorine atoms.

One molecule of bromine contains two bromide ions.

One molecule of bromine contains two bromine atoms.

Dot and cross diagrams

The ions in this equation can be drawn as dot and cross diagrams (see pages 76–77).

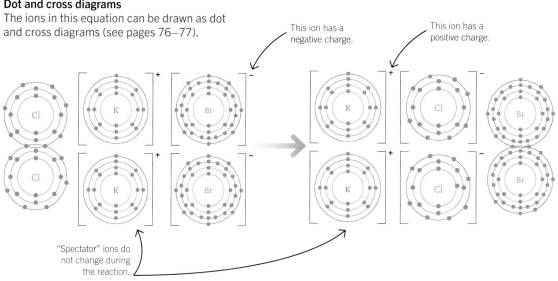

This ion has a negative charge.

This ion has a positive charge.

"Spectator" ions do not change during the reaction.

Metal Displacement Reactions

In a displacement reaction between metals, a more reactive metal can displace a less reactive metal from its compound (see page 144). The thermite reaction (see page 149) is one example of this kind of reaction.

Key Facts

✓ Metals and metal compounds can undergo displacement reactions.

✓ A more reactive metal can displace a less reactive metal from its compound.

✓ Thermite reactions and the displacement of iron inside a blast furnace are examples of displacement reactions.

Displacement of copper

Copper is a fairly unreactive metal, and forms a bright blue solution with sulfate ions called copper sulfate. If a more reactive metal, such as each of these ribbons of magnesium, aluminum, and zinc, are added to separate samples of copper sulfate, the copper is displaced from the solution. The more reactive metal dissolves in the clear solution that is left behind.

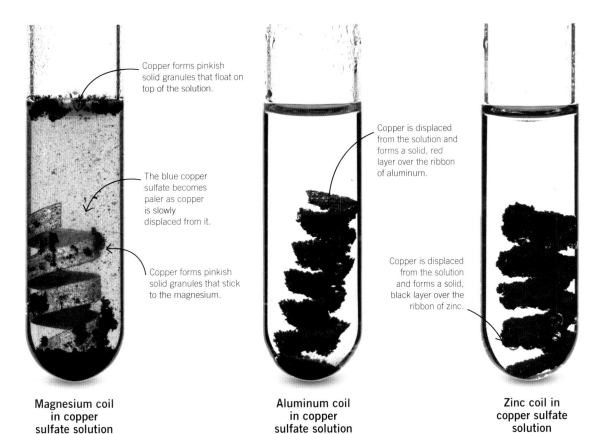

Copper forms pinkish solid granules that float on top of the solution.

The blue copper sulfate becomes paler as copper is slowly displaced from it.

Copper forms pinkish solid granules that stick to the magnesium.

Copper is displaced from the solution and forms a solid, red layer over the ribbon of aluminum.

Copper is displaced from the solution and forms a solid, black layer over the ribbon of zinc.

Magnesium coil in copper sulfate solution

Aluminum coil in copper sulfate solution

Zinc coil in copper sulfate solution

Electrolysis

Electrolysis is the use of an electric current to split compounds into elements. In industry, electrolysis is used to produce pure metals. Ions (see page 73) must be free to move for electrolysis to work, so the ion-bearing substance must be either molten or dissolved in a solution. The molten substance or dissolved solution is called the electrolyte.

Key Facts

✓ Electrolysis is the use of electricity to split up compounds.

✓ Electrolysis is used in industry to produce pure metals.

✓ The substance must either be molten or dissolved to undergo electrolysis.

Equipment for electrolysis

Electrolysis needs a power source, such as a battery. This is connected to two electrodes that are placed in the electrolyte.

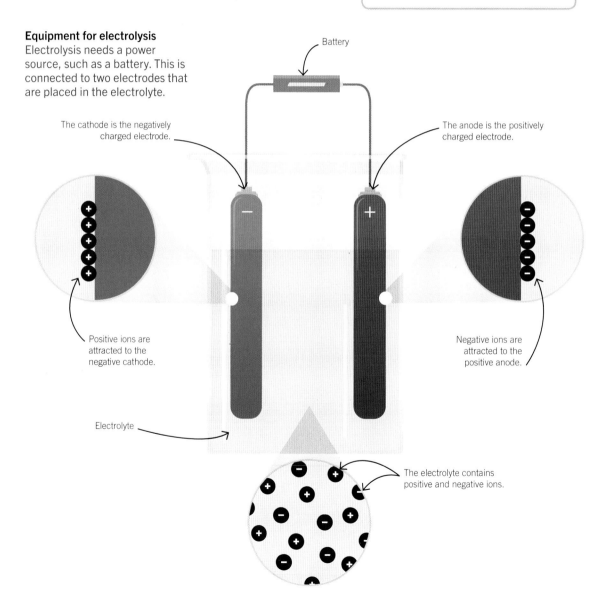

Battery

The cathode is the negatively charged electrode.

The anode is the positively charged electrode.

Positive ions are attracted to the negative cathode.

Negative ions are attracted to the positive anode.

Electrolyte

The electrolyte contains positive and negative ions.

Extracting Metals with Electrolysis

Electrolysis is used to separate pure metals out of compounds that contain metals. For this to work, the ions in the compound have to be free to move, so the ore must be molten. Metals produced by electrolysis are pure.

Key Facts

✓ Electrolysis can be used to separate metals from their ores (metal compounds).

✓ The metal ore must be molten so its ions are free to move.

✓ Metals produced by electrolysis are pure.

Separating lead using electrolysis

In the lab, lead bromide can be separated into lead and bromine by electrolysis using a power supply, electrodes, a crucible, and a Bunsen burner.

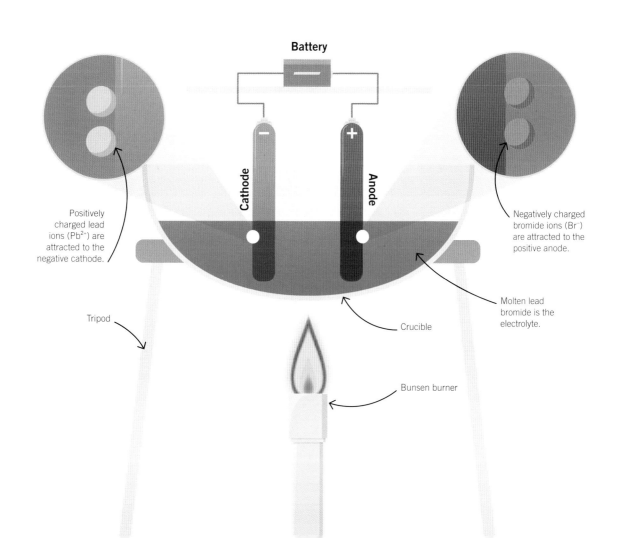

Battery

Cathode

Anode

Positively charged lead ions (Pb^{2+}) are attracted to the negative cathode.

Negatively charged bromide ions (Br^-) are attracted to the positive anode.

Molten lead bromide is the electrolyte.

Tripod

Crucible

Bunsen burner

Half Equations

During electrolysis (see page 153), electrons are lost at the anode (positive electrode) and electrons are gained at the cathode (negative electrode). We can write half equations for what happens at the anode and the cathode. Two half equations can be combined to make an ionic equation, and they also include electrons.

Key Facts

✓ Half equations can be used to describe what happens at each electrode during electrolysis.

✓ Half equations include electrons.

✓ Two half equations can be combined to form an ionic equation.

Ionic equation
Electrolysis of lead bromide can be shown as the following ionic equation.

$$Pb^{2+} + 2Br^- \longrightarrow Pb + Br_2$$

At the anode
At the anode, each bromide ion loses one electron to form bromine.

Anode

$$2Br^- \longrightarrow Br_2 + 2e^-$$

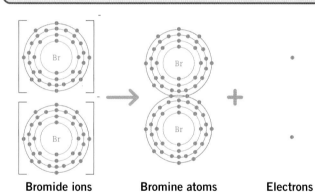

Bromide ions   Bromine atoms   Electrons

At the cathode
At the cathode, each lead ion gains two electrons to form lead.

Cathode

$$Pb^{2+} + 2e^- \longrightarrow Pb$$

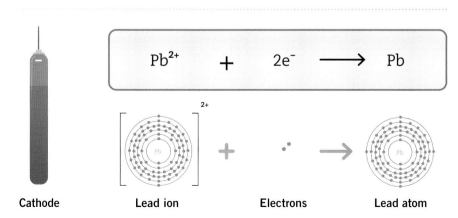

Lead ion   Electrons   Lead atom

Extracting Aluminum in Industry

Aluminum ore is called bauxite (contains aluminum oxide, Al_2O_3). Because aluminum is more reactive than carbon, it can't be separated from oxygen in the same way as iron (see page 148). Instead, electrolysis is used.

Industrial electrolysis

In factories, electrolysis of metal ores is performed in a large steel tank that can withstand high temperatures. Bauxite is mixed with a substance called cryolite to create a mixture with a lower melting point, allowing electrolysis to be performed.

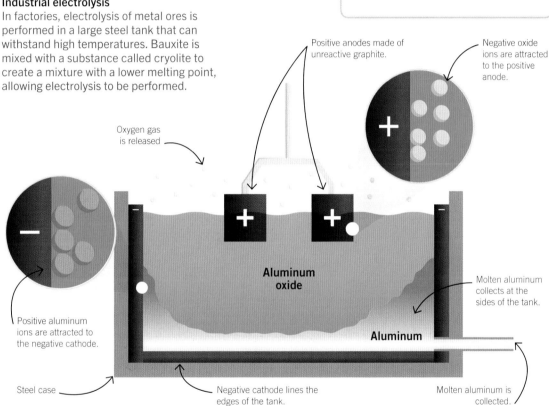

Positive anodes made of unreactive graphite.

Negative oxide ions are attracted to the positive anode.

Oxygen gas is released

Aluminum oxide

Molten aluminum collects at the sides of the tank.

Positive aluminum ions are attracted to the negative cathode.

Aluminum

Steel case

Negative cathode lines the edges of the tank.

Molten aluminum is collected.

Uses of Aluminum

Pure aluminum is a very useful substance. It's used to make planes because it's not very dense, and its protective oxide layer (see page 264) prevents aluminum foil from reacting with chemicals in food.

Planes

Foil

Electrolysis of Water

In water (H_2O), a tiny number of molecules break up into H^+ and OH^- ions. Because of this, electrolysis can be used to split water into hydrogen gas (H_2) and oxygen gas (O_2). Historically, this experiment was used to prove that water is a compound and not a single element, and that its formula is H_2O.

Key Facts

✓ Electrolysis breaks water up into H^+ and OH^- ions.

✓ Electrolysis can be used to split water into hydrogen gas (H_2) and oxygen gas (O_2).

Separating water in the laboratory
By using a battery and inert (unreactive) electrodes, electrolysis can be performed in the laboratory to separate water molecules.

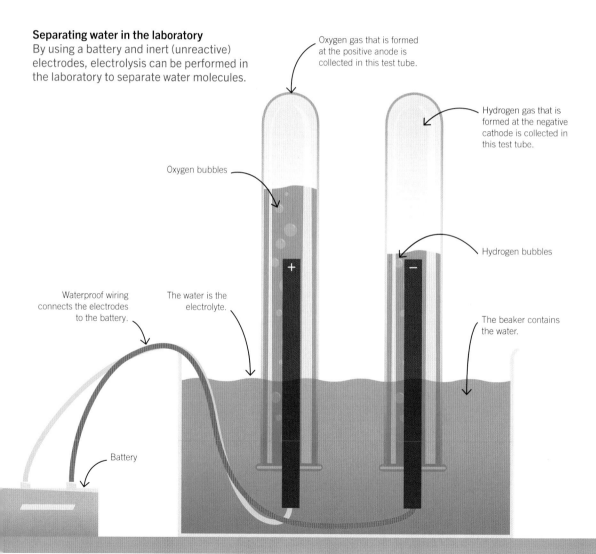

Oxygen gas that is formed at the positive anode is collected in this test tube.

Hydrogen gas that is formed at the negative cathode is collected in this test tube.

Oxygen bubbles

Hydrogen bubbles

Waterproof wiring connects the electrodes to the battery.

The water is the electrolyte.

The beaker contains the water.

Battery

Electrolysis Experiments

Electrolysis can be performed in the laboratory using an electrochemical cell. You should make a hypothesis (see page 10) predicting what will be produced at the anode or the cathode, depending on what electrolyte you choose to test. You may also need to draw the experiment (see page 174).

Electrolysis of water
You need an electrochemical cell (battery, anode, and cathode), test tubes, and a beaker to perform electrolysis to separate oxygen and hydrogen in water. After, tests can be conducted to confirm their presence in the test tubes (see pages 229 and 231).

🔍 Predicting What Happens

When a pure, molten substance is used as the electrolyte, a metal will form at the cathode and a metal at the cathode. However, electrolysis of salts will produce many products at the anode and cathode.

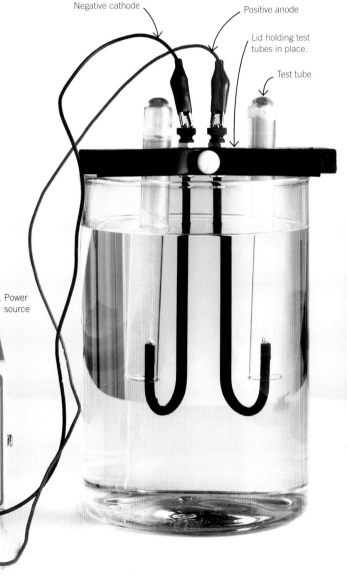

Negative cathode

Positive anode

Lid holding test tubes in place.

Test tube

Power source

DC
V

Voltage

Power

Output
1.5V - 15V DC
— 1.5A +

Electrolysis of Aqueous Solutions

Electrolysis can separate a substance if it is dissolved in water (an aqueous solution). Here, hydrogen ions (H^+) and hydroxide ions (OH^-) are attracted to each electrode (see page 157), as well as other elements.

Key Facts

✓ Electrolysis works with substances dissolved in water (aqueous solutions).

✓ Aqueous solutions contain hydrogen and hydroxide ions, as well as ions from the dissolved substance.

✓ Oxygen may discharge at the anode and/or hydrogen at the cathode.

Examples of electrolysis
These solutions can be separated using electrolysis in industry.

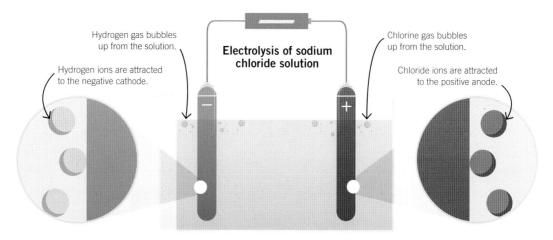

Hydrogen gas bubbles up from the solution.

Hydrogen ions are attracted to the negative cathode.

Electrolysis of sodium chloride solution

Chlorine gas bubbles up from the solution.

Chloride ions are attracted to the positive anode.

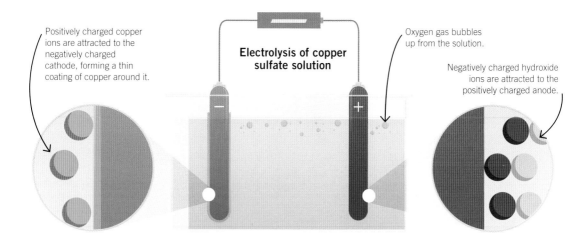

Positively charged copper ions are attracted to the negatively charged cathode, forming a thin coating of copper around it.

Electrolysis of copper sulfate solution

Oxygen gas bubbles up from the solution.

Negatively charged hydroxide ions are attracted to the positively charged anode.

Electroplating

Electroplating uses electrolysis (see page 153) to coat items with a layer of metal. This is done to change its appearance or to protect it from rust (see page 264). For example, utensils made out of (inexpensive) nickel alloys can be plated with silver. Silver looks more appealing and is less reactive, so the cutlery lasts longer.

📌 **Key Facts**

✓ **Electroplating is used to coat items with a layer of metal.**

✓ **Electroplating changes a metal's appearance and protects it.**

✓ **A common example is plating items made from nickel alloys with a layer of silver.**

Silver-plated spoons
Electrolysis can be performed to coat spoons with a layer of silver.

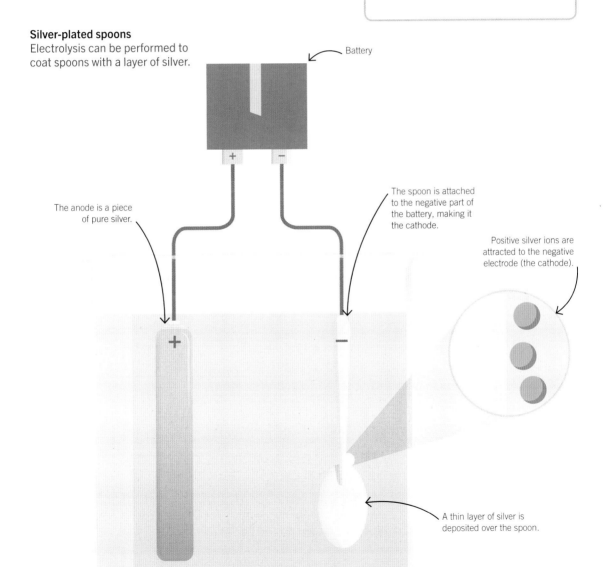

Battery

The anode is a piece of pure silver.

The spoon is attached to the negative part of the battery, making it the cathode.

Positive silver ions are attracted to the negative electrode (the cathode).

A thin layer of silver is deposited over the spoon.

Energy Changes

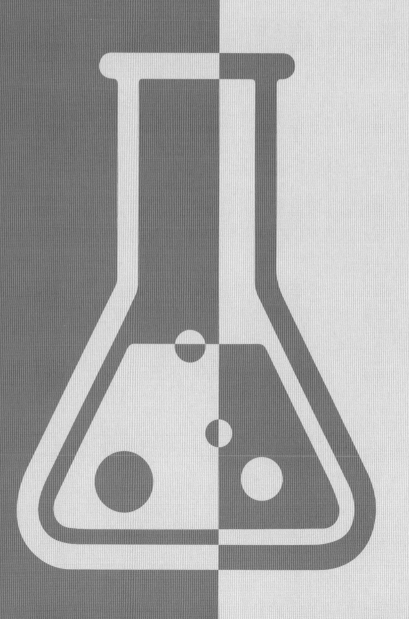

Chemical Reactions

Chemical reactions involve changes in energy. The starting substances in chemical reactions are called reactants. They react to form new substances called products. In many reactions, two reactants make one or two different products. However, some reactions involve just one reactant, while others may make three or more different products.

Changes in reactions

Chemical reactions have these features in common.

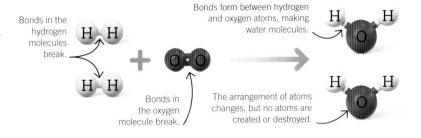

Gases or solids may be formed during the reaction.

Mass is conserved —the total mass before and after the reaction is the same.

The temperature of the reaction mixture may go up or down.

The color of the reaction mixture may change.

Key Facts

✓ **Atoms are only rearranged in reactions, so the total mass stays the same.**

✓ **Energy is transferred to or from the surroundings.**

✓ **The energy change in the reaction mixture is equal and opposite to the energy change in the surroundings.**

✓ **Evidence for reactions includes temperature changes, color changes, gases produced, or solids being formed.**

⚙ How Chemical Reactions Work

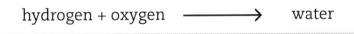

hydrogen + oxygen ⟶ water

In a chemical reaction, bonds between atoms in the reactants break. Atoms are not created or destroyed but new bonds form, making products with atoms arranged differently. For example, hydrogen reacts with oxygen to make water.

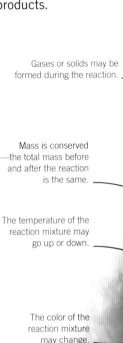

Bonds in the hydrogen molecules break.

Bonds in the oxygen molecule break.

Bonds form between hydrogen and oxygen atoms, making water molecules.

The arrangement of atoms changes, but no atoms are created or destroyed.

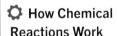

Combustion

Combustion is a rapid chemical reaction between a fuel and oxygen that gives out energy as heat and light. These reactions can be described as "burning." Heat is usually needed to start combustion reactions and they stop if cooled rapidly, or when the oxygen or fuel runs out.

Burning sugar
The gas used in a Bunsen burner is mostly methane, which reacts with oxygen in the air. A flame or spark is needed to start the reaction, but after that the burning continues until the gas is turned off, stopping the supply of fuel.

The yellow flame indicates that carbon particles (soot) are present.

The air hole on the Bunsen burner is closed, meaning less oxygen is available, but there's still enough for combustion to occur.

 Key Facts

✓ Combustion occurs when a fuel reacts rapidly with oxygen, producing heat and light.

✓ Combustion is often described as burning.

✓ Combustion requires a fuel and oxygen. Heat is usually needed to start combustion reactions.

⚙ The Fire Triangle

The fire triangle on the right shows the three things needed to start a fire and keep it going. If one side is missing, a fire goes out. This concept is used in firefighting, and different fires can be put out in different ways.

Covering a fire with sand, carbon dioxide, or a fire blanket stops oxygen in the air from getting to the fuel.

Removing the fuel works but can be difficult. If there's a gas supply it can be turned off, and in forest fires, a section of trees can be cleared to make a firebreak.

Water is very good at absorbing heat. It's used to put simple house fires or bonfires out.

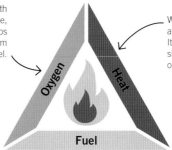

Oxygen

Heat

Fuel

Oxidation

Oxygen is very reactive and combines with many metals and nonmetals to form compounds called oxides. When a substance gains oxygen, scientists call the reaction oxidation. More generally, oxidation refers to the loss of electrons (see page 149). Combustion (see page 163) is an example of an oxidation reaction.

Burning magnesium

Magnesium reacts strongly with oxygen in the air to form magnesium oxide. A bright, white flame is produced in this combustion reaction, which is useful in emergency flares, photographic flash bulbs, and fireworks.

(see page 149)
(see page 163)

A brilliant white light is produced as magnesium reacts vigorously with oxygen in the air.

White magnesium oxide is formed.

Key Facts

✓ Oxidation is a reaction in which a substance gains oxygen and generally loses electrons.

✓ Metals and nonmetals can react with oxygen to form oxides.

✓ Oxidation occurs when substances burn (during combustion).

⚙ Metal Oxides and Nonmetal Oxides

Metals, such as magnesium, react with oxygen to form metal oxides.

$$\text{magnesium} + \text{oxygen} \longrightarrow \text{magnesium oxide}$$

$$2Mg + O_2 \longrightarrow 2MgO$$

Nonmetals can also react with oxygen. These reactions produce nonmetal oxides. For example, carbon will react with oxygen to form carbon dioxide.

$$\text{carbon} + \text{oxygen} \longrightarrow \text{carbon dioxide}$$

$$C + O_2 \longrightarrow CO_2$$

Thermal Decomposition

Some substances chemically decompose (break down) when they're heated. This is called thermal decomposition, which is an endothermic process (see page 167) as constant heat is required.

Heating copper(II) carbonate
Copper(II) carbonate ($CuCO_3$) is a bright green solid. When it's heated, it thermally decomposes to form carbon dioxide gas and copper(II) oxide, which is a black solid.

Black copper(II) oxide, a solid, forms in the test tube.

Limewater (calcium hydroxide solution) turns milky in the presence of carbon dioxide.

Key Facts

✓ Thermal decomposition occurs when a single substance breaks down into two or more products as it's heated.

✓ Metal carbonates commonly undergo thermal decomposition reactions.

✓ Thermal decomposition is endothermic (it absorbs heat from the surroundings).

⚙ The Thermal Decomposition of Metal Carbonates

Some metal carbonates, such as copper (II) carbonate, decompose when heated to form a metal oxide and carbon dioxide.

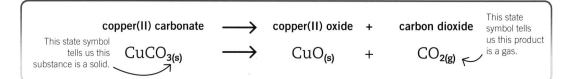

$$\text{metal carbonate} \longrightarrow \text{metal oxide} + \text{carbon dioxide}$$

copper(II) carbonate $\longrightarrow$ copper(II) oxide + carbon dioxide

This state symbol tells us this substance is a solid.

$$CuCO_{3(s)} \longrightarrow CuO_{(s)} + CO_{2(g)}$$

This state symbol tells us this product is a gas.

Exothermic Reactions

Reactions can be exothermic or endothermic. In an exothermic reaction, energy is transferred from the reacting substances to the surroundings. This usually happens as heat escaping, so the temperature of the surroundings increases. The combustion of a fuel is a good example of an exothermic reaction.

Combustion

Explosions are combustion reactions (see page 163) which occur when burning substances react rapidly with oxygen. They happen at high temperatures and transfer energy to the surroundings as sound, heat, and light.

(see page 163)

Flames can be seen during combusrion reactions.

The explosion is very bright because energy is transferred to the surroundings in the form of light.

Key Facts

✓ Common exothermic reactions are combustion, neutralization, and displacement reactions.

✓ Exothermic reactions transfer energy to the surroundings.

✓ Energy is transferred mostly via heat.

✓ Heating increases the temperature of the surroundings.

⚙ How Exothermic Reactions Work

Exothermic reactions transfer the energy stored in chemical bonds to the surroundings. Here, potassium reacts with water to produce potassium hydroxide and hydrogen gas.

1. Potassium is added to water and produces potassium hydroxide and hydrogen gas.

2. Increased heating occurs, causing the hydrogen to ignite with a lilac flame.

3. The hot metal gives off sparks and disappears with a small explosion at the end of the reaction.

Endothermic Reactions

In an endothermic reaction, energy is transferred from the surroundings to the reacting substances. For reactions in solutions, this causes the temperature of the solution to decrease. Reactions can be exothermic or endothermic, but fewer reactions are endothermic. Photosynthesis, thermal decomposition reactions, and electrolysis are endothermic reactions.

Sodium bicarbonate

The reaction between sodium hydrogen carbonate (sodium bicarbonate) and a dilute acid, in this case citric acid solution, is an endothermic reaction.

Sodium hydrogen carbonate powder is added to the solution.

Bubbles of carbon dioxide are given off during the reaction.

A dilute acid, such as citric acid, is added to the sodium hydrogen carbonate.

The temperature of the reaction mixture goes down.

Key Facts

✓ In endothermic reactions, energy is transferred from the surroundings to the reactants.

✓ Endothermic reactions only continue while energy is supplied.

✓ The temperature of the reaction mixtures in the solution decreases.

✓ Thermal decomposition, melting ice, and electrolysis are endothermic reactions.

⚙ How Endothermic Reactions Work

Dissolving can be an exothermic or endothermic process, depending on what is being dissolved. The dissolving of ammonium chloride in water is an endothermic process and is used in cold packs.

2. When the pack is squeezed, the compartments break and the two substances mix together.

1. The ammonium chloride and water are in separate compartments in the cold pack.

3. As the two substances react, the mixture quickly becomes cold.

Energy Transfer: Solutions

Exothermic reactions in solution cause the temperature of a reaction mixture to increase. Endothermic reactions in solution cause the temperature to decrease. You can tell whether a reaction is exothermic or endothermic by measuring the temperature change—this is called calorimetry. Neutralization reactions (see page 135) are typically exothermic.

Energy transfer in a neutralization reaction
You can investigate energy transfer by observing the reaction of hydrochloric acid and sodium hydroxide and monitoring the temperature. See the box on the right for how these results can be used to figure out the energy transferred.

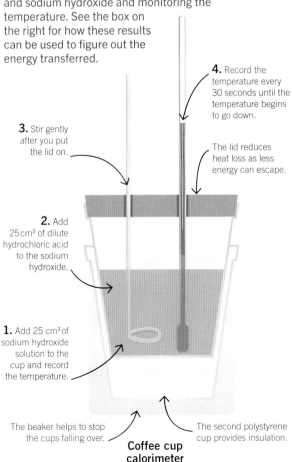

4. Record the temperature every 30 seconds until the temperature begins to go down.

3. Stir gently after you put the lid on.

The lid reduces heat loss as less energy can escape.

2. Add 25 cm³ of dilute hydrochloric acid to the sodium hydroxide.

1. Add 25 cm³ of sodium hydroxide solution to the cup and record the temperature.

The beaker helps to stop the cups falling over.

The second polystyrene cup provides insulation.

Coffee cup calorimeter

Key Facts

✓ In an exothermic reaction, the temperature of the solution goes up.

✓ In an endothermic reaction, the temperature of the solution goes down.

✓ The energy transfer can be measured— this is called calorimetry.

✓ Energy is lost to the surroundings, so the reaction mixture is well insulated.

An Example

Question
25 cm³ of hydrochloric acid reacts with 25 cm³ of sodium hydroxide solution. The temperature increases by 20°C. Calculate the energy change. (c = 4.2 J/g/°C)

Method
1. Calculate the mass of water. 1 cm³ = 1 g so total volume = 25 cm³ + 25 cm³ = 50 cm³
Mass = 50 g

2. Use the equation below to calculate the energy change. The specific heat capacity is the heat energy needed to raise the temperature of 1 g of water by 1°C.

$$Q = mc\Delta T$$

Q   = energy change (J)
m   = mass of water (g)
c   = specific heat capacity of water
ΔT   = temperature change (°C)

Q = mcΔT
     = 50 × 4.2 × 20
     = 4,200 J

3. As the temperature has increased, the reaction is exothermic (so Q will be negative).

Answer
The energy change for the reaction = −4,200 J

Energy Transfer: Combustion

All combustion reactions are exothermic (see page 166). They transfer energy to the surroundings, mainly by heating. You can use a spirit burner to heat a container of water and figure out the energy transferred to the water.

Energy transfer in a combustion reaction

You can investigate energy transfer by burning fuel to heat water and looking at the mass of fuel burned against the temperature increase. See the example box on the right for how these results can be used to figure out the energy change.

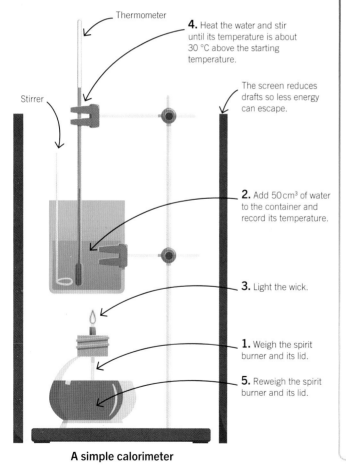

Thermometer

4. Heat the water and stir until its temperature is about 30 °C above the starting temperature.

The screen reduces drafts so less energy can escape.

Stirrer

2. Add 50 cm³ of water to the container and record its temperature.

3. Light the wick.

1. Weigh the spirit burner and its lid.

5. Reweigh the spirit burner and its lid.

A simple calorimeter

Key Facts

✓ Energy transfer can be measured by burning fuel to heat water and measuring the temperature change.

✓ Measuring the energy transferred to water by heating is called calorimetry.

✓ Energy transfer can be calculated if you know the mass of fuel used and the resulting increase in temperature.

An Example

Question

0.59 g of a fuel is burned, increasing the temperature of 50 cm³ of water by 31°C. Calculate the energy change in kJ/g of fuel used. (c = 4.2 J/g/°C)

Method

1. Calculate the mass of water.
1 cm³ = 1 g so mass = 50 cm³ = 50 g

2. Use the equation below to calculate the energy change in J.

$$Q = mc\Delta T$$

Q = energy change (J)
m = mass of water (g)
c = specific heat capacity of water
ΔT = temperature change (°C)

Q = 50 × 4.2 × 31 = 6,510 J

3. Convert J to kJ.
6,510 J = 6,510/1,000 = 6.51 kJ

4. Divide kJ by the mass of fuel used to find the energy change in kJ/g.
6.51 kJ /0.59 g = 11 kJ/g

Answer

The energy change = 11 kJ/g

Exothermic Reaction Profiles

Bond forming is an exothermic process because it releases energy. Bond breaking is an endothermic process because it needs energy. When bonds form in products during exothermic reactions, more energy is released than what is needed to break bonds in the reactants.

A reaction profile for an exothermic reaction
The energy level of the reactants is higher than that of the products. Energy is given out to the surroundings over the course of the reaction.

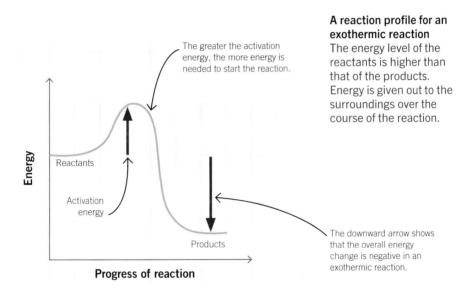

The greater the activation energy, the more energy is needed to start the reaction.

The downward arrow shows that the overall energy change is negative in an exothermic reaction.

⚙ How Bond Forming Works

Energy is given out when chemical bonds form. Depending on the substances involved, these may be metallic bonds, ionic bonds (see page 74), or covalent bonds (as shown in this diagram).

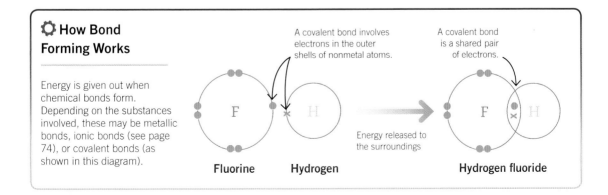

A covalent bond involves electrons in the outer shells of nonmetal atoms.

A covalent bond is a shared pair of electrons.

Energy released to the surroundings

Endothermic Reaction Profiles

Bond breaking is an endothermic process because it needs energy. Bond forming is an exothermic process because it releases energy. In endothermic reactions, more energy is needed to break bonds in the reactants than is released when bonds form in the products.

Key Facts

✓ In endothermic reactions, the energy level of the products is higher than the reactants.

✓ Activation energy is shown by an upward arrow that goes higher than the products.

✓ Overall energy change is shown by an upward arrow.

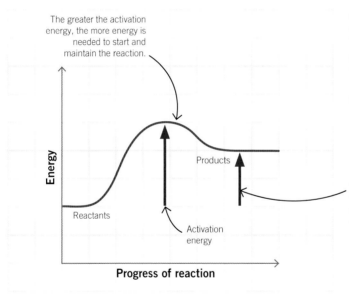

The greater the activation energy, the more energy is needed to start and maintain the reaction.

Products

Reactants

Activation energy

Energy

Progress of reaction

A reaction profile for an endothermic reaction
The energy level of the products is higher than the reactants. Energy is taken in from the surroundings during the reaction.

This upward arrow shows that the overall energy change is positive in an endothermic reaction.

⚙ How Bond Breaking Works

Energy is needed to break chemical bonds. Depending on the substances involved, these may be metallic bonds, ionic bonds (see page 74), or covalent bonds (as shown in the diagram).

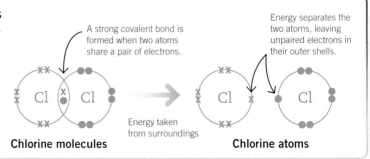

A strong covalent bond is formed when two atoms share a pair of electrons.

Energy separates the two atoms, leaving unpaired electrons in their outer shells.

Cl   Cl

Energy taken from surroundings

Cl   Cl

Chlorine molecules   Chlorine atoms

Calculating Energy Changes

Energy is needed to break bonds and is released when bonds form. The amount of energy involved is called the bond energy. You can calculate the energy change involved in a reaction using the bond energies of the bonds in the reactants and products.

Bond energies
Bond energies are measured in kilojoules per mole of bonds broken. The greater the bond energy, the stronger the bond.

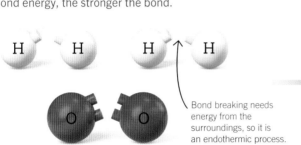

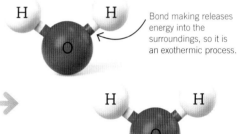

Bond making releases energy into the surroundings, so it is an exothermic process.

Bond breaking needs energy from the surroundings, so it is an endothermic process.

Reactants

Product

⚙ The Energy Change of a Reaction

> **energy change = bond energies of reactants – bond energies of products**

Question
Using the equation above and information in the table on the right, what is the energy change when hydrogen reacts with chlorine?

Bond	Bond energy (kj/mol)
H–H	436
Cl–Cl	242
H–Cl	431

Figuring it out
1. Balanced equation: $H_2 + Cl_2 \longrightarrow 2HCl$
2. Showing all bonds: H–H + Cl–Cl $\longrightarrow$ 2(H–Cl)
3. Bond energies of reactants: 436 + 242 = 678 kJ/mol
4. Bond energies of products: 2 × 431 = 862 kJ/mol
5. Energy change = 678 – 862 = -184 kJ/mol

Answer
The energy change is –184 kJ/mol.
The energy change has a negative value.
This shows that the reaction is exothermic.

Simple Voltaic Cells

A chemical cell contains chemicals that react to generate electricity. A simple voltaic cell can be made by pressing two pieces of metal with different reactivities (see page 144) into a lemon, and connected to a voltmeter. Electron transfer during the different chemical reactions generates a potential difference, also known as a voltage.

Simple cells

A simple voltaic (also known as "galvanic") cell can be made by connecting two different metals (electrodes), in contact with a source of electrolyte, to a high-resistance voltmeter. One of the metals used must be more reactive than the other.

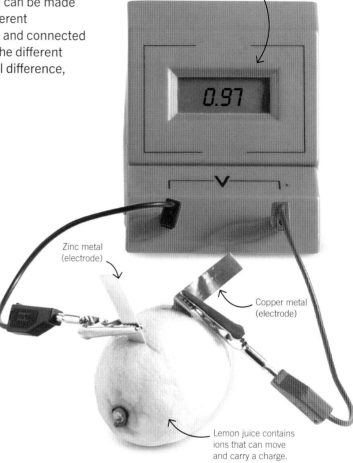

The voltmeter measures and displays the potential difference (voltage).

0.97

Zinc metal (electrode)

Copper metal (electrode)

Lemon juice contains ions that can move and carry a charge.

Key Facts

✓ **A voltage can be produced from two pieces of metal with different reactivities and a piece of fruit.**

✓ **The metals act as electrodes and the fruit juice acts as an electrolyte (a liquid containing charged particles).**

✓ **The different chemical reactions result in a potential difference, otherwise known as a voltage.**

Electrolytes

An electrolyte is a liquid containing ions that can carry an electrical charge. Juices of fruits and vegetables can act as electrolytes.

Citrus fruits
Oranges, lemons, and grapefruits contain citric acid, a source of hydrogen ions.

Potatoes
These contain phosphoric acid, which can act as an electrolyte.

Liquids
Dilute solutions of salts or acids, such as vinegar, work well as an electrolyte.

Voltaic Cells

It's not practical to use fruit and vegetables to generate a voltage (see page 173), so you can set up a simple voltaic cell using specific chemicals and electrodes. A simple voltaic cell consists of two electrodes in electrolyte solutions (commonly salts of the same metal), wires, a voltmeter, and a salt bridge.

Key Facts

✓ **A simple voltaic cell can be made by placing two pieces of metal of different reactivities into electrolyte solutions and connecting them with a voltmeter.**

✓ **Zinc is more reactive than copper, which results in a potential difference (voltage).**

✓ **The bigger the difference between the reactivity of the metals used, the larger the voltage.**

A zinc and copper voltaic cell

Zinc metal is placed in a beaker containing zinc sulfate solution, while copper metal is placed in a beaker containing copper sulfate solution. The concentration of the solutions affects the voltage.

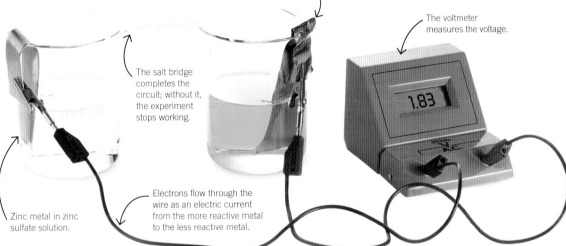

Copper metal in copper sulfate solution.

The voltmeter measures the voltage.

The salt bridge completes the circuit; without it, the experiment stops working.

Zinc metal in zinc sulfate solution.

Electrons flow through the wire as an electric current from the more reactive metal to the less reactive metal.

⚙ How Voltaic Cells Work

Voltaic cells use chemical reactions that involve the transfer of electrons to produce energy. Because of the reactivities of the metals, electrons are released at one terminal, while at the other they're gained. This causes a flow of electrons around the circuit.

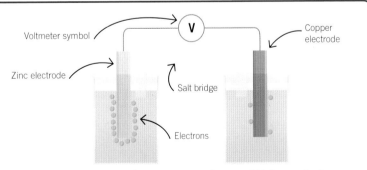

Voltmeter symbol

Zinc electrode

Salt bridge

Copper electrode

Electrons

Zinc is more reactive than copper, which means it gives up its electrons more readily. Zinc becomes the negative terminal of the cell.

Copper metal is less reactive than zinc, therefore copper ions tend to gain electrons. The copper becomes the positive terminal.

Batteries

A battery is a container with one or more voltaic cells inside it (see page 174). Most batteries have an outer casing of metal or plastic, and two terminals that allow them to be connected in a circuit. Inside, chemical energy is converted into electrical energy, which can be used to power devices for days, weeks, or even years.

Alkaline batteries

Alkaline batteries are commonly used to power electrical devices, such as flashlights, toys, and remote controls. They can be single-use or rechargeable.

Key Facts

✓ **A battery contains one or more voltaic cells.**

✓ **In nonrechargeable batteries, the chemicals are eventually used up and the batteries must be replaced.**

✓ **In rechargeable batteries, the reaction is reversed by connecting the battery to an external power source, which allows the chemicals to re-form and the batteries to be used over and over again.**

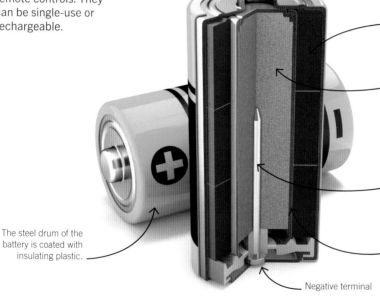

Positive terminal

Manganese dioxide powder is mixed with powdered carbon. This is the cathode.

Zinc powder is mixed with potassium hydroxide. This is the anode.

A metallic pin (typically brass) collects the electric charge, which then flows to and powers the device.

The steel drum of the battery is coated with insulating plastic.

The separator keeps the different chemicals apart.

Negative terminal

⚙ Common Battery Types

There are several different types of commercially available batteries and they contain different chemicals. Their names usually give a clue as to what they contain.

Battery type	Contents	Uses
Alkaline	Zinc Manganese dioxide Potassium hydroxide	Small electrical devices, such as toys and remote controls
Lead-acid	Lead dioxide Lead Sulfuric acid	Cars
Lithium-ion	Graphite Lithium cobalt oxide Organic lithium solution	Cell phones and laptops

Fuel Cells

A fuel cell uses the chemical reaction between a fuel and oxygen (or air) to produce a potential difference. The fuel is oxidized but, unlike combustion (see page 163), the reaction is an electrochemical one. The potential difference causes a current to flow when the fuel cell is part of a complete circuit, which can be used to power an electric motor.

Key Facts

✓ A fuel is oxidized by an electrochemical reaction with oxygen (or air).

✓ Hydrogen and methanol are common fuels for fuel cells.

✓ A potential difference is produced by the reaction, causing a current to flow.

A model fuel-cell car
The electric motor in this model car is powered by a miniature hydrogen–oxygen fuel cell.

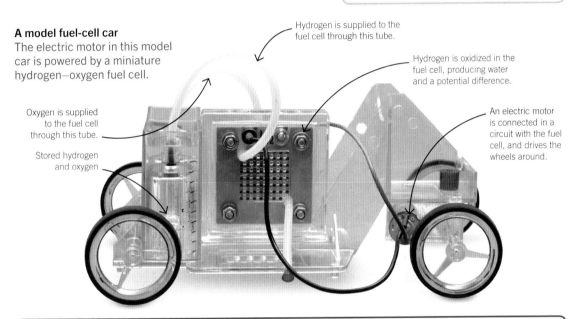

Hydrogen is supplied to the fuel cell through this tube.

Hydrogen is oxidized in the fuel cell, producing water and a potential difference.

Oxygen is supplied to the fuel cell through this tube.

Stored hydrogen and oxygen

An electric motor is connected in a circuit with the fuel cell, and drives the wheels around.

⚙ Comparing Fuel Cells and Batteries

Fuel cells and batteries both use electrochemical reactions to produce a potential difference. However, fuel cells need a fuel but batteries do not. There are other differences too.

Fuel cells	Batteries
The potential difference stays the same while the fuel cell is working.	The potential difference gradually decreases over time with use.
Have large reserves of fuel so last a long time.	Have small reserves of chemicals so need to be recharged or disposed of.
Cannot be recharged.	Some types are rechargeable but many are disposable.
Expensive to make.	Cheap to make.

Inside a Fuel Cell

At the anode (negative electrode) in a hydrogen–oxygen fuel cell, hydrogen is oxidized to hydrogen ions and electrons. The ions reach the other side of the cell through a membrane, and the electrons flow there through an external circuit. At the cathode (positive electrode) oxygen reacts with hydrogen ions and electrons and is reduced to water.

Key Facts

✓ In a hydrogen–oxygen fuel cell, hydrogen reacts with oxygen to produce water.

✓ Hydrogen loses electrons and is oxidized to hydrogen ions.

✓ Oxygen reacts with hydrogen ions and electrons and is reduced to water.

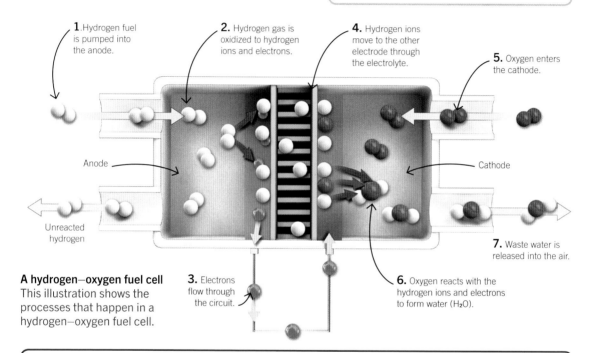

1.Hydrogen fuel is pumped into the anode.

2. Hydrogen gas is oxidized to hydrogen ions and electrons.

4. Hydrogen ions move to the other electrode through the electrolyte.

5. Oxygen enters the cathode.

Anode

Cathode

Unreacted hydrogen

7. Waste water is released into the air.

A hydrogen–oxygen fuel cell
This illustration shows the processes that happen in a hydrogen–oxygen fuel cell.

3. Electrons flow through the circuit.

6. Oxygen reacts with the hydrogen ions and electrons to form water (H_2O).

⚙ Reactions in the Hydrogen–Oxygen Fuel Cell

The overall reaction in the hydrogen–oxygen fuel cell is:

hydrogen	+	oxygen	$\longrightarrow$	water
$2H_2$	+	O_2	$\longrightarrow$	$2H_2O$

This overall reaction can be separated into two reactions, which take place at each side of the cell. For more on half equations, see page 154.

Anode reaction Hydrogen gas loses electrons and is oxidized to hydrogen ions. The half equation for this is:

$$2H_2 \longrightarrow 4H^+ + 4e^-$$

Cathode reaction Oxygen reacts with hydrogen ions and electrons and is reduced to water. The half equation for this is:

$$O_2 + 4H^+ + 4e^- \longrightarrow 2H_2O$$

The Rate and Extent of Chemical Change

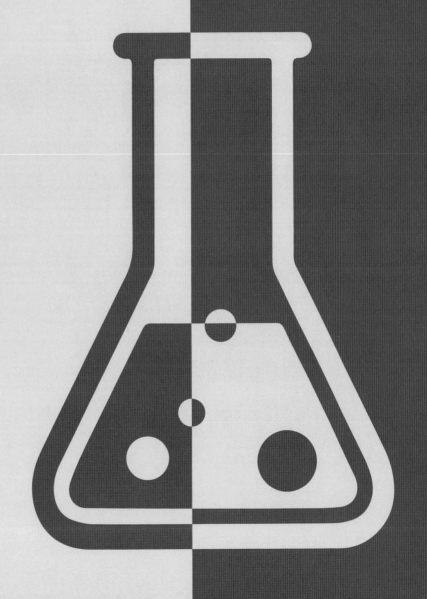

Rates of Reaction

The rate of a chemical reaction is a measure of how quickly it happens. You can describe the rate of a reaction as how quickly reactants are used up, or how quickly products are formed. Reactions happen at different rates, depending on the type of reaction and the conditions.

Key Facts

✓ The rate of a chemical reaction is the rate at which reactants are used up or products are formed.

✓ Some reactions happen slowly while other reactions happen quickly.

✓ Rusting is a slow reaction but explosions are very fast reactions.

The rusting of iron
Rusting happens when iron reacts with substances in the environment (see page 264). It is a slow reaction that can take days, months, or years to complete.

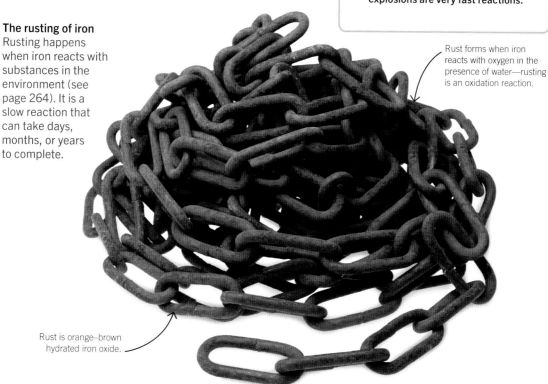

Rust forms when iron reacts with oxygen in the presence of water—rusting is an oxidation reaction.

Rust is orange–brown hydrated iron oxide.

🔍 Reaction Rates

Different reactions happen at different rates. Some reactions happen very slowly while other reactions happen very quickly.

Slow
The formation of crude oil from the remains of dead organisms takes millions of years.

Moderate
The reaction between magnesium and dilute acid takes a few seconds to several minutes.

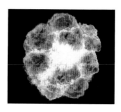

Fast
The reaction of a fuel with oxygen is almost instantaneous during combustion (see page 163).

Collision Theory

 Key Facts

Collision theory explains chemical reactions and the rate at which they happen. A chemical reaction between two substances can only happen if their particles collide, and if the collision has enough energy. The more successful collisions that happen in a given time, the faster the reaction.

✓ Chemical reactions only happen if the reactant particles collide with enough energy.

✓ A collision that results in a chemical reaction is called a successful collision.

✓ The greater the rate of successful collisions, the greater the rate of reaction.

✓ The reacting particles in chemical reactions can be atoms, ions, or molecules.

Successful collisions
Moving particles collide with each other. A reaction can happen if they have enough energy. Collisions that cause a reaction are called successful collisions.

An unsuccessful collision

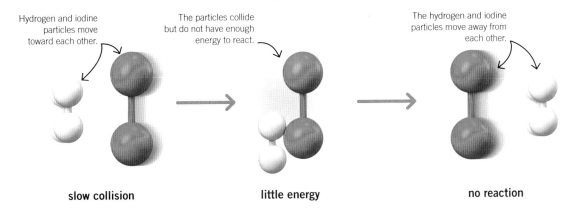

Hydrogen and iodine particles move toward each other.

The particles collide but do not have enough energy to react.

The hydrogen and iodine particles move away from each other.

slow collision   **little energy**   **no reaction**

A successful collision

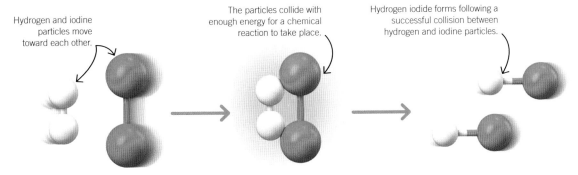

Hydrogen and iodine particles move toward each other.

The particles collide with enough energy for a chemical reaction to take place.

Hydrogen iodide forms following a successful collision between hydrogen and iodine particles.

fast collision   **a lot of energy**   **reaction happens**

Reaction Rates and Temperature

The higher the temperature, the faster the rate of reaction. As the particles in a reaction mixture gain energy, they move around faster and collide with each other more frequently. This means that successful collisions are more frequent.

Key Facts

✓ Chemical reactions go faster as the temperature increases.

✓ Reactant particles move faster and collide more frequently.

✓ More particles have the activation energy or higher.

✓ There are more successful collisions in a given time.

Reducing copper oxide
When heated, copper oxide reacts with hydrogen to produce copper and water.

Excess hydrogen escapes from a hole in the tube and is deliberately ignited so that it cannot build up and cause an explosion.

Hydrogen gas flows into a tube containing copper oxide powder.

The higher the temperature, the more frequent successful collisions occur, and the greater the rate of reaction.

The Bunsen burner flame heats the copper oxide, increasing its temperature.

How Particles Move

The activation energy is the minimum amount of energy that particles must have for them to react. A collision that results in a reaction is described as successful. As the temperature increases, collisions happen more often, and more of these are successful.

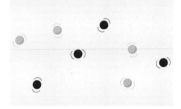

Low temperature and low reaction rate
Infrequent collisions with only a small proportion that are successful.

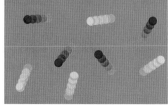

High temperature and high reaction rate
More frequent collisions and with a high proportion that are successful.

Reaction Rates and Concentration

The higher the concentration of a reactant in solution, the greater the rate of reaction. More particles in the solution means the solution becomes more crowded and the particles collide more often. Similarly, in a gas, increasing the pressure means that the particles are closer together and collide more frequently.

Key Facts

✓ Chemical reactions go faster as the concentration or pressure increases.

✓ More reactant particles occupy the same volume, so they are more crowded.

✓ Particles collide more frequently when they are more crowded.

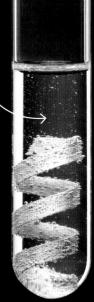

The low rate of bubbling in the lowest concentration of acid shows that the rate of reaction is low.

The higher rate of bubbling in a higher concentration of acid shows that the rate of reaction is greater.

The highest rate of bubbling in the highest concentration of acid shows that the rate of reaction is greatest.

Magnesium reacting with acid Magnesium reacts with hydrochloric acid of different concentrations to produce magnesium chloride and hydrogen.

⚙ How Particles Move

Concentration is a measure of how many dissolved particles occupy a given volume. Gas pressure is caused by the force of particle collisions with the container walls. The greater the rate of collisions, the greater the gas pressure.

Low concentration or low pressure
Particles are not crowded so they do not collide often.

High concentration or high pressure
Particles are more crowded so they collide more often.

Reaction Rates and Surface Area

The greater the surface area of a solid reactant, the greater the reaction rate. Smaller pieces have a larger surface area to volume ratio. This means more particles are exposed on the surface and these collide more often with the smaller pieces.

Calcium carbonate and hydrochloric acid
When a single piece of chalk (calcium carbonate) is broken up into lumps, the reaction rate is visibly greater.

Key Facts

✓ Surface area to volume ratio increases as the size of a solid reactant decreases.

✓ Powders have a much larger surface area to volume ratio than lumps.

✓ Reactions are faster with powders because more particles are exposed on the surface so there are more frequent successful collisions.

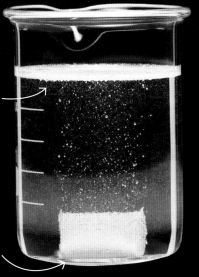

Bubbles are released when dilute hydrochloric acid reacts with calcium carbonate.

This large piece of chalk has a relatively small surface area to volume ratio. Most of its particles are on the inside rather than on its surface, so are not available to react.

These smaller lumps of calcium carbonate have the same mass as the large piece, but more particles are on the surfaces and available to react

⚙ Breaking Up Solids

Particles of a solid reactant are only available to react if they are on the surface. When a solid is divided or ground into a powder, more reactant particles are exposed on the surface so there are more frequent successful collisions and the rate of reaction increases.

Large lumps
Low rates of collisions so low rates of reaction.

Small lumps
High rates of collisions so high rates of reaction.

Reaction Rates and Catalysts

A catalyst is a substance that increases the rate of a reaction, but does not get used up. It works by reducing the activation energy needed, but a catalyst does not alter the products and is unchanged chemically and in mass at the end of the reaction. Enzymes are proteins that act as biological catalysts.

Hydrogen peroxide
Hydrogen peroxide very slowly decomposes to water and oxygen. Potassium iodide acts as a catalyst to speed up this reaction.

Key Facts

- ✓ Catalysts speed up reactions without being used up.
- ✓ Catalysts provide alternative reaction pathways with lower activation energies than the uncatalyzed reactions.
- ✓ Different reactions need different catalysts.
- ✓ Enzymes are biological catalysts.

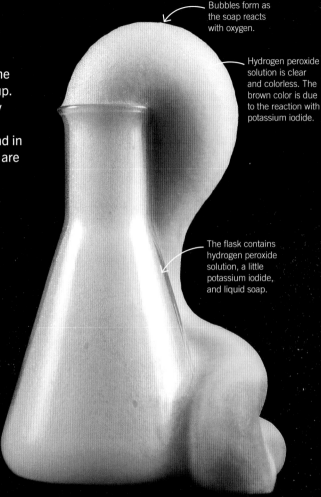

Bubbles form as the soap reacts with oxygen.

Hydrogen peroxide solution is clear and colorless. The brown color is due to the reaction with potassium iodide.

The flask contains hydrogen peroxide solution, a little potassium iodide, and liquid soap.

⚙ How Catalysts Work

The activation energy is the minimum amount of energy needed for a reaction to occur. Catalysts provide an alternative reaction pathway with a lower activation energy. As this reduces the amount of energy needed for a collision, the rate of successful collisions increases.

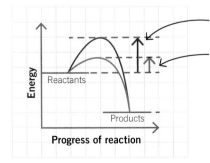

Energy
Reactants
Products
Progress of reaction

Higher activation energy without a catalyst.

Lower activation energy with a catalyst.

A reaction profile for an exothermic reaction For more on exothermic reaction profiles, see page 170.

Rate of Reaction Graphs

As a reaction happens, the quantity of reactants goes down and the quantity of products goes up. The changes in these quantities can be shown in a graph of quantity against time. The gradient of the line in these graphs gives you the rate of reaction.

✓ Graphs of quantity of reactant or product against time give the rate of reaction.

✓ The greater the gradient, the higher the reaction rate.

✓ Mean reaction rate is the quantity of reactant used or product formed divided by time.

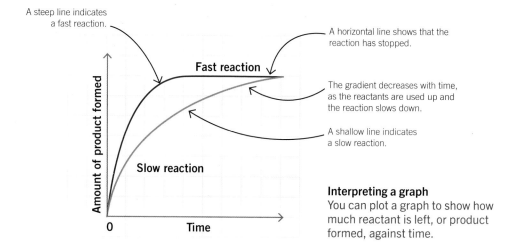

A steep line indicates a fast reaction.

A horizontal line shows that the reaction has stopped.

The gradient decreases with time, as the reactants are used up and the reaction slows down.

A shallow line indicates a slow reaction.

Interpreting a graph
You can plot a graph to show how much reactant is left, or product formed, against time.

⚙ Mean Rate of Reaction

You can calculate the mean rate of reaction if you know the quantity of reactant used or product formed, and the time taken. Quantity can be the mass, volume, or number of moles of substance.

Figuring it out

$$\text{mean rate of reaction} = \frac{\text{quantity of reactant used or product produced}}{\text{time taken}}$$

Mean rate of reaction $= \dfrac{14.4\,\text{cm}^3}{8\,\text{s}} = 1.8\,\text{cm}^3/\text{s}$

Question
What is the mean rate of reaction if 14.4 cm³ of gas is produced in 8 seconds?

Answer
The mean rate of reaction is 1.8 cm³/s.

Reaction Rates and the Volume of Gas

The volume of a gas is conveniently measured using a gas syringe. These are made of glass and usually measure 100 cm³ in intervals of 1 cm³. They are more convenient than other apparatus, such as an upturned measuring cylinder in a trough of water.

Key Facts

✓ Gas syringes are used to measure gas volumes.

✓ The rate of reaction is determined by recording the volume of gas produced and the time.

✓ The gradient of a graph of volume against time gives the rate of reaction.

Calcium carbonate and hydrochloric acid
Bubbles of carbon dioxide gas are given off when calcium carbonate reacts with dilute hydrochloric acid.

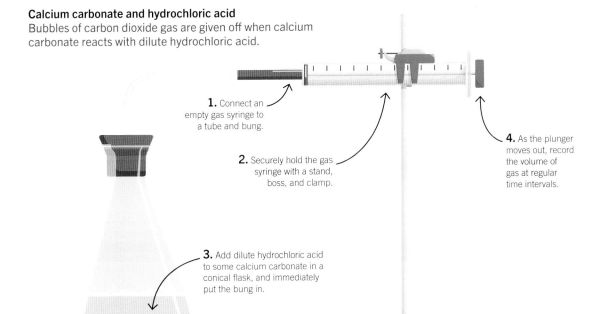

1. Connect an empty gas syringe to a tube and bung.

2. Securely hold the gas syringe with a stand, boss, and clamp.

4. As the plunger moves out, record the volume of gas at regular time intervals.

3. Add dilute hydrochloric acid to some calcium carbonate in a conical flask, and immediately put the bung in.

⚙ **How to Determine the Rate of Reaction**

To determine a rate of reaction, you can record the volume at regular intervals, or the time at regular volumes. Then plot a graph of volume of gas against time. For more on rate of reaction graphs, see page 185.

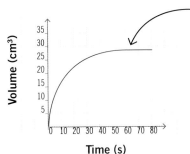

The greater the volume in a given time interval, the steeper the curve and the greater the reaction rate.

Volume (cm³)

35
30
25
20
15
10
5

0 10 20 30 40 50 60 70 80

Time (s)

Reaction Rates and Changes in Mass

In the lab, you can measure the mass using a top pan balance. Carbon dioxide is a dense gas, so you can measure its loss from a reaction mixture. Although the total mass of reactants and products stays the same, the reaction mixture loses mass as the gas escapes into the surroundings.

Key Facts

✓ Balances measure masses.

✓ The rate of reaction is determined by recording the mass of the reaction mixture and apparatus, and the time.

✓ The gradient of a graph of loss in mass against time gives the rate of reaction.

1. Place a flask of dilute hydrochloric acid and calcium carbonate on the balance.

2. Record the starting mass and then the mass at regular intervals of time.

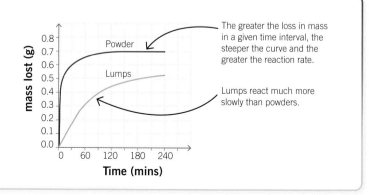

Calcium carbonate and hydrochloric acid
Carbon dioxide escapes when calcium carbonate reacts with dilute hydrochloric acid. This causes the reaction mixture to lose mass.

⚙ How to Determine the Rate of Reaction

To determine a rate of reaction, you record the mass at regular intervals. At each time interval, you calculate the loss in mass from the start, then plot a graph of your results. Lumps react more slowly than powders because they have a lower surface area to volume ratio (see page 183).

The greater the loss in mass in a given time interval, the steeper the curve and the greater the reaction rate.

Lumps react much more slowly than powders.

Powder

Lumps

mass lost (g) — 0.0 0.1 0.2 0.3 0.4 0.5 0.6 0.7 0.8

Time (mins) — 0 60 120 180 240

Reaction Rates and Precipitation

A precipitate is an insoluble substance formed when two solutions react together. Solutions are clear but a precipitate makes the mixture cloudy. Eventually the reaction mixture becomes so cloudy that you cannot see through it. You can measure a reaction rate by finding how long this takes.

Key Facts

✓ A reaction mixture turns cloudy if it produces a precipitate.

✓ It will become too cloudy to see through after a while.

✓ The longer this takes, the lower the rate of reaction.

The disappearing cross experiment
Sodium thiosulfate solution reacts with dilute hydrochloric acid. A yellow precipitate of sulfur forms in the reaction, which makes the reaction mixture cloudy. Use a stopwatch to time the reaction.

1. Draw a cross on a piece of paper. Place a beaker or flask of sodium thiosulfate solution on the paper.

2. Add dilute hydrochloric acid and start the stopwatch. The reaction mixture begins to turn cloudy.

3. Keep looking through the liquid. Stop timing when the cross just disappears from sight. Record the reading to the nearest whole second.

⚙ Calculating the Rate of Reaction

The experiment gives the reaction time. This is inversely proportional to the rate of reaction—the shorter the time, the greater the rate. To get easy numbers for a graph, divide 1,000 by the reaction time.

$$\text{rate of reaction} = \frac{1{,}000}{\text{time}}$$

Question
In a disappearing cross experiment, the reaction time is 20 s. Calculate the rate of reaction.

Figuring it out

$$\text{rate of reaction} = \frac{1{,}000}{20s} = 50 \text{ /s}$$

Answer
The rate of reaction is 50 /s.

Reaction Rates and Acid Concentration

For a dissolved reactant, the more concentrated the solution is, the more frequently collisions happen and the greater the rate of reaction. You can investigate the effect of concentration by repeating the same experiment, just changing the concentration of one reactant each time.

Key Facts

✓ Reaction rate increases as the concentration of a reactant increases.

✓ Reaction rate can be measured by seeing how quickly a reactant is used up or a product formed.

✓ Only the concentration should be changed when investigating concentration.

Calcium carbonate and hydrochloric acid
On page 186, the volume of carbon dioxide gas given off when calcium carbonate reacts with dilute hydrochloric acid was measured. This reaction can be repeated at different concentrations of hydrochloric acid. The mass and size of the calcium carbonate pieces should be kept the same, and also the volume and temperature of the acid.

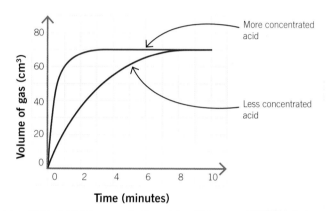

⚙ Interpreting the Results

Question

Plot graphs of volume of gas against time (see page 185) and determine the mean rates of reaction for each concentration of acid. What is the effect of increasing acid concentration on the rate of reaction?

Figuring it out

1. Look at the graph above to see when the reaction finishes (the line goes flat).

More concentrated acid: 3 minutes
Less concentrated acid: 8 minutes

2. Calculate the mean rates of reaction and compare the rates.

$$\text{mean rate of reaction} = \frac{\text{volume of gas (cm}^3\text{)}}{\text{reaction time (min)}}$$

More concentrated acid: $\frac{70}{3} = 23.33\,\text{cm}^3/\text{min}$

Less concentrated acid: $\frac{70}{8} = 8.75\,\text{cm}^3/\text{min}$

Answer

Increasing the acid concentration increases the rate of reaction.

Calculating Reaction Rates

You can represent a reaction by measuring the amount of a reactant or product at various times, then plotting a graph of your results. The line on the graph lets you calculate a mean rate of reaction, and the rate of the reaction at a particular instant.

 Key Facts

✓ You can use graphs to calculate mean rates of reaction between any two times.

✓ The rate at a particular time is equal to the gradient.

✓ As soon as the graph line goes flat, the reaction finishes.

🖻 Calculating a Mean Rate

You can calculate the mean rate of reaction between two times, for example between 20 s and 80 s. Draw lines crossing these two times, figure out the two volumes, then carry out the calculation below.

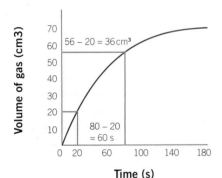

Question
Calculate the mean rate between 20 s and 80 s.

Figuring it out

$$\frac{\text{change in volume}}{\text{change in time}} = \frac{(56\,\text{cm}^3 - 20\,\text{cm}^3)}{(80\,\text{s} - 20\,\text{s})}$$

$$= \frac{36\,\text{cm}^3}{60\,\text{s}} = 0.6\,\text{cm}^3/\text{s}$$

Answer
The mean rate of reaction is 0.6 cm³/s.

🖻 Calculating the Rate at a Given Time

You can calculate the rate of reaction at a given time by drawing a tangent, for example at 80 s. Find two points on the line that you can read easily, then carry out the calculation below.

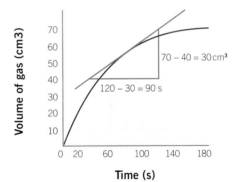

Question
Calculate the rate of reaction at 80 s.

Figuring it out

$$\frac{\text{change in volume}}{\text{change in time}} = \frac{30\,\text{cm}^3}{90\,\text{s}} = 0.33\,\text{cm}^3/\text{s}$$

Answer
The rate of reaction at 80 s is 0.33 cm³/s.

Reversible Reactions

Some chemical reactions are reversible. Some reactions are easily reversed by changing reaction conditions such as the temperature, pressure, and concentration. These reversible reactions are shown in chemical equations by using the symbol ⇌ instead of →.

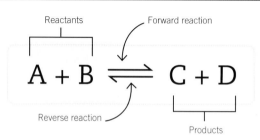

Key Facts

✓ A reversible reaction has a forward reaction and a reverse reaction.

✓ The symbol ⇌ is used to show a reversible reaction.

✓ The dehydration of hydrated blue copper sulfate is easily reversed.

The dehydration and rehydration of copper sulfate

Hydrated copper sulfate contains water, which can be driven off by heating. The change is reversible.

Hydrated copper sulfate is blue.

Anhydrous copper sulfate is white.

Heating hydrated copper sulfate removes water, forming anhydrous copper sulfate.

Blue hydrated copper sulfate.

White anhydrous copper sulfate.

When water is added, white anhydrous copper sulfate is rehydrated to blue hydrated copper sulfate.

🔍 Reversible Reactions Equations

Equations for reversible reactions use the symbol ⇌ instead of an arrow. This shows that the reaction can go in either direction. The products can react to form the reactants again. Here's the equation for the reversible reaction above. The dot (·) separates the two parts of the formula.

Reactants

Forward reaction

$$A + B \rightleftharpoons C + D$$

Reverse reaction

Products

hydrated copper sulfate	⇌	anhydrous copper sulfate	+	water
$CuSO_4.5H_2O_{(s)}$	⇌	$CuSO_{4(s)}$	+	$5H_2O_{(l)}$

Equilibrium

A reversible reaction in a closed system (where no substances can get in or out) reaches equilibrium. At equilibrium, the forward and reverse reactions still happen but their rate is equal. This means that the concentrations of the reactants and products are constant, though not necessarily equal.

Key Facts

✓ Reversible reactions reach equilibrium in closed systems where nothing can enter or leave.

✓ At equilibrium, the forward and reverse reactions happen at the same rate.

✓ The concentrations of the reactants and products are constant.

Two gases at equilibrium
Brown nitrogen dioxide (NO_2) and colorless dinitrogen tetroxide (N_2O_4) reach equilibrium in a sealed container.

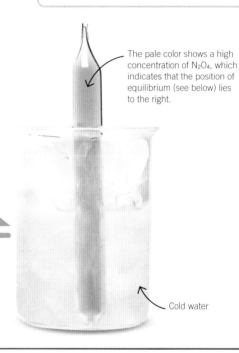

The pale color shows a high concentration of N_2O_4, which indicates that the position of equilibrium (see below) lies to the right.

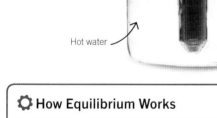

The dark color shows a high concentration of NO_2, which indicates that the position of equilibrium (see below) lies to the left.

Hot water

Cold water

⚙ How Equilibrium Works

Equilibrium is reached when the forward and reverse reactions happen at the same rate. The position of equilibrium is a measure of the concentration at equilibrium. If the equilibrium lies to the right, there are more products than reactants, and if it lies to the left, there are more reactants than products.

The forward reaction slows down as reactants are used up.

reactants ⇌ products

The reverse reaction speeds up as products are formed.

nitrogen dioxide		dinitrogen tetroxide
NO_2	⇌	N_2O_4

Energy Transfer in Reversible Reactions

All chemical reactions involve energy transfers to or from the surroundings. In a reversible reaction, if the forward reaction is exothermic (see page 166), the reverse reaction will be endothermic (see page 167). The opposite is also true—if the forward reaction is endothermic, the reverse reaction will be exothermic.

Key Facts

✓ In reversible reactions, one direction is exothermic and the other is endothermic.

✓ The same amount of energy is transferred to or from the surroundings.

✓ The reaction between anhydrous copper(II) sulfate and water is reversible.

Copper(II) sulfate and water
The reaction between anhydrous copper(II) sulfate and water is reversible.

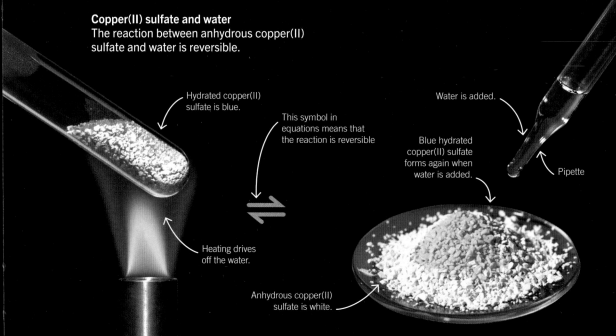

Hydrated copper(II) sulfate is blue.

This symbol in equations means that the reaction is reversible

Water is added.

Blue hydrated copper(II) sulfate forms again when water is added.

Pipette

Heating drives off the water.

Anhydrous copper(II) sulfate is white.

⚙ Energy Changes

In reversible reactions, one direction is exothermic and one is endothermic. The same amount of energy is transferred, but whether it is transferred to or from the surroundings is different.

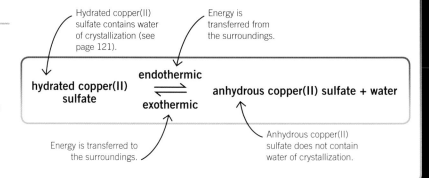

Hydrated copper(II) sulfate contains water of crystallization (see page 121).

Energy is transferred from the surroundings.

hydrated copper(II) sulfate ⇌ anhydrous copper(II) sulfate + water

endothermic

exothermic

Energy is transferred to the surroundings.

Anhydrous copper(II) sulfate does not contain water of crystallization.

Equilibrium and Temperature

Reversible reactions are exothermic in one direction and endothermic in the other direction. Temperature increases shift the position of equilibrium (see page 192) in the direction of the endothermic reaction. The opposite is also true—temperature decreases shift the position of equilibrium in the direction of the exothermic reaction.

Key Facts

✓ In reversible reactions, a temperature increase shifts the position of equilibrium in the endothermic direction.

✓ A temperature decrease shifts the position of equilibrium in the exothermic direction.

✓ The concentrations of reacting substances change when the position of equilibrium changes.

Nitrogen dioxide gas

In a sealed flask, the reaction between brown nitrogen dioxide (NO_2) and colorless dinitrogen tetroxide (N_2O_4) reaches equilibrium. If the temperature decreases, the equilibrium moves in the direction of the exothermic reaction, reducing the concentration of brown NO_2. The opposite happens if the temperature increases.

Higher concentration of colorless dinitrogen tetroxide (N_2O_4).

Flask in ice water

Higher concentration of brown nitrogen dioxide (NO_2).

Flask at room temperature

nitrogen dioxide	exothermic ⟶	dinitrogen tetroxide
$2NO_2$	⟵ endothermic	N_2O_4

Equilibrium and Pressure

When the reaction conditions of a reversible reaction change, the position of equilibrium moves to oppose the change (see page 192). In a reaction involving gases, an increase in pressure causes the position of equilibrium to move in the direction of the fewest molecules of gas.

Key Facts

✓ The position of equilibrium can change if the pressure is changed.

✓ The position of equilibrium moves in the direction of the fewest molecules of gas, as seen in the balanced symbol equation.

Reacting nitrogen and dinitrogen tetroxide
Nitrogen dioxide (NO_2) and dinitrogen tetroxide (N_2O_4) reach equilibrium in a sealed syringe: $2NO_2(g) \rightleftharpoons N_2O_4(g)$.

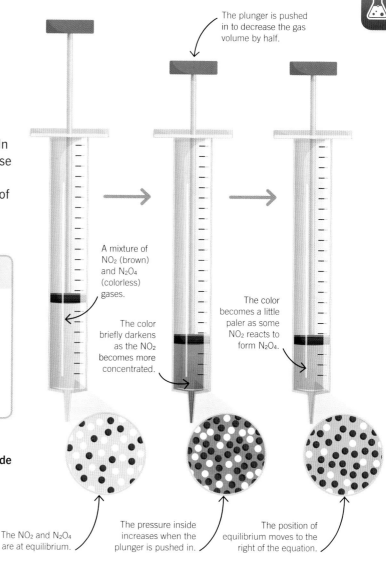

The plunger is pushed in to decrease the gas volume by half.

A mixture of NO_2 (brown) and N_2O_4 (colorless) gases.

The color briefly darkens as the NO_2 becomes more concentrated.

The color becomes a little paler as some NO_2 reacts to form N_2O_4.

The NO_2 and N_2O_4 are at equilibrium.

The pressure inside increases when the plunger is pushed in.

The position of equilibrium moves to the right of the equation.

⚙ Pressure Changes and Equilibrium

You can predict how a pressure change will affect the position of equilibrium. If the pressure is increased, the position of equilibrium will move in the direction of the fewest molecules of reacting gas. Here, there are fewer molecules on the right, so if the pressure is increased, the position of equilibrium moves to the right of the equation, increasing the amount of sulfur trioxide.

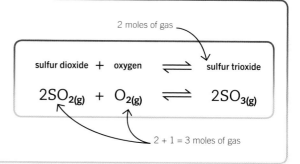

2 moles of gas

sulfur dioxide + oxygen ⇌ sulfur trioxide

$$2SO_{2(g)} + O_{2(g)} \rightleftharpoons 2SO_{3(g)}$$

2 + 1 = 3 moles of gas

Equilibrium and Concentration

When the conditions of a reversible reaction change, the position of equilibrium moves to oppose the change (see page 192). If the concentration of a reactant is increased, the position of equilibrium moves to decrease it by producing more product. If the concentration of a product is decreased, the position of equilibrium moves to make more of it.

Cobalt compounds

A pink cobalt compound reacts with hydrochloric acid to form a blue cobalt compound and water. Adding more water or hydrochloric acid changes the concentration and affects the position of equilibrium.

Key Facts

✓ The equilibrium changes if the concentration of a solution is changed.

✓ If the concentration of a reactant is increased, the equilibrium moves to decrease it.

✓ If the concentration of a product is decreased, the equilibrium moves to make more of it.

This red solution has a high concentration of the pink compound and a low concentration of the blue compound.

This purple solution has a high concentration of the blue compound and a low concentration of the pink compound.

⚙ The Effect of Concentration on Equilibrium

If a reactant concentration is increased, the system moves to counteract the change by producing more of the product. If a product concentration is decreased, the system responds by reducing the concentration of the reactant.

| pink cobalt compound | + | chloride ions | ⇌ | blue cobalt compound | + | water |

When hydrochloric acid is added, it increases the chloride ion concentration and the equilibrium moves to the right of the equation.

When water is added, it decreases the chloride ion concentration and the equilibrium moves to the left of the equation.

Organic Chemistry

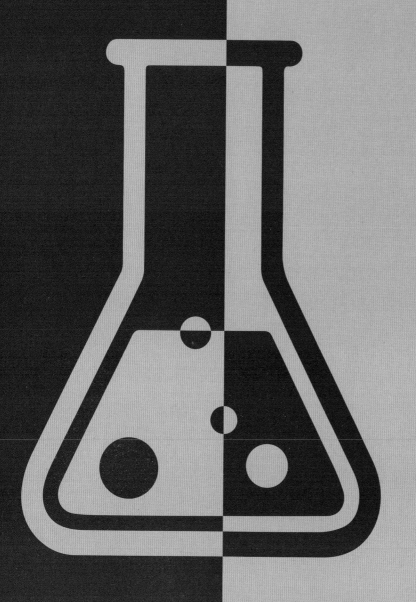

Organic Compounds

Organic compounds contain carbon and at least one other element. Their chemical properties are due to an atom, bond, or group of atoms called the functional group. A homologous series is a "family" of organic compounds with the same functional group and general formula. They include alkanes, alkenes, alcohols, carboxylic acids, and esters.

Key Facts

✓ A functional group is an atom or group of atoms that give organic compounds their typical reactive properties.

✓ They are: alkenes $C=C$, alcohols $-OH$, carboxylic acids $-COOH$, esters $-COO-$.

✓ Members of a homologous series have the same functional group and general formula.

Functional groups

The general structure of the compounds in a homologous series is easier to see if the functional group is shown attached to the letter R. R stands for an atom or group of atoms that can be part of an organic compound.

In alkanes, R stands for a hydrogen atom, or carbon atoms joined to hydrogen atoms.

R—C—H

Alkanes

R C=C H R

Alkenes have the functional group C=C.

R—O—H

Alcohols have the functional group –OH.

R—C—O—H

Carboxylic acids have the functional group –COOH.

R—C—O—R

Esters have the functional group –COO–.

🔍 Homologous Series Formulas

The number of carbon atoms in a general formula is represented by *n*. This is used to calculate the number of hydrogen atoms.

The general formula for alkanes is C_nH_{2n+2}

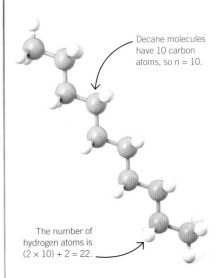

Decane molecules have 10 carbon atoms, so n = 10.

The number of hydrogen atoms is $(2 \times 10) + 2 = 22$.

A ball-and-stick model of decane

The molecular formula for decane is $C_{10}H_{22}$

Naming Organic Compounds

Organic compounds have systematic names that follow a system of stems and suffixes. The stem is the start of the name and the suffix is the end. The stem comes from the number of carbon atoms and the suffix comes from the homologous series and its functional group.

Key Facts

✓ The name of an organic compound is based on its number of carbon atoms and its functional group.

✓ The number of carbon atoms is represented by the name's stem.

✓ The homologous series and functional group is represented by the name's suffix (ending).

Counting carbon atoms
The stem (start of name) is based on the number of carbon atoms in the compound.

Number of carbon atoms	1	2	3	4	5	6
Stem of the name	meth- or methan-	eth- or ethan-	prop- or propan-	but- or butan-	pent- or pentan-	hex-or hexan

Suffixes
The suffix comes at the end of the name. It tells you which homologous series and functional group the substance belongs to.

Homologous series	Suffix	Example	
alkane	-ane	methane	CH_4
alkene	-ene	ethene	$CH_2=CH_2$
alcohol	-ol	propanol	$CH_3CH_2CH_2OH$
carboxylic acid	-anoic acid	butanoic acid	$CH_3CH_2CH_2COOH$
ester	Prefix (from the alcohol): -yl Suffix (from the ester): -oate	ethyl ethanoate	$CH_3COOCH_2CH_3$

Naming alkene isomers
Alkenes with four or more carbon atoms have isomers (see page 210). Their molecular formula is the same, but the functional group is in different positions.

$$CH_2=CHCH_2CH_3 \longleftarrow \qquad \longrightarrow CH_3CH=CHCH_3$$

but-1-ene

Both are C_4H_8

but-2-ene

Hydrocarbons

Hydrocarbons are compounds containing hydrogen and carbon atoms only. Their atoms are joined together by covalent bonds. Alkanes and alkenes are two types of hydrocarbons. Alkanes have C–C bonds but no C=C bonds, so they are described as saturated. Alkenes have one C=C bond, so they are described as unsaturated.

Key Facts

✓ Hydrocarbons are the simplest organic compounds.

✓ Hydrocarbon molecules only contain carbon and hydrogen atoms.

✓ Carbon and hydrogen atoms are joined to each other by single covalent bonds.

✓ Alkanes are saturated hydrocarbons because they have no C=C bonds.

The first four alkanes

In order of increasing numbers of carbon atoms, the first four alkanes are methane, ethane, propane, and butane. Their general formula is C_nH_{2n+2}, where n is the number of carbon atoms in the molecule.

		Condensed formula	Molecular formula	Structural formula
	Methane	CH_4	CH_4	H–C–H with H above and H below
	Ethane	C_2H_6	CH_3CH_3	H–C–C–H structure
	Propane	C_3H_8	$CH_3CH_2CH_3$	H–C–C–C–H structure
	Butane	C_4H_{10}	$CH_3CH_2CH_2CH_3$	H–C–C–C–C–H structure

Alkane Properties

Crude oil consists of hydrocarbons, which are compounds containing hydrogen and carbon only. Most of these hydrocarbons are alkanes. Alkane molecules only have single carbon–carbon bonds. The alkanes show trends in their physical properties as the number of carbon atoms in their molecules increases.

 Key Facts

✓ Alkanes are hydrocarbons with no carbon–carbon double bonds in their molecules.

✓ As the number of carbon atoms in alkane molecules increases, the viscosity of the alkane increases.

✓ As the number of carbon atoms in alkane molecules increases, the volatility and flammability of the alkane decreases.

Viscosity
The viscosity of a substance is a measure of how runny it is. The more carbon atoms there are in an alkane molecule, the more viscous the substance is.

Crude oil has a high viscosity so it is not very runny.

Volatility
The volatility of a substance is a measure of how easily it evaporates or boils. The more carbon atoms there are in an alkane molecule, the less volatile the substance is, and the higher its boiling point. Propane is a volatile alkane, with only three carbon atoms.

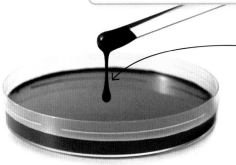

Propane is used in bottled gas. It has a low boiling point so is a gas at room temperature.

Flammability
The flammability of a substance is a measure of how easily it is set on fire. The more carbon atoms there are in an alkane molecule, the less flammable the substance is, and the more difficult it is to ignite.

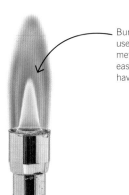

Bunsen burners use natural gas (mainly methane). Methane ignites easily as its molecules only have one carbon atom.

Hydrocarbon Combustion

The burning of a fuel is called combustion. It is an oxidation reaction because atoms in the fuel bond with oxygen, and an exothermic reaction because energy is transferred to the surroundings. Hydrocarbon fuels burn completely in oxygen to produce carbon dioxide and water.

Key Facts

✓ Complete combustion happens in a plentiful supply of oxygen.

✓ Hydrocarbons produce carbon dioxide and water during complete combustion.

✓ Useful fuels release a lot of energy during combustion.

Complete combustion

Some rockets use a liquid methane fuel. Carbon in the methane combines with oxygen to make carbon dioxide. Hydrogen in the methane combines with oxygen to make water. The maximum amount of energy is released during complete combustion.

This glowing flame is composed of exhaust particles heated by the reaction.

$$\text{hydrocarbon} + \text{oxygen} \longrightarrow \text{carbon dioxide} + \text{water}$$

⚙ The Complete Combustion of Methane

Methane (CH_4) is the main hydrocarbon in natural gas. Here is one way to write a balanced equation for its complete combustion, following the general equation above.

1. Write the formulas for the reactants and products, with plus signs and an arrow.

$$CH_4 + O_2 \longrightarrow CO_2 + H_2O$$

2. Methane has four hydrogen atoms, so two water molecules are needed on the right.

$$CH_4 + O_2 \longrightarrow CO_2 + 2H_2O$$

3. Four oxygen atoms on the right means two oxygen molecules are needed on the left.

$$CH_4 + 2O_2 \longrightarrow CO_2 + 2H_2O$$

Crude Oil

Crude oil was formed over hundreds of thousands of years from the ancient remains of living things in the sea. These were covered by layers of mud and heated under pressure in the absence of air. Over millions of years, the remains changed to oil and the mud changed to sedimentary rock above it.

Extracting crude oil

Oil fields form where rock covers the oil. To extract crude oil, a hole is drilled from an oil rig through the rock. The oil may reach the surface itself if it is under pressure, but it may need to be pumped out.

Key Facts

✓ Crude oil is a fossil fuel.

✓ It is made over millions of years from the ancient remains of marine organisms.

✓ Crude oil is a finite resource because it is made extremely slowly, or is not being made at all now.

✓ It is a nonrenewable resource, and will run out one day if we keep on using it.

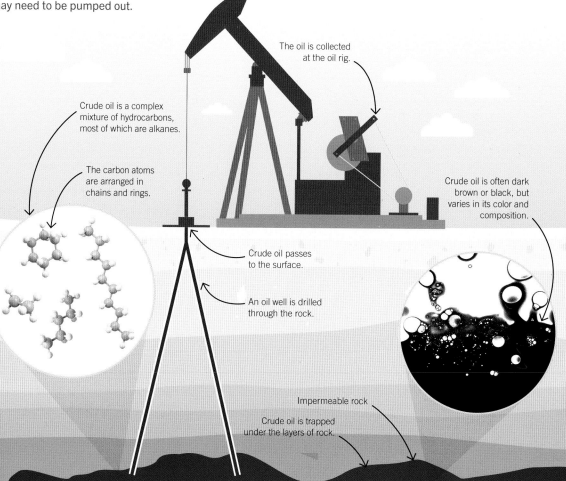

The oil is collected at the oil rig.

Crude oil is a complex mixture of hydrocarbons, most of which are alkanes.

The carbon atoms are arranged in chains and rings.

Crude oil is often dark brown or black, but varies in its color and composition.

Crude oil passes to the surface.

An oil well is drilled through the rock.

Impermeable rock

Crude oil is trapped under the layers of rock.

Fractional Distillation

Fractional distillation is a process used to separate mixtures of liquids. It relies on the substances in the mixture having different boiling points. When heated, the mixture releases some of the substances as a vapor, which cools and condenses back into a liquid state. The different substances do this at different temperatures.

Fraction distillation of crude oil

Depending on the size of their molecules, the hydrocarbons in oil are solid, liquid, or gas at room temperature. Fractional distillation separates oil into "fractions." A "fraction" is a mixture of molecules with similar boiling points.

Key Facts

✓ Fractional distillation separates crude oil into useful mixtures.

✓ Fractions are called "fractions" because they are only part of the original crude oil.

✓ Hydrocarbons in a fraction have a similar boiling point and number of carbon atoms.

✓ Going up the column, fractions become less viscous, easier to ignite, and have lower boiling points.

Substances that are gases at room temperature collect at the top of the column.

The higher up the column, the runnier and easier to ignite the fractions become.

The vapor cools as it rises, with each substance condensing back into liquid at a different temperature.

The fractionating column has a temperature gradient —hottest at the bottom and coolest at the top.

Crude oil is heated strongly in an industrial oil refinery.

A mixture of liquids and gases enters the fractionating column.

Crude oil

1–4 carbon atoms
Highly flammable gases

Refinery gases
Heating and cooking

4–12 carbon atoms
Highly flammable liquids with
very low viscosity

Gasoline
Fuel for cars

7–14 carbon atoms
Very flammable liquids with low viscosity

Naphtha
Feedstock for the
petrochemical industry

11–15 carbon atoms
Flammable liquids with low viscosity

Kerosene
Fuel for aircraft

14–19 carbon atoms
Flammable but viscous liquids

Diesel oil
Fuel for some trains
and cars

18–30 carbon atoms
Very viscous liquids, difficult to ignite

Fuel oil
Fuel for large ships and
some power stations

30+ carbon atoms
Solids at room temperature

Asphalt
Waterproofing roofs and
surfacing roads

Cracking

Alkane molecules with long chains of carbon atoms can be decomposed by heating over a suitable catalyst (see page 206). This process is called cracking. It's used industrially to produce alkanes with shorter chains, which are more useful as fuels. Cracking also produces alkenes, which are used to make addition polymers (see page 213).

Oil fractions
Fractional distillation separates oil into "fractions" (see page 204). The fractions shown here are in order of decreasing carbon chain length. The demand for fractions with shorter hydrocarbon molecules is greater than the supply of them.

Key Facts

✓ As the chain length decreases, hydrocarbons become more flammable and flow more easily.

✓ Hydrocarbons with shorter chains are more useful as fuels than those with longer chains.

✓ Cracking converts longer alkane molecules into shorter alkanes and alkenes.

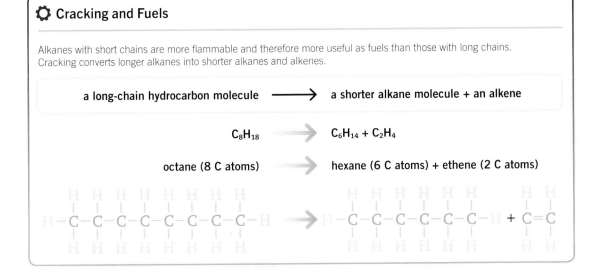

Viscous substances are not runny. They are thick liquids or solids like tar.

Fractions with the longest hydrocarbon molecules, such as asphalt, are viscous, difficult to ignite, and not in great demand.

Fractions with shorter hydrocarbon molecules, such as fuel oil, are in high demand.

Cracking converts less useful fractions into more useful fractions, such as gasoline.

⚙ Cracking and Fuels

Alkanes with short chains are more flammable and therefore more useful as fuels than those with long chains. Cracking converts longer alkanes into shorter alkanes and alkenes.

| a long-chain hydrocarbon molecule $\longrightarrow$ a shorter alkane molecule + an alkene |

$$C_8H_{18} \implies C_6H_{14} + C_2H_4$$

octane (8 C atoms) $\implies$ hexane (6 C atoms) + ethene (2 C atoms)

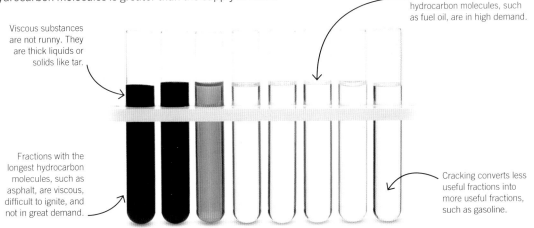

Cracking Paraffin

Paraffin oil is a colorless liquid. It can be used to demonstrate cracking (see page 206) in the laboratory. Its vapor is passed over a hot catalyst, causing its alkane molecules to break down into shorter alkanes and alkenes. Some of these new substances are liquids at room temperature, but others are gases.

Key Facts

✓ Cracking is a process in which longer alkanes are broken down into shorter alkanes, which are useful as fuels.

✓ Cracking also produces alkenes for making addition polymers.

✓ Cracking lets refineries match the supply of short-chain alkanes to industrial demand.

✓ Paraffin oil is cracked by heating over a catalyst.

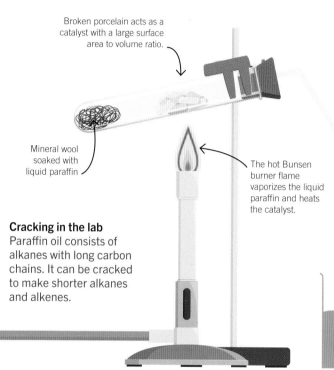

Broken porcelain acts as a catalyst with a large surface area to volume ratio.

Mineral wool soaked with liquid paraffin

The hot Bunsen burner flame vaporizes the liquid paraffin and heats the catalyst.

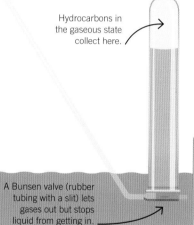

Alkane molecules in the paraffin oil are decomposed to form shorter alkanes and alkenes.

Hydrocarbons in the gaseous state collect here.

Cracking in the lab
Paraffin oil consists of alkanes with long carbon chains. It can be cracked to make shorter alkanes and alkenes.

A Bunsen valve (rubber tubing with a slit) lets gases out but stops liquid from getting in.

⚙ Supply and Demand

Fractional distillation gives a greater supply of fractions with larger hydrocarbon molecules than the demand for them. Cracking converts these less useful "heavy" fractions into more useful "light" fractions, allowing an oil refinery to match its supply with demand.

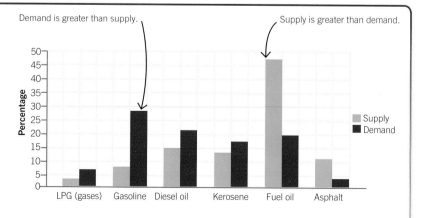

Demand is greater than supply.

Supply is greater than demand.

Percentage

Supply
Demand

LPG (gases) Gasoline Diesel oil Kerosene Fuel oil Asphalt

Alkenes

The alkenes form a homologous series of hydrocarbons (see page 198) with the functional group C=C. They have similar chemical properties and the general formula C_nH_{2n}. The formula of each successive alkene differs by CH_2. The C=C bond allows alkenes to take part in addition reactions, so they are more reactive than alkanes.

 Key Facts

✓ The alkenes are a homologous series of hydrocarbons.

✓ Their molecules contain a carbon–carbon double bond.

✓ The C=C bond makes alkenes more reactive than alkanes.

✓ The general formula for alkenes is C_nH_{2n}.

The first four alkenes
The first four alkenes are ethene, propene, butene, and pentene. Butene and pentene both have position isomers where the C=C bond occupies different positions on the carbon chain.

		Condensed formula	Molecular formula	Structural formula
	Ethene	C_2H_4	$CH_2{=}CH_2$	
	Propene	C_3H_6	$CH_3CH{=}CH_2$	
	Butene	C_4H_8	$CH_3CH_2CH{=}CH_2$	
	Pentene	C_5H_{10}	$CH_3CH_2CH_2CH{=}CH_2$	

Addition Reactions

In an addition reaction, two substances react together to produce just one product. Alkenes have a C=C bond that lets them take part in addition reactions. Alkenes react with hydrogen to form alkanes, and with bromine to form dibromo compounds. They can also react together to form addition polymers.

Key Facts

✓ Alkenes can undergo addition reactions because they have a C=C bond.

✓ Only one product forms when an addition reaction happens.

✓ Addition with hydrogen forms alkanes.

✓ Addition with halogens forms halogenoalkanes.

C=C bonds
In all addition reactions involving alkenes, the C=C bond becomes a C–C bond, and an atom or group of atoms bonds to each of the two carbon atoms.

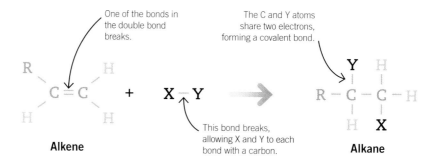

The addition of hydrogen
When heated in the presence of a nickel catalyst (see page 184), alkenes take part in addition reactions with hydrogen, to form alkanes. For example, ethene reacts with hydrogen to form ethane.

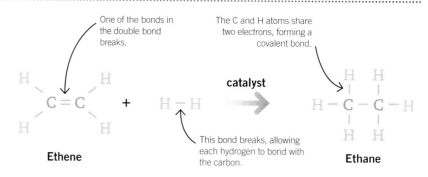

The addition of halogens
Alkenes take part in addition reactions with halogens (see page 70), such as chlorine, bromine, and iodine. Reactions with chlorine form dichloro-compounds, such as dichloropropane.

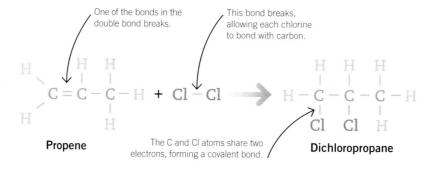

Isomers

Isomers have the same molecular formula but different structural formulas, and some of their properties, such as boiling point, may differ. The molecular formula tells you how many atoms of each element are in one of its molecules. The structural formula takes into account the arrangement of the atoms.

Key Facts

✓ Isomers are compounds with the same molecular formula but different structures.

✓ Isomers may differ in their carbon chains, the position of their functional group, or the type of functional group.

✓ Alkenes and alcohols can have position isomers.

Chain isomers of alkanes
Chain isomers occur when the carbon atoms are joined together in different positions. Butane and methylpropane both have the formula C_4H_{10}, but their carbon atoms are arranged differently.

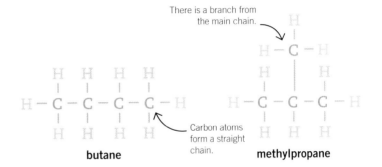

There is a branch from the main chain.

Carbon atoms form a straight chain.

butane

methylpropane

Position isomers of alkenes
Position isomers occur when the functional group of the molecule occupies different positions on the carbon chain. But-1-ene and but-2-ene both have the formula C_4H_8 but their functional groups are in different positions.

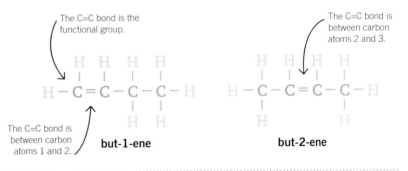

The C=C bond is the functional group.

The C=C bond is between carbon atoms 1 and 2.

but-1-ene

The C=C bond is between carbon atoms 2 and 3.

but-2-ene

Position isomers of alcohols
Alcohols have the functional group –OH. This can be attached to different atoms on the carbon chain. Propan-1-ol and propan-2-ol both have the formula C_3H_7OH.

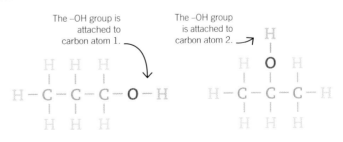

The –OH group is attached to carbon atom 1.

The –OH group is attached to carbon atom 2.

propan-1-ol

propan-2-ol

Combustion of Alkenes

The alkenes are a homologous series of hydrocarbons (see page 208). If there is an excess of oxygen, they burn completely to form carbon dioxide and water. If there is not enough oxygen, incomplete combustion happens. While this still produces water and carbon dioxide, carbon and carbon monoxide (a toxic gas) are also produced.

The black soot consists of carbon particles, which can blacken buildings and cause breathing problems.

Toxic carbon monoxide gas is produced during incomplete combustion.

A smoky yellow flame instead of a blue flame indicates incomplete combustion.

Key Facts

✓ When alkenes undergo complete combustion, they form carbon dioxide and water.

✓ Incomplete combustion happens when there is insufficient oxygen.

✓ Instead of carbon dioxide, carbon monoxide and carbon are produced during incomplete combustion.

The combustion of cyclohexene
Cyclohexene (C_6H_{10}) is an alkene in the liquid state at room temperature. This image shows its incomplete combustion.

⚙ How the Incomplete Combustion of Alkenes Works

For a given number of hydrogen atoms, alkenes have more carbon atoms than alkanes. Due to the strength of the C=C bond, they are more likely to undergo incomplete combustion in air. Here is the equation for the incomplete combustion of alkenes.

Water is produced.

$$\text{alkene} + \text{oxygen} \longrightarrow \text{carbon monoxide} + \text{carbon} + \text{water}$$

Toxic carbon monoxide is produced during incomplete combustion.

Carbon is produced as black particles, or soot.

Testing for Alkenes

All alkene molecules contain C=C bonds. These bonds allow alkenes to take part in addition reactions (see page 209). Alkane molecules do not contain C=C bonds, so they cannot take part in addition reactions. Bromine water, a halogen (see page 70), is used to test whether a compound is an alkene or alkane.

Bromine water
The test for alkenes works with bromine and bromine water. Bromine is corrosive and toxic, so very dilute bromine water is safer.

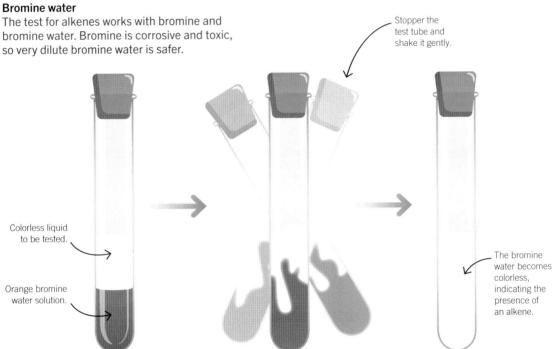

Stopper the test tube and shake it gently.

Colorless liquid to be tested.

Orange bromine water solution.

The bromine water becomes colorless, indicating the presence of an alkene.

Addition reactions of alkenes
The reaction with bromine above is an addition reaction. Alkenes react with bromine because they have a C=C bond. Ethene is an alkene that is widely used in the chemical industry.

One of the bonds breaks and each C and Br atom forms a covalent bond.

The colorless compound formed has two bromine atoms as the name suggests.

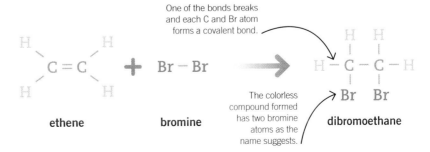

ethene   bromine   dibromoethane

Addition Polymers

Polyethylene is an example of an addition polymer. It is made from ethylene molecules that have been joined end to end during an addition polymerization reaction. Only one product forms in addition reactions (see page 209), so only the polymer is made. You can represent polymer molecules using structural formulas of their repeating unit (see page 214) .

(see page 209) (see page 214)

> ### Key Facts
>
> ✓ Polymer molecules are large molecules made from smaller molecules called monomers.
> ✓ Monomers for addition polymers frequently contain C=C bonds.
> ✓ The polymer is the only product made during addition polymerization.
> ✓ The repeating unit of a polymer is figured out from the structure of its monomer.

Polyethylene
This ball-and-stick model shows part of a polyethylene molecule.

One of the bonds in a double bond can open up and join onto other ethene molecules.

Addition polymerization
Polymerization reactions can be shown using structural formulas. Each line between two atoms represents a covalent bond. Here, three ethylene monomers form a section of polyethylene.

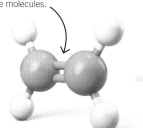

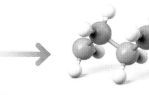

Three ethylene molecules

Polyethylene

Repeating units
A polymer molecule consists of repeating units, like a train consists of cars. Polymer molecules contain many of these units, so n is used instead of the actual number.

n is a very large number of monomers.

These bonds connect to the next monomers.

n ethylene molecules

n repeating units of polyethylene

Representing Addition Polymers

A polymer molecule can contain thousands of atoms. It would be too difficult to draw a diagram to show a whole molecule. Instead, polymers are represented by their repeating unit. You can figure out the repeating unit of a polymer from its monomer, and the monomer from the repeating unit.

Key Facts

✓ The monomer and the repeating unit of a polymer have the same number and arrangement of atoms.

✓ The C=C bond in a monomer becomes a single bond in the repeating unit.

✓ A polymer's name is the word "poly" followed by the name of the monomer in parentheses.

Monomer to repeating unit
A polymer's monomer and repeating unit have the same number of atoms of each element. The atoms have the same arrangement but the bonding is slightly different.

The C=C bond opens up to form a C–C bond in the repeating unit.

Draw a long bond each side of where the C=C bond was.

Draw parentheses passing through each long bond.

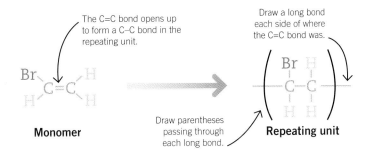

Monomer

Repeating unit

Repeating unit to monomer
A polymer's repeating unit and monomer have the same number of atoms of each element. The atoms have the same arrangement but the bonding is slightly different.

Remove outside bonds and parentheses.

Add a double bond.

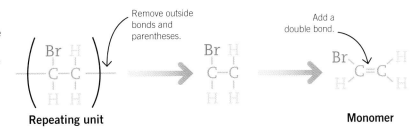

Repeating unit

Monomer

🔍 From Propene to Poly(propylene)

You use the monomer and repeating unit to show the equation for making a polymer.

n stands for any very large number.

n **propene monomers**

A long bond drawn in the repeating unit represent the bond that attaches to the next repeating unit.

You need to use the letter n in an equation but not when showing an individual monomer or repeating unit.

n **repeating units of poly(propylene) polymer**

Alcohols

The alcohols are a homologous series of organic compounds (see page 198). They contain the functional group −OH, which is responsible for their typical chemical properties. The simplest alcohol, methanol, is toxic but is used as a fuel on its own or mixed with gasoline. Ethanol is found in alcoholic drinks and is a useful biofuel.

Key Facts

✓ The alcohols form a homologous series of organic compounds.

✓ Alcohols contain the functional group −OH, giving them their typical chemical properties.

✓ The names of alcohols end in "-ol."

✓ The general formula for alcohols is $C_nH_{2n+1}OH$.

The first four alcohols
This table shows information for the first four alcohols. The −OH group is always at the end of a carbon chain.

		Condensed formula	Molecular formula	Structural formula
	Methanol	CH_3OH	CH_3OH	H−C−O−H
	Ethanol	C_2H_5OH	CH_3CH_2OH	H−C−C−O−H
	Propanol	C_3H_7OH	$CH_3CH_2CH_2OH$	H−C−C−C−O−H
	Butanol	C_4H_9OH	$CH_3(CH_2)_3OH$	H−C−C−C−C−O−H

Properties of Alcohols

Alcohols with short carbon chains mix completely with water, forming neutral mixtures. Like hydrocarbons, alcohols burn completely in excess air or oxygen to form carbon dioxide and water (see page 200). They can be oxidized to carboxylic acids by heating with oxidizing agents.

Key Facts

✓ Alcohols with short carbon chains mix completely with water.

✓ Complete combustion produces carbon dioxide and water.

✓ Alcohols can be oxidized to carboxylic acids.

Solubility in water
Methanol, ethanol, propanol, and butanol mix completely with water to form neutral, clear, and colorless solutions.

H_2O

C_2H_5OH

Water is a clear, colorless liquid.

Ethanol is a clear, colorless liquid.

Flammable
Alcohols are flammable. They undergo complete combustion (see page 163) in a plentiful supply of oxygen to produce carbon dioxide and water. They undergo incomplete combustion in a limited supply of oxygen or air. This produces carbon monoxide, carbon, and water.

A smoky yellow flame indicates incomplete combustion.

Oxidation
Oxidation is the gain of oxygen by a substance. Alcohols can be oxidized by burning them. They can also be oxidized using potassium manganate(VII).

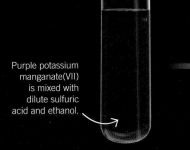

Purple potassium manganate(VII) is mixed with dilute sulfuric acid and ethanol.

Once heated, the color fades as colorless ethanoic acid is produced.

Uses of Ethanol

The alcohols are a homologous series of compounds with the −OH functional group (see page 198). Ethanol is the alcohol found in alcoholic drinks. It is a useful solvent that can dissolve some substances that water cannot. Ethanol is also used as an antiseptic and fuel.

> **Key Facts**
>
> ✓ Ethanol is useful as a solvent to dissolve other substances.
>
> ✓ Ethanol kills bacteria so it is useful as an antiseptic.
>
> ✓ Ethanol burns in air and is useful as a fuel.

Solvents
Ethanol dissolves oil and grease, which water cannot do. It is a useful solvent in paints, cleaning products, perfumes, and varnish.

Ethanol is a solvent in paints.

Paints

Antiseptics
Antiseptics are substances that kill bacteria. Ethanol is a good antiseptic. It is used in antiseptic hand gels and foams.

Ethanol wipes are used to sterilize the skin before giving an injection.

Antiseptic skin wipes

Fuels
Most ethanol is bioethanol, which is manufactured by fermentation. It is a useful fuel, either on its own or mixed with gasoline.

Ethanol is used as a fuel in spirit burners.

Fuel

Alcoholic drinks
Alcoholic drinks such as beer and wine contain ethanol (about 4% and 12% respectively). Distillation increases its concentration for drinks such as vodka and whisky (about 40%).

Beer contains ethanol and is made by the fermentation of grains, such as malted barley.

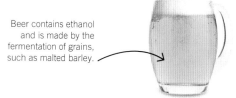

Beer

The Production of Ethanol

Fermentation is a type of anaerobic respiration (a process that happens in the absence of oxygen). It produces ethanol and carbon dioxide from carbohydrates (see page 226) dissolved in water. Yeast cells contain the enzymes needed for fermentation to happen.

An airlock allows carbon dioxide out but stops air from getting in.

Fermentation

Fermentation produces ethanol on an industrial scale for use as a biofuel. It is also used to make beer, wine, and other alcoholic drinks.

The mixture of water, sugars, and yeast is kept at about 70–85°F (20–30°C).

Yeast die and sink to the bottom when the ethanol concentration gets too high for them.

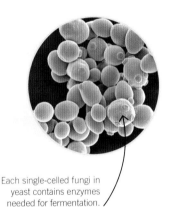

Each single-celled fungi in yeast contains enzymes needed for fermentation.

Homemade wine

Key Facts

✓ Ethanol can be made by the fermentation of sugars at moderate temperatures and pressures.

✓ Fermentation also produces carbon dioxide.

✓ Ethanol can be made by the hydration of ethene, an addition reaction, at high temperatures and pressures.

enzymes in yeast

sugar ⟶ ethanol + carbon dioxide

⚙ Hydration of Ethene

Ethene reacts with steam to form ethanol in an addition reaction (see page 209). This is a reversible reaction that needs a phosphoric acid catalyst, and high temperatures and pressures.

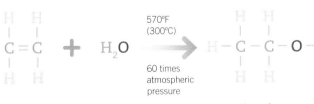

570°F (300°C)

60 times atmospheric pressure

ethene   water   ethanol

Carboxylic Acids

The carboxylic acids form a homologous series of organic compounds (see page 198). They all contain the $-COOH$ functional group, which gives them similar reactive properties. Their formulas differ by a $-CH_2-$ group, which changes from one carboxylic acid to the next. The names of carboxylic acids end in "-anoic acid."

Key Facts

✓ The carboxylic acids form a homologous series.

✓ Their molecules all contain a $-COOH$ functional group.

✓ Their names are derived from the total number of carbon atoms, and end in "-anoic acid."

✓ The general formula for carboxylic acids is $C_nH_{2n+1}COOH$, where n is any whole number from 0 upward.

The first four carboxylic acids
This table shows information for the first four carboxylic acids. The $-COOH$ group is always at the end of a carbon chain.

		Condensed formula	Molecular formula	Structural formula
	methanoic acid	HCOOH	HCOOH	
	ethanoic acid	CH_3COOH	CH_3COOH	
	propanoic acid	C_2H_5COOH	CH_3CH_2COOH	
	butanoic acid	C_3H_7COOH	$CH_3CH_2CH_2COOH$	

Carboxylic Acid Reactions

Carboxylic acids are weak acids. They undergo the typical reactions of acids with reactive metals and with carbonates. These reactions are slower than similar reactions involving strong acids of equal concentration (see page 137). The names of the salts formed by carboxylic acids end in "-anoate."

Key Facts

✓ Carboxylic acids are weak acids because they only partially ionize in solution.

✓ They react with metal carbonates to produce salts, water, and carbon dioxide.

✓ They react with metals to produce salts and hydrogen.

Reaction with carbonates
Carboxylic acids react with carbonates to form salts, water, and carbon dioxide.

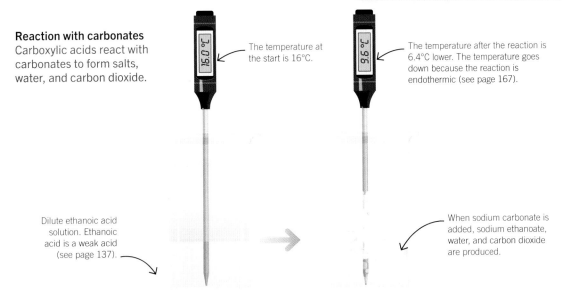

The temperature at the start is 16°C.

The temperature after the reaction is 6.4°C lower. The temperature goes down because the reaction is endothermic (see page 167).

Dilute ethanoic acid solution. Ethanoic acid is a weak acid (see page 137).

When sodium carbonate is added, sodium ethanoate, water, and carbon dioxide are produced.

🗐 Reactions with Carbonates

Like other acids, carboxylic acids react with carbonates to produce salt, water, and carbon dioxide (see page 140).

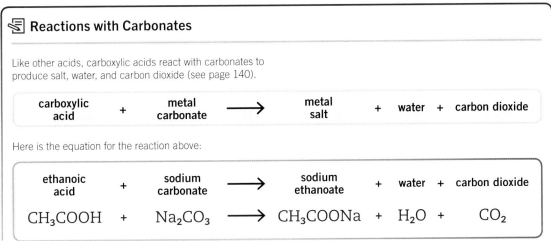

| carboxylic acid | + | metal carbonate | → | metal salt | + | water | + | carbon dioxide |

Here is the equation for the reaction above:

| ethanoic acid | + | sodium carbonate | → | sodium ethanoate | + | water | + | carbon dioxide |

$$CH_3COOH + Na_2CO_3 \longrightarrow CH_3COONa + H_2O + CO_2$$

Esters

Esters are organic compounds (see page 198) produced by the reactions between alcohols and carboxylic acids. They all contain the −COO− functional group. Esters have fruity smells, which make them useful in the production of perfumes and flavorings. Ethyl ethanoate is a good solvent and is used in nail polish remover and glues.

 Key Facts

✓ Esters are organic compounds with a −COO− functional group.

✓ They are named after the alcohol and carboxylic acid that formed them.

✓ Sulfuric acid is used as a catalyst when making esters.

Making esters
Esters are made by reacting alcohols with carboxylic acids. Sulfuric acid is added as a catalyst (see page 184) and the reaction mixture is warmed.

$$\text{alcohol + carboxylic acid} \xrightarrow{\text{sulfuric acid catalyst}} \text{ester + water}$$

Making ethyl ethanoate
Ethyl ethanoate is an ester. It is made by reacting ethanol with ethanoic acid.

| ethanol | + | ethanoic acid | ⟶ | ethyl ethanoate | + | water |

$$C_2H_5OH \; + \; CH_3COOH \longrightarrow CH_3COOC_2H_5 \; + \; H_2O$$

(structural reaction diagram with sulfuric acid catalyst)

Ester Smells

Esters have fruity smells, so they are used in perfumes. Esters occur naturally in plants, and manufactured esters are used as artificial flavorings. The table shows some examples.

Alcohol	Carboxylic acid	Ester	Smell
ethanol	ethanoic acid	ethyl ethanoate	pear drops
propanol	hexanoic acid	propyl hexanoate	blackberries
butanol	ethanoic acid	butyl ethanoate	apples
butanol	butanoic acid	butyl butanoate	pineapples

Condensation Polymers

Addition polymers such as polyethylene contain one type of repeating monomer (see page 213). Their monomers have C=C bonds and only the polymer is made. Condensation polymers, such as polyesters and polyamides (see page 223), have two types of repeating monomer, each of which has two functional groups (see page 198). When the monomers join, water is produced as a by-product.

Key Facts

✓ Condensation polymers have two types of monomer.

✓ These monomers do not need C=C bonds to produce a polymer but they do need two functional groups.

✓ One water molecule is produced for each ester link formed in a polyester.

Nylon

Nylon is a condensation polymer formed from two monomers. One is a diamine with two $-NH_2$ groups (see page 223). The other is a dicarboxylic acid with two $-COOH$ groups (see page 223).

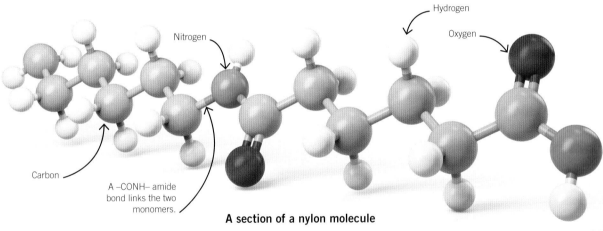

A section of a nylon molecule

Hydrogen
Oxygen
Nitrogen
Carbon
A –CONH– amide bond links the two monomers.

⚙ How Condensation Polymerization Works

In a condensation reaction, two monomers join together to make a polymer. They are called condensation reactions as a water molecule forms for each repeating unit made. This diagram shows the condensation reaction between a carboxylic acid and an alcohol to form an ester (see page 221) and water.

Groups of atoms between the two functional groups

A water molecule (H_2O) is formed.

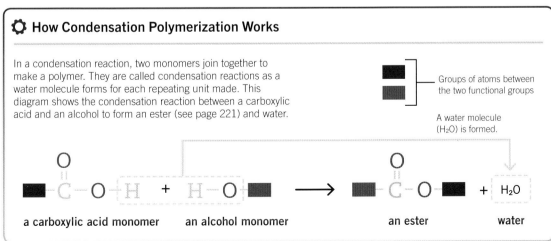

a carboxylic acid monomer   an alcohol monomer   an ester   water

Polyesters and Polyamides

Polyesters and polyamides are both examples of condensation polymers (see page 222). During a polymerization reaction, two water molecules form as a by-product for every repeating unit made. Polyesters are formed from a dicarboxylic acid and a diol, and polyamides from a dicarboxylic acid and a diamine.

Key Facts

✓ Polyesters and polyamides are condensation polymers.

✓ Polyesters are formed from a dicarboxylic acid and a diol.

✓ Polyamides are formed from a dicarboxylic acid and a diamine.

✓ Water is a by-product of condensation polymerization.

Polyesters
Polyesters form when dicarboxylic acid molecules (with one —COOH group at each end) react with diol molecules (with —OH groups at each end) to form ester bonds (—COO) and give off water. This creates the structure of the repeating unit below.

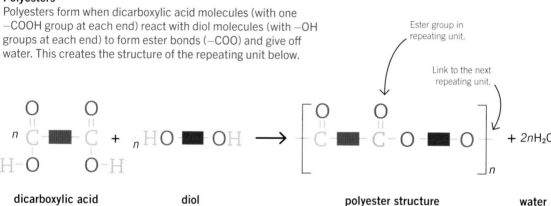

Ester group in repeating unit.

Link to the next repeating unit.

dicarboxylic acid   diol   polyester structure   water

Polyamides
Polyamides form when dicarboxylic acid molecules react with diamine molecules to form amide bonds (—CONH) and give off water. This creates the structure of the repeating unit below.

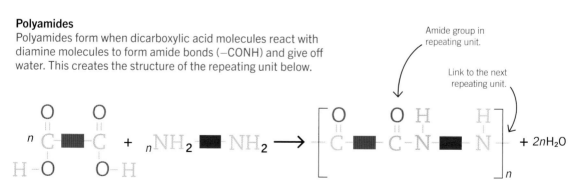

Amide group in repeating unit.

Link to the next repeating unit.

dicarboxylic acid   diamine   polyamide structure   water

DNA

DNA is the genetic material found in the nucleus of a cell. It is a natural condensation polymer made from four different nucleotide monomers. The two strands in a DNA molecule wrap around each other to form a double helix shape.

Key Facts

✓ **DNA consists of two strands coiled around each other in a double helix.**

✓ **Each strand is made of nucleotides.**

✓ **A nucleotide consists of a sugar, a phosphate group, and a base (G, C, A, or T).**

DNA double helix
DNA is a natural condensation polymer formed from monomers called nucleotides. Each nucleotide contains one of four different bases (G, C, A, or T).

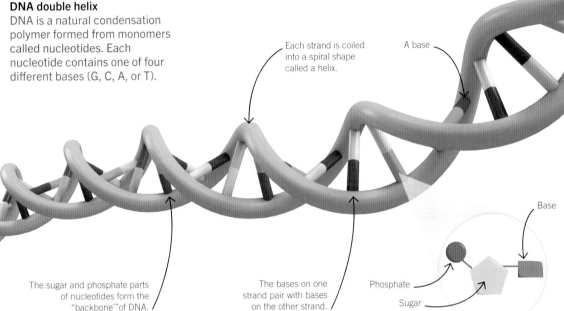

Each strand is coiled into a spiral shape called a helix.

A base

The sugar and phosphate parts of nucleotides form the "backbone'"of DNA.

The bases on one strand pair with bases on the other strand.

Base

Phosphate

Sugar

A nucleotide

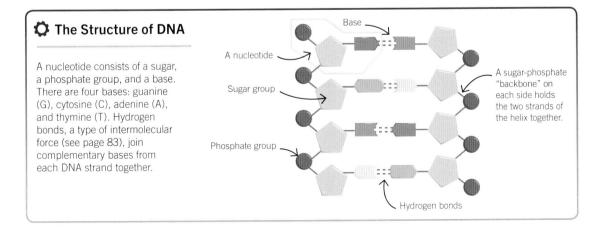

⚙ The Structure of DNA

A nucleotide consists of a sugar, a phosphate group, and a base. There are four bases: guanine (G), cytosine (C), adenine (A), and thymine (T). Hydrogen bonds, a type of intermolecular force (see page 83), join complementary bases from each DNA strand together.

Base

A nucleotide

Sugar group

Phosphate group

A sugar-phosphate "backbone" on each side holds the two strands of the helix together.

Hydrogen bonds

Proteins

Proteins are condensation polymers (see page 222) formed from many amino acid monomers. Amino acids have a −COOH functional group at one end and a −NH2 functional group at the other. These groups react, linking the amino acids by bonds called peptide links. There are 20 standard amino acids. Different types of proteins include enzymes, hair, and transport proteins.

📌 Key Facts

✓ Proteins are condensation polymers.

✓ They are made from amino acids and contain peptide links.

✓ Different proteins consist of different combinations and numbers of amino acids.

✓ All enzymes are proteins.

Insulin

Insulin molecules consist of two chains joined together, one with 21 amino acids and the other with 30 amino acids.

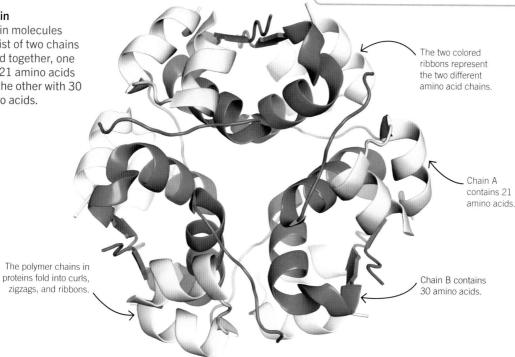

The two colored ribbons represent the two different amino acid chains.

Chain A contains 21 amino acids.

Chain B contains 30 amino acids.

The polymer chains in proteins fold into curls, zigzags, and ribbons.

⚙ The Structure of a Protein

Proteins are condensation polymers made from amino acid monomers. Amino acid molecules have a different functional group at each end. They react to form peptide bonds that are a type of amide bond (−CONH).

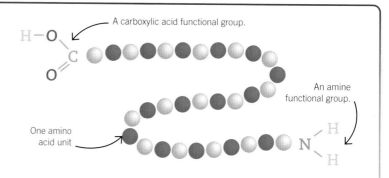

A carboxylic acid functional group.

One amino acid unit

An amine functional group.

Carbohydrates

Carbohydrates are compounds containing carbon, hydrogen, and oxygen. Starch and glycogen are complex carbohydrates that consist of thousands of glucose molecules joined together. Glucose and fructose are simple sugars (monosaccharides). These can join together to make disaccharides such as sucrose, which is table sugar.

Cellulose fibers
Cellulose is a complex carbohydrate found in plant cell walls. It forms fibers like this (seen using an electron microscope). A single fiber contains many cellulose molecules twisted around each other.

Key Facts

✓ Carbohydrates are compounds containing carbon, hydrogen, and oxygen.

✓ Starch is a complex carbohydrate made from many glucose molecules joined together.

✓ Sucrose consists of two simple sugars joined together.

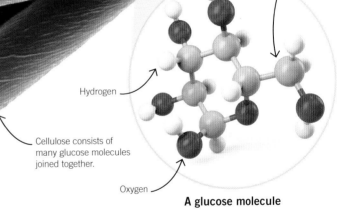

Carbon

Hydrogen

Cellulose consists of many glucose molecules joined together.

Oxygen

A glucose molecule

⚙ Complex Carbohydrates

A complex carbohydrate molecule consists of simple sugar molecules joined together. Starch and cellulose are made from glucose and are carbohydrates—an important source of energy.

Each starch molecule can contain thousands of glucose units.

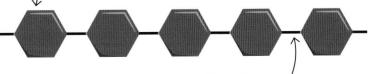

A section of starch

The bond between two glucose units.

Hydrolysis of Polymers

Proteins (see page 225) and complex carbohydrates such as starch are examples of natural condensation polymers (see page 222). They consist of many monomer units joined together. Water is produced as a by-product during polymerization. The reverse process, breaking down the polymer into its monomers again, is called hydrolysis.

Key Facts

✓ Proteins and complex carbohydrates can be broken down to their monomers.

✓ This is called hydrolysis.

✓ Hydrolysis needs enzymes or hot concentrated acid.

✓ Chromatography using locating agents is useful in separating and identifying the products of hydrolysis.

Hydrolysis of proteins

Protease enzymes can hydrolyze proteins to amino acids by breaking the bonds between molecules. Hot concentrated hydrochloric acid can do the same, but more slowly.

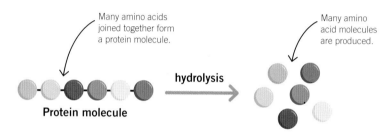

Many amino acids joined together form a protein molecule.

Protein molecule

hydrolysis

Many amino acid molecules are produced.

Amino acids

Hydrolysis of complex carbohydrates

Carbohydrase enzymes can hydrolyze complex carbohydrates to simple sugars by breaking the bonds between molecules. For example, starch can be hydrolyzed to glucose.

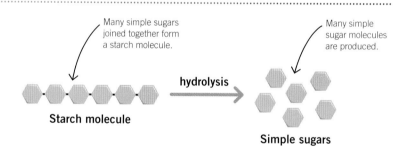

Many simple sugars joined together form a starch molecule.

Starch molecule

hydrolysis

Many simple sugar molecules are produced.

Simple sugars

✿ Separation and Identification by Chromatography

Chromatography allows the separation of different soluble substances in a mixture. It can be used to identify amino acids and simple sugars when their R_f values on a chromatogram are calculated (see pages 44–45). Locating agents are sprayed onto the chromatogram to make these substances visible.

Amino acids and simple sugars are colorless.

The spots become colored and visible when a locating agent is sprayed onto the chromatogram.

Without locating agent

With locating agent

Chemical
Analysis

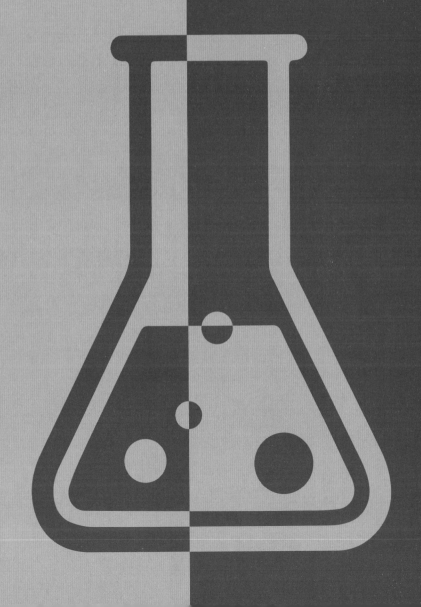

Testing for Oxygen

Oxygen is a colorless, odorless gas, and so can be difficult to detect. It is needed for a substance to combust (burn), and bringing a substance that can combust into contact with more oxygen will make it burn even more easily and brightly. You can use this to detect oxygen's presence.

Key Facts

✓ Oxygen is a colorless and odorless gas, so it's hard to detect.

✓ Oxygen is required for a substance to combust.

✓ You can test for the presence of oxygen by relighting a glowing splint.

🔎 Why Test for Oxygen?

Testing for the presence of oxygen is important, because oxygen-rich air is a fire hazard. Underground vaults, tunnels, or sewers are confined spaces that may have high levels of oxygen in the air. People working in these spaces may need to test for high oxygen levels to confirm these spaces are safe to work in.

Setting up the experiment
Add 3 grams of manganese oxide to a conical flask. Measure 20 cm³ of hydrogen peroxide with a measuring cylinder. Connect the conical flask to a basin of water using the two delivery tubes.

1. Pour 20 cm³ of clear hydrogen peroxide solution into the flask containing manganese oxide powder using the thistle funnel.

4. Light a wooden splint, and blow it out to leave a glowing ember. Quickly open the test tube and place the splint into the test tube. If oxygen was successfully collected, the lit splint will reignite.

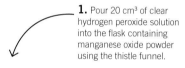

Delivery tube

3. Oxygen gas is collected over water in a test tube. Repeat this step twice with two other test tubes.

Thistle funnel

Two-hole stopper

Wooden splint

2. Manganese oxide powder inside conical flask reacts with hydrogen peroxide solution.

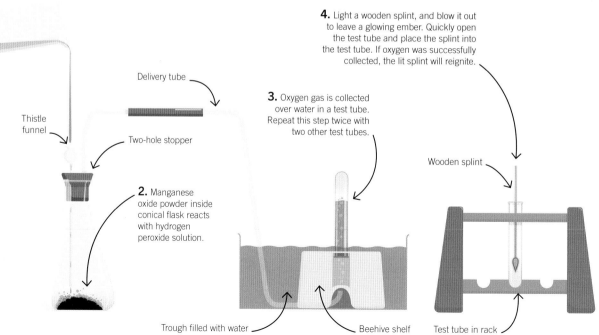

Trough filled with water

Beehive shelf

Test tube in rack

Testing for Carbon Dioxide

Carbon dioxide is a nontoxic, colorless, odorless gas. It is fairly unreactive, but it is slightly soluble and forms a weakly acidic solution. It can be detected in the laboratory using either a splint, limewater, or universal indicator.

Key Facts

✓ Carbon dioxide is a colorless, odorless, and nontoxic gas.

✓ Carbon dioxide gas extinguishes a lit splint, turns limewater milky, or turns universal indicator red upon reaction.

Setting up the experiment
Add calcium carbonate to a conical flask. Measure 50 cm³ of hydrochloric acid. Connect the conical flask to a basin of water using the two delivery tubes.

1. Pour 50 cm³ of hydrochloric acid using the thistle funnel into the conical flask containing calcium carbonate.

3. Carbon dioxide gas is collected over water in an upside down test tube. Repeat this step twice with two other test tubes.

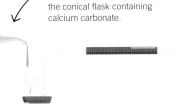

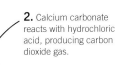

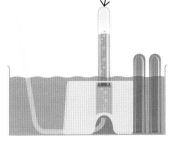

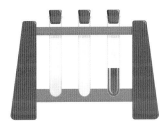

2. Calcium carbonate reacts with hydrochloric acid, producing carbon dioxide gas.

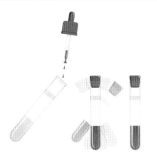

Splint
Place a lit splint in one of the test tubes, and the carbon dioxide gas will extinguish it.

Limewater
Add limewater using a pipette to one of the test tubes and shake well. Carbon dioxide will turn the limewater milky.

Universal indicator
Add five drops of universal indicator to one of the test tubes and shake well. Carbon dioxide is slightly acidic, so it will turn red.

Testing for Hydrogen

Hydrogen (H$_2$) is a nontoxic, colorless, and odorless gas (see page 55). It is highly explosive, so testing for its presence in the laboratory must be conducted carefully, following safety procedure.

Key Facts

✓ Hydrogen is a nontoxic, colorless, and odorless gas.

✓ Hydrogen can react explosively with other elements such as oxygen.

✓ Hydrogen can be detected in the lab by listening for a squeaky "pop" when a lit splint is placed near hydrogen gas.

Testing for Ammonia

Ammonia gas smells really bad and is dangerous for your eyes. If you hold damp red litmus paper over a test tube containing ammonia, it will turn blue. Be sure to follow safety procedures when carrying out this experiment.

Litmus paper

Test solution

Bunsen burner

Setting up the experiment

Add zinc to a conical flask. Measure 50 cm^3 of hydrochloric acid. Connect the conical flask to a basin of water using the two delivery tubes.

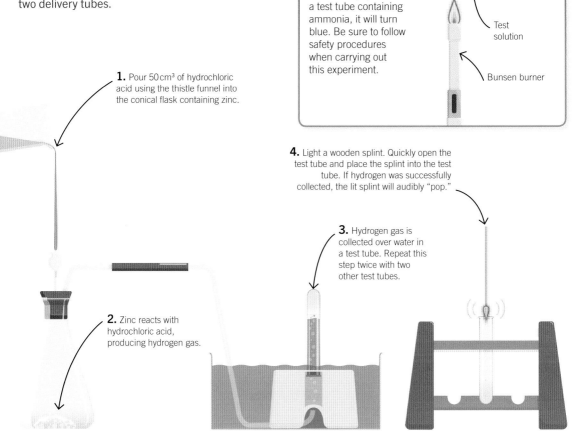

1. Pour 50 cm^3 of hydrochloric acid using the thistle funnel into the conical flask containing zinc.

2. Zinc reacts with hydrochloric acid, producing hydrogen gas.

3. Hydrogen gas is collected over water in a test tube. Repeat this step twice with two other test tubes.

4. Light a wooden splint. Quickly open the test tube and place the splint into the test tube. If hydrogen was successfully collected, the lit splint will audibly "pop."

Testing for Cations
Flame Tests

Cations are positive ions (see page 73) that form after they lose one or more of their outer electrons. Metal atoms form cations, and their charges depend on the number of electrons they lose. For example, Na^+ (sodium) has lost one electron, and Ca^{2+} (calcium) has lost two electrons.

Flame tests
The bright colors are produced by the presence of different metal cations in a solid substance.

Key Facts

✓ Cations are positive ions that form when atoms lose electrons.

✓ Most cations are metal ions.

✓ When metal cations are held within a flame they produce unique colors.

✓ Colors in flame tests help identify metals.

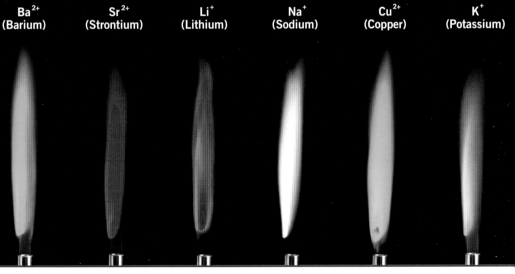

| Ba^{2+} (Barium) | Sr^{2+} (Strontium) | Li^+ (Lithium) | Na^+ (Sodium) | Cu^{2+} (Copper) | K^+ (Potassium) |

⚙ How Flame Tests Work

Flame tests can be done in the laboratory. All you need is a metal wire and a Bunsen burner. Clean and moisten the wire, and then dip it into the substance you want to test. Then, place it slowly and carefully in the blue part of a Bunsen burner's flame. The flame will then change color to represent the ion present in the substance. Some ions may produce the same color in the flames, in this case, a different test can be used (see page 233).

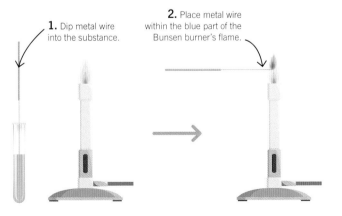

1. Dip metal wire into the substance.

2. Place metal wire within the blue part of the Bunsen burner's flame.

Testing for Cations
Precipitation Reactions

Precipitates are small, insoluble particles that float or sink in a solution. A precipitate forms when a dissolved substance in a solution reacts with another substance added to a solution to produce an insoluble solid.

Using sodium hydroxide
If you add a few droplets of alkaline sodium hydroxide to a solution containing a metal; in some cases, a metal hydroxide precipitate forms.

Key Facts

✓ Cations are positive ions that form when atoms lose electrons.

✓ Some metal ions can be identified using precipitation reactions.

✓ A precipitate is an insoluble solid formed when two solutions react.

✓ A precipitate's color depends on the metal ion.

✓ Sodium hydroxide and ammonia solutions can be used to create precipitates with some metals.

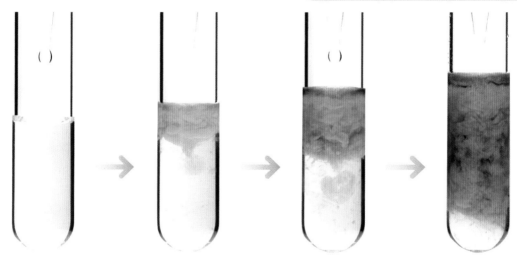

1. One mol of sodium hydroxide is added to 0.2 mol of iron(II) ammonium sulfate.

2. A cloudy green-white precipitate slowly begins to form.

3. The precipitate solidifies and expands as more iron(II) in the solution reacts with hydroxide.

4. The precipitate turns brown as oxygen oxidizes the iron at the top of the solution.

⚙ Colored Precipitates

Precipitation reactions can be done in the laboratory. All you need is either sodium hydroxide or ammonia solutions, and a pipette. The precipitate's color will tell you what metal ion is in the solution.

| Al^{3+} | Cu^{2+} | Co^{2+} | Fe^{3+} | Fe^{2+} | Zn^{2+} |
| Aluminum | Copper | Cobalt | Iron (III) | Iron (II) | Zinc |

Testing for Anions
Carbonates and Sulfates

Anions are negative ions (see page 73) that form when atoms gain one or more electrons in their outer shell. Nonmetal atoms form anions, and their charge depends on the number of electrons they gain. For example, carbonate ions (CO_3^{2-}) have gained two electrons.

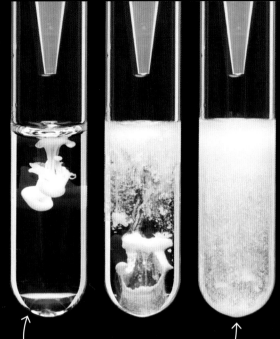

Test tube containing zinc sulfate solution.

White precipitate forms in zinc sulfate solution.

 Key Facts

✓ Anions are negative ions that form when atoms gain electrons.

✓ Carbonate ions are common in rocks such as limestone chalk and marble.

✓ Add dilute acid to test for the presence of carbonate ions in a solution.

✓ Add dilute hydrochloric acid and barium chloride solution to a sulfate solution to create a white precipitate.

Testing for sulfate ions

Add dilute hydrochloric acid, followed by barium chloride, to a solution. If sulfate ions are present in the solution, a white precipitate will form. For example, barium chloride added to zinc sulfate will form a misty white precipitation.

⚙ Testing for Carbonate Ions

Carbonate ions are commonly found in rocks such as limestone chalk. To test for carbonate ions, add dilute hydrochloric acid. If carbonate ions are present, the hydrochloric acid will react with them to produce bubbles of carbon dioxide. The solution will then turn milky.

Limewater becomes milky once carbon dioxide has been added.

Bubbles of carbon dioxide gas are given off when dilute acid is added to limewater.

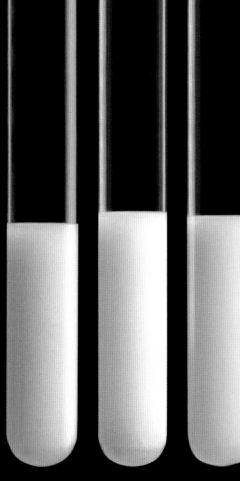

Testing for Anions
Halides and Nitrates

Anions are negative ions (see page 73) that form when atoms gain one or more electrons in their outer shell. The elements chlorine, bromine, and iodine in Group 7 (see page 70) can all form anions called halides. Nitrogen, an element in Group 5, can also form anions called nitrates.

Testing for halides
When a few drops of dilute silver nitrate are added to a solution containing halides, the halides react with the nitrate to form a cloudy precipitate. The color of the precipitate identifies which Group 7 element is present.

Chloride ions produce white precipitate

Bromide ions produce cream precipitate

Iodide ions produce yellow precipitate

 Key Facts

✓ Anions are negative ions formed by gaining electrons.

✓ Chlorine, bromine, and iodine elements form anions called halides.

✓ Nitrogen and oxygen form anions called nitrates.

⚙ Testing for Nitrates

Nitrates are negatively charged ions of nitrogen oxide, shown using the formula NO_3^-. To test for their presence in some solutions, add sodium hydroxide solution and aluminum powder, then heat the mixture. This reduces the ions, producing ammonia gas. Use damp litmus paper or damp universal indicator paper to test for the presence of ammonia gas.

Damp litmus paper turns blue

Damp universal indicator paper turns blue

Testing for Chlorine

Chlorine is a gas (sometimes colored yellow–green), with a strong smell. The element is usually found combined with other elements in compounds (see page 33), such as sodium chloride (common salt) and many other consumer products. On its own, chlorine is used as a disinfectant in water to kill germs, or as a bleach where it removes the color from materials such as wool and paper.

Key Facts

✓ Chlorine is a yellow–green gas.

✓ Chlorine is used as a disinfectant and a bleach.

✓ Chlorine's presence can be tested for using moist litmus paper, which turns red and then white in chlorine's presence.

Using litmus paper
Wet blue litmus paper (see page 134) can be used to test for the presence of chlorine gas.

Litmus paper is blue.

1. Hold wet blue litmus paper above a test tube that holds chlorine gas.

2. The litmus paper turns red at first, indicating that chlorine is acidic.

3. Chlorine gas then bleaches the red litmus paper white.

Test tube containing chlorine gas.

Testing for Water

Water is one of the most important compounds on Earth. Without water, there would be no life. Cobalt chloride paper is an indicator that can be used as a test for the presence of water. It's a useful test to check for moisture in the air or water leaks.

Key Facts

✓ Water is essential for life.
✓ Cobalt chloride paper changes from blue to pink when near water.
✓ Cobalt chloride paper indicates if there is water present—not if it's pure (see page 38).

Using cobalt chloride paper
Soak a strip of paper in cobalt chloride solution and leave it to dry until it turns blue. Then, hold it over a substance you believe contains water. If water is present, the paper will turn pink. This reaction is reversible (see page 191)—redrying the paper will turn it back to blue.

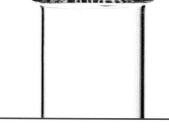

1. Cobalt chloride paper is blue.

2. Cobalt chloride paper turns pink when it's near water.

🔍 **Adding Water**

Water can be detected using other methods. Anhydrous (without water) copper sulfate is a fine, white powder that has had its water evaporated from it. When water is added, the anhydrous copper sulfate reacts with it and turns from white to blue, indicating water is present. It becomes hydrated (with water) copper sulfate.

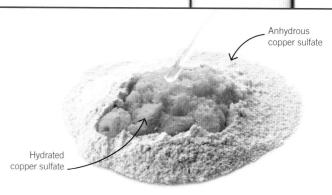

Anhydrous copper sulfate

Hydrated copper sulfate

Adding water to copper sulfate

Flame Emission Spectroscopy

White light is a spectrum (collection) of colors: red, orange, yellow, green, blue, indigo, and violet. The light produced by metal ions during a flame test (see page 232) are not single colors, but a mixture of certain colors from this spectrum. Flame emission spectroscopy is used to separate the emitted colors to produce a spectrum (collection of colors) for each element (see opposite page).

Key Facts

✓ White light is made up of a spectrum of colors.

✓ The light produced in flame tests is made up of a mixture of colors.

✓ Spectroscopy separates this light into its different colors.

✓ Spectroscopy produces a spectrum (collection) of colors for each element.

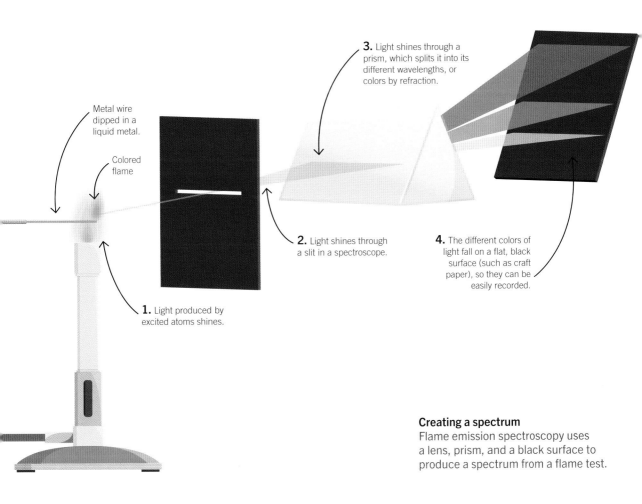

3. Light shines through a prism, which splits it into its different wavelengths, or colors by refraction.

Metal wire dipped in a liquid metal.

Colored flame

2. Light shines through a slit in a spectroscope.

4. The different colors of light fall on a flat, black surface (such as craft paper), so they can be easily recorded.

1. Light produced by excited atoms shines.

Creating a spectrum
Flame emission spectroscopy uses a lens, prism, and a black surface to produce a spectrum from a flame test.

Interpreting Spectroscopy Charts

When atoms are heated, their electrons get excited and jump to different electron shells (see page 28). This produces different wavelengths of light that have different colors. Each element has its own unique set of colors (like a fingerprint) called its spectrum.

Key Facts

✓ Each element has a unique spectrum.

✓ Each line in a spectrum represents the wavelength of the color the element produces in a flame.

✓ Spectra can be used to detect the presence of elements in substances.

Elemental spectra charts
The elements hydrogen, helium, neon, sodium, and mercury all have unique spectra charts.

⚙ Advantages of Instrumental Analysis

Instrumental analysis is the use of technology, rather than manual effort, to analyze data. There are a number of advantages to instrumental analysis. It saves time, improves the accuracy of results, and can detect smaller quantities of elements in substances.

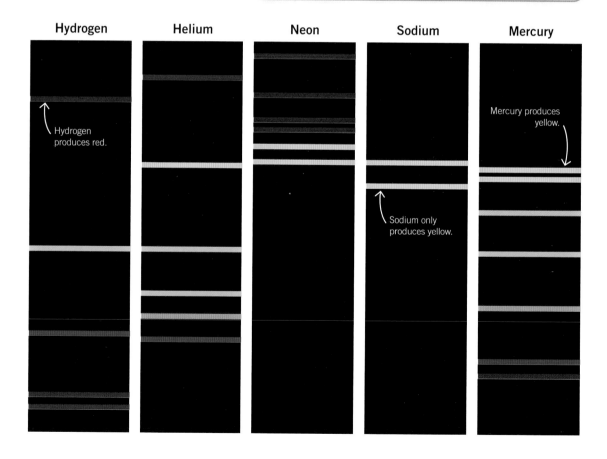

Hydrogen
Hydrogen produces red.

Helium

Neon

Sodium
Sodium only produces yellow.

Mercury
Mercury produces yellow.

Chemistry
of the Earth

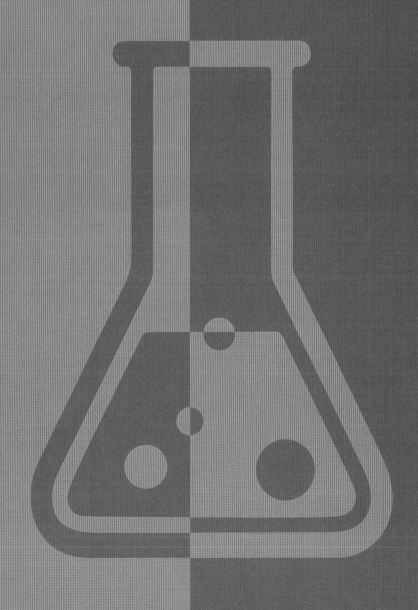

Earth's Structure

Earth is made up of many layers. The crust is made of solid rock and a variety of minerals and metal ores. Below that lies the mantle, a layer that is naturally molten rock. Some parts of the mantle move very slowly because of convection currents. Earth's core has two layers—its outer core is a mixture of liquid metals, and its inner core is mostly solid iron.

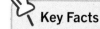
Key Facts

✓ Earth's crust is solid and thin.

✓ A variety of minerals and metal ores are found in the crust.

✓ The mantle is partially molten and large, but some parts can flow slowly like liquid.

✓ The outer core is liquid.

✓ The inner core is solid.

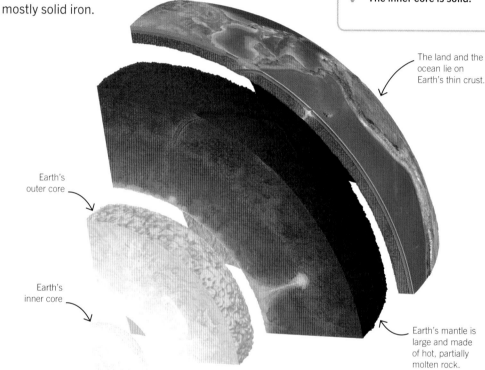

The land and the ocean lie on Earth's thin crust.

Earth's outer core

Earth's inner core

Earth's mantle is large and made of hot, partially molten rock.

Earth

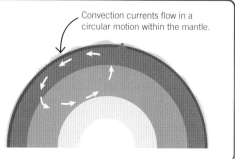

⚙ Convection Currents

Convection currents cause the parts of the mantle that meet the crust to flow very slowly, similar to a liquid. Radioactive (see page 60) processes from the mantle and heat from the core cause these convection currents. They are circular, and rise and fall over millions of years.

Convection currents flow in a circular motion within the mantle.

Tectonic Plates

Earth's crust and the upper layer of the mantle is broken up into sections called tectonic plates. Carried by convection currents in the lower layer of the mantle, these plates move slowly in different directions at about 1 cm a year—the same rate that fingernails grow.

Key Facts

✓ Earth's crust and upper mantle is broken into many tectonic plates.

✓ Tectonic plates move very slowly because of mantle currents below them.

✓ Earthquakes happen if tectonic plates move suddenly.

✓ Volcanoes are common where tectonic plates meet.

Broken crust
Earth's upper layers, including the crust, are split into many tectonic plates, like pieces of a puzzle. A plate boundary is where plates meet.

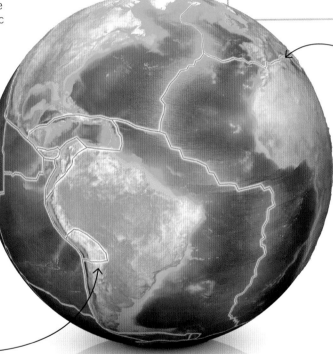

Volcanoes are common at plate boundaries where two plates are colliding or moving away from each other.

Mountain ranges such as the Andes have been pushed up as one tectonic plate moves into another.

⚙ Earthquakes

Earthquakes occur at the boundaries between tectonic plates, when the plates slide against, beneath, or next to each other. Earthquakes can cause great damage and be extremely dangerous.

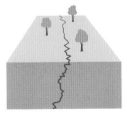

1. Two neighboring tectonic plates that move in opposite directions may become stuck.

2. Pressure builds as the mantle currents continue to carry the stuck plates in different directions.

3. Eventually, the plates become unstuck, causing the ground to shift very quickly, causing an earthquake.

Rocks

Rocks are classified into three main groups: metamorphic, igneous, and sedimentary. The type of rock depends on the way it was formed. All rocks are a mixture of elements and compounds called minerals that form naturally in Earth's crust. Minerals may form crystals in a range of shapes and colors.

Key Facts

✓ There are three types of rock: sedimentary, metamorphic, and igneous.

✓ Rocks are a mixture of elements and compounds called minerals.

✓ Crystals are formed from minerals, and their size depends on how quickly molten magma has cooled.

Visible, uneven banding that shows which direction this gneiss rock was compressed.

Black igneous rock called obsidian is shiny.

Light brown sandstone rock is rough.

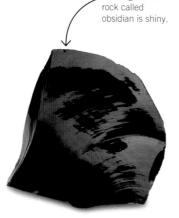

Metamorphic rock
When rocks undergo heat and pressure in Earth's crust, they form metamorphic rocks.

Igneous rock
When rocks in Earth's crust melt, they become magma. Once they cool and solidify, they form igneous rocks.

Sedimentary rock
Tiny grains of rock carried by rivers into the ocean are compacted by many layers above them to form sedimentary rock.

🔍 Inside Minerals

The mineral halite forms crystals of sodium and chlorine ions. The ions have combined to create a repeating, three-dimensional structure called a crystal.

Halite crystal

Sodium chloride atomic structure

Sodium ion

The Rock Cycle

Rocks are constantly changing. Over millions of years, they can be exposed to heat, pressure, weathering, and erosion. This cycle is called the rock cycle, and it transforms rocks from one type to another.

Key Facts

✓ Metamorphic, igneous, and sedimentary rocks can change into another.

✓ The rock cycle happens above and beneath the Earth's surface.

✓ The rock cycle happens over the course of millions of years.

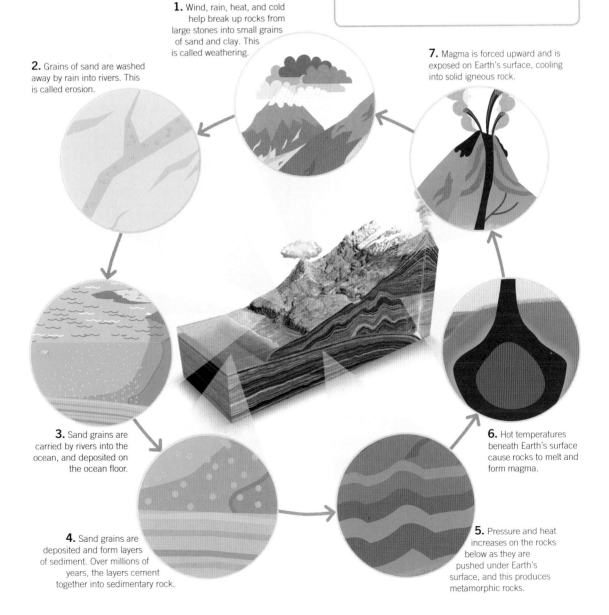

1. Wind, rain, heat, and cold help break up rocks from large stones into small grains of sand and clay. This is called weathering.

2. Grains of sand are washed away by rain into rivers. This is called erosion.

7. Magma is forced upward and is exposed on Earth's surface, cooling into solid igneous rock.

3. Sand grains are carried by rivers into the ocean, and deposited on the ocean floor.

6. Hot temperatures beneath Earth's surface cause rocks to melt and form magma.

4. Sand grains are deposited and form layers of sediment. Over millions of years, the layers cement together into sedimentary rock.

5. Pressure and heat increases on the rocks below as they are pushed under Earth's surface, and this produces metamorphic rocks.

The Atmosphere

The mixture of gases surrounding our planet is called the atmosphere. The composition of gases in the atmosphere was formed over billions of years, producing a mixture that sustains life on Earth.

Gases
These are the main gases found in the atmosphere.

Key Facts

✓ **The atmosphere is a mixture of gases that surrounds Earth.**

✓ **The atmosphere has formed over billions of years.**

✓ **The atmosphere contains 78% nitrogen, 21% oxygen, less than 1% argon, and tiny amounts of carbon dioxide and other gases.**

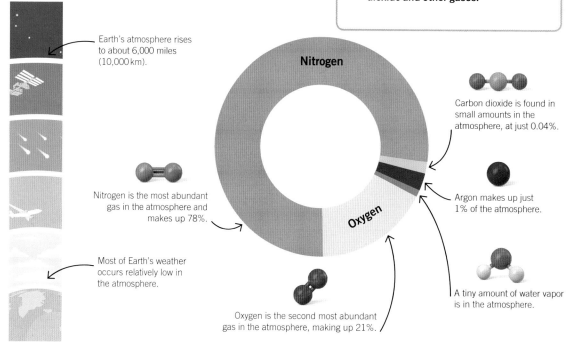

Earth's atmosphere rises to about 6,000 miles (10,000 km).

Nitrogen

Carbon dioxide is found in small amounts in the atmosphere, at just 0.04%.

Nitrogen is the most abundant gas in the atmosphere and makes up 78%.

Argon makes up just 1% of the atmosphere.

Oxygen

Most of Earth's weather occurs relatively low in the atmosphere.

A tiny amount of water vapor is in the atmosphere.

Oxygen is the second most abundant gas in the atmosphere, making up 21%.

⚙ The Early Atmosphere

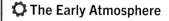

When Earth formed 4.5 billion years ago, it was very hot and volcanoes covered its surface. The early atmosphere was formed from the gases released by volcanic eruptions. Then, the atmosphere was mostly made of carbon dioxide gas. However, over billions of years, the amount of oxygen rose to the levels we have today.

Gases released by volcanic eruptions.

Water vapor condensed and falls as rain.

Carbon dioxide absorbed by ocean.

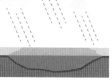

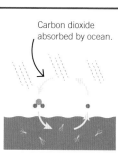

1. Billions of years ago, volcanoes released carbon dioxide, ammonia, methane, and water vapor.

2. Earth cooled, allowing water vapor to condense into clouds. Rain fell, and formed the first oceans.

3. Microorganisms, algae, and plants evolved in the oceans. Over millions of years, they absorbed carbon dioxide and released oxygen.

Measuring Oxygen

The amount of oxygen in the air can be measured by passing a known volume of air over hot copper filings. The copper reacts with the oxygen, removing it from the air, and forms solid copper oxide.

How to measure oxygen
Scientists can set up an experiment using two syringes and stands, a Bunsen burner, and copper filings to measure how much oxygen is in the air.

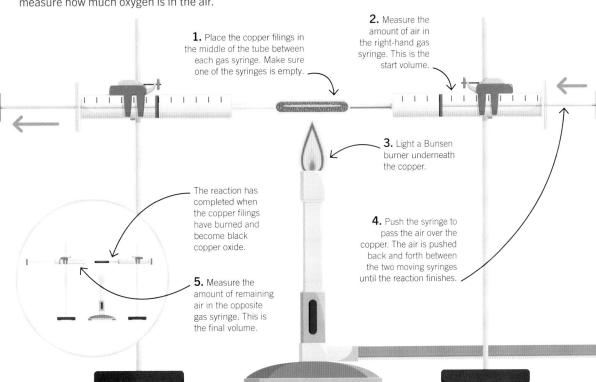

1. Place the copper filings in the middle of the tube between each gas syringe. Make sure one of the syringes is empty.

2. Measure the amount of air in the right-hand gas syringe. This is the start volume.

3. Light a Bunsen burner underneath the copper.

The reaction has completed when the copper filings have burned and become black copper oxide.

4. Push the syringe to pass the air over the copper. The air is pushed back and forth between the two moving syringes until the reaction finishes.

5. Measure the amount of remaining air in the opposite gas syringe. This is the final volume.

Calculating the Percentage of Oxygen

Take the measurements you collected at steps 2 and 5 of the experiment and use this formula to calculate the percentage of oxygen in the air.

$$\frac{\text{start volume} - \text{final volume}}{\text{start volume}} \times 100$$

The Carbon Cycle

In the carbon cycle, the element carbon (see page 66) moves through Earth and all living things. Biological processes, such as photosynthesis in plants and respiration in all living things, keeps levels of carbon dioxide in Earth's atmosphere constant.

Stored carbon
Carbon is stored in plants, animals, the ocean, and in Earth's crust and atmosphere—but it moves around due to a variety of processes.

Key Facts

✓ Carbon passes through living things and organic matter.

✓ Photosynthesis in plants absorbs carbon dioxide from the atmosphere.

✓ Carbon is taken in by animals when they eat.

✓ Respiration in plants and animals releases carbon dioxide.

Carbon dioxide gas is in the atmosphere. Plants, animals, the oceans, and human activity influence levels of carbon dioxide.

Energy from the Sun is used by plants during photosynthesis.

Plants absorb carbon dioxide during photosynthesis. The carbon is transformed into glucose.

Animals release carbon dioxide when they respire.

Carbon dioxide dissolves into the oceans. Animal life in the ocean also releases carbon.

Large amounts of carbon dioxide are released into the atmosphere by burning hydrocarbons in fossil fuels.

Animals take in carbon in carbohydrates (see page 226) and protein (see page 225) when they eat plants.

Carbon dioxide is released when dead animals decay. Poop also contains carbon.

Dead aquatic life releases carbon into the surrounding rocks.

Over millions of years, dead plants eventually become fossil fuels, which contain hydrocarbons.

Carbon dioxide is released from fossil fuels when they are dug up.

The Greenhouse Effect

Tiny amounts of certain gases in the atmosphere help trap the Sun's energy and keep Earth warm. This is called the greenhouse effect. Without these gases and this effect, Earth would have an average temperature of −0.4°F (−18°C), and most organisms wouldn't be able to survive.

Key Facts

✓ The greenhouse effect keeps Earth warm and allows it to support life.

✓ Greenhouse gases trap heat energy radiating from the Sun.

✓ The main greenhouse gases are carbon dioxide, methane, and water vapor.

Keeping warm

Earth's atmosphere acts like a greenhouse, keeping its surface warm.

Sun

Some heat is reflected back into space.

2. Infrared radiation is reflected back off Earth's surface.

3. Some of the infrared radiation is reflected off greenhouse gases back to Earth's surface.

Some heat is reflected back into space.

1. Infrared radiation transfers heat energy from the Sun through Earth's atmosphere.

4. Earth's surface also radiates heat.

5. Heat absorbed by greenhouse gases radiates back to Earth's surface.

The atmosphere

Earth

🔍 Greenhouse Gases

All the greenhouse gases are made up of small molecules—groups of atoms held together by covalent bonds (see page 80). Methane is one of the most potent greenhouse gases because its molecules are able to trap more heat than other gases.

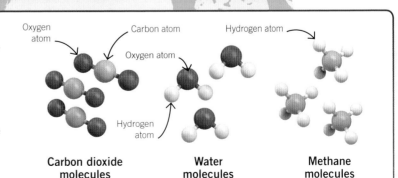

Oxygen atom

Carbon atom

Oxygen atom

Hydrogen atom

Hydrogen atom

Carbon dioxide molecules

Water molecules

Methane molecules

Human Activity

Humans have caused levels of greenhouse gases in the atmosphere to rise over the past 300 years. These gases are released when fossil fuels are burned for energy to power our homes and fuel our cars. Humans also disturb the natural carbon cycle (see page 247) by preventing carbon dioxide, a greenhouse gas (see page 248), from being absorbed from the atmosphere.

Negative activities

Human activities that contribute to high levels of greenhouse gases include burning fossil fuels, landfill sites, deforestation, and a rising number of farm animals.

Key Facts

✓ Human activity causes levels of greenhouse gases in the atmosphere to rise.

✓ Burning fossil fuels releases greenhouse gases into the atmosphere.

✓ Deforestation means that there are fewer plants to absorb carbon dioxide from the atmosphere.

✓ Rising demand for meat means more domestic animals releasing methane, a potent greenhouse gas.

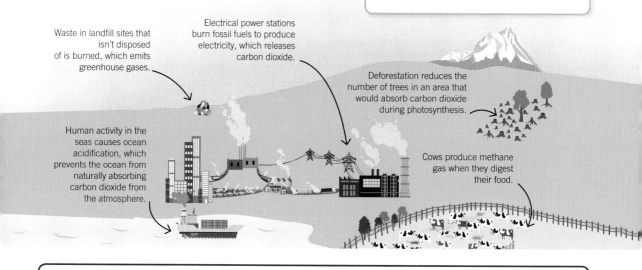

Waste in landfill sites that isn't disposed of is burned, which emits greenhouse gases.

Electrical power stations burn fossil fuels to produce electricity, which releases carbon dioxide.

Deforestation reduces the number of trees in an area that would absorb carbon dioxide during photosynthesis.

Human activity in the seas causes ocean acidification, which prevents the ocean from naturally absorbing carbon dioxide from the atmosphere.

Cows produce methane gas when they digest their food.

🔍 Levels of Carbon Dioxide in the Atmosphere

Since 1960, scientists have found that the carbon dioxide level in the atmosphere has risen very sharply. Populations are increasing and the demand for energy is rising. More fossil fuels are burned, releasing carbon dioxide.

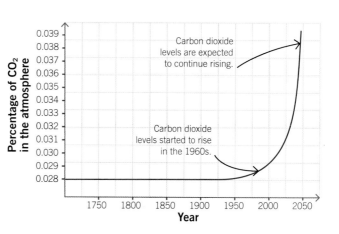

Carbon dioxide levels are expected to continue rising.

Carbon dioxide levels started to rise in the 1960s.

Percentage of CO_2 in the atmosphere

0.039
0.038
0.037
0.036
0.035
0.034
0.033
0.032
0.031
0.030
0.029
0.028

1750 1800 1850 1900 1950 2000 2050

Year

Global Warming

The Earth's average temperature has risen by about 1°C in the last 100 years. This rise is caused by humans increasing levels of greenhouse gases in the atmosphere, making the greenhouse effect (see page 248) stronger. This rise seems small, however it has caused significant climate change.

Key Facts

✓ Human activity is causing global warming by increasing the greenhouse effect.

✓ This causes global temperatures to rise.

✓ Global warming is causing climate change.

The greenhouse effect

Human activity increases the levels of greenhouse gases in the atmosphere. This means the greenhouse effect is much stronger, and global temperatures rise.

Sun

1. Heat from the Sun enters Earth's atmosphere.

2. Higher levels of greenhouse gases trap more of the Sun's heat, raising global temperatures.

3. Burning fossil fuels releases carbon dioxide and water vapor into the atmosphere.

The atmosphere

Earth

🔍 Extreme Weather

Weather is the day-to-day conditions of temperature, sunlight, and rainfall. Climate is weather patterns over years and decades. Climate change is happening because of global warming, and is leading to flooding, droughts, and violent storms.

Higher numbers of floods are happening because higher global temperatures cause polar ice caps to melt, raising sea levels.

Deserts are spreading because higher global temperatures mean already arid areas become even hotter and drier.

Storms are more common because higher global temperatures mean heavier rainfall and unpredictable weather in tropical areas.

Carbon Footprints

Carbon footprints measure the amount of greenhouse gases released into the atmosphere by either a person, a product, or a company. A person's carbon footprint may be high if they ate a lot of meat or drove a lot (see page 249), or low if they cycled to work every day. Diesel cars have a high carbon footprint because they burn fuel and release greenhouse gases from their exhaust pipes.

Key Facts

✓ A carbon footprint is the amount of greenhouse gases that are put into the atmosphere.

✓ Carbon footprints can be measured for people, products, or companies.

✓ Carbon footprints are difficult to check and measure.

Reducing carbon footprints
There are many things that can contribute to a person's carbon footprint. Understanding their own footprint can help someone reduce it.

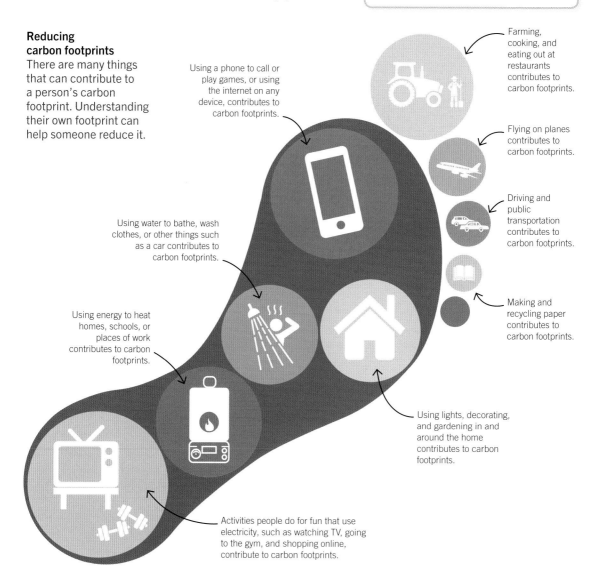

Using a phone to call or play games, or using the internet on any device, contributes to carbon footprints.

Farming, cooking, and eating out at restaurants contributes to carbon footprints.

Flying on planes contributes to carbon footprints.

Driving and public transportation contributes to carbon footprints.

Making and recycling paper contributes to carbon footprints.

Using water to bathe, wash clothes, or other things such as a car contributes to carbon footprints.

Using energy to heat homes, schools, or places of work contributes to carbon footprints.

Using lights, decorating, and gardening in and around the home contributes to carbon footprints.

Activities people do for fun that use electricity, such as watching TV, going to the gym, and shopping online, contribute to carbon footprints.

Carbon Capture

Governments have more power and resources than individuals when it comes to reducing carbon footprints and combating global warming (see page 250). They can increase tax on fossil fuels to reduce their use, but this is not enough. Scientists have designed a way to capture the carbon dioxide that is released when fossil fuels are burned and store it underground. This is called carbon capture.

(see page 250)

Carbon capture

Power stations, factories, and refineries emit a lot of carbon dioxide into the atmosphere. Governments implement carbon capture technology to reduce the levels of carbon dioxide they emit.

Key Facts

✓ Reducing individual personal carbon footprints helps, but is not enough to prevent global warming.

✓ Governments need to pass laws to reduce greenhouse gas emissions.

✓ Carbon capture diverts carbon dioxide that is released after burning fossil fuels.

✓ The removed carbon dioxide is stored underground.

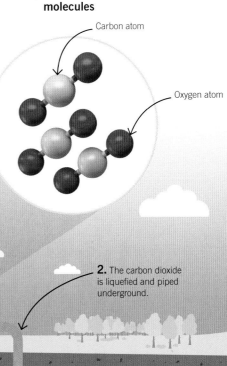

Carbon dioxide molecules

Carbon atom

Oxygen atom

1. Carbon dioxide gas is captured during chemical reactions with substances called amines.

2. The carbon dioxide is liquefied and piped underground.

3. The carbon dioxide is stored underground in holes in the rocks.

Nuclear Energy

Some governments encourage the use of alternative energy sources instead of fossil fuels. Nuclear energy is one type of clean energy, because no greenhouse gases are released in its supply. However, nuclear power stations where nuclear energy is "made" produce a lot of dangerous radioactive waste (see page 60).

Key Facts

✓ Governments can encourage the use of alternative energy sources.

✓ Alternative energy sources don't increase levels of greenhouse gases.

✓ Nuclear energy doesn't produce greenhouse gases.

✓ There are dangers associated with nuclear power.

Nuclear fission

During nuclear fission, a neutron is fired at a large atom to break it up. This also releases lots of energy. Nuclear fission is used in nuclear power stations to produce heat, which is harnessed to produce electricity.

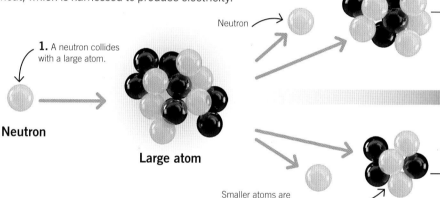

Neutron

1. A neutron collides with a large atom.

Neutron

Large atom

2. Atom splits into smaller atoms and neutrons.

energy

3. Huge amounts of heat is released, which is used to generate electricity.

Smaller atoms are radioactive waste.

Nuclear fusion

During nuclear fusion, two isotopes (see page 31) of hydrogen molecules (see page 55) are smashed together to form one larger nucleus of helium to release a huge amount of energy. This is how energy is produced in the Sun. Scientists have not yet found a way to control nuclear fusion and use the energy produced safely on Earth.

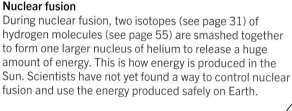

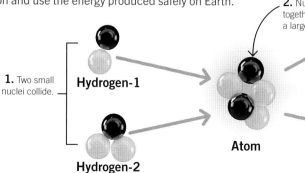

3. Helium is a product of the reaction.

2. Nuclei fuse together to form a larger nuclei.

Helium atom

1. Two small nuclei collide.

Hydrogen-1

Hydrogen-2

Atom

energy

4. Huge amounts of energy are released.

Neutron

Air Pollution

Most vehicles are still fueled by fossil fuels, such as gasoline and diesel. The combustion of these hydrocarbon fuels (see page 202) releases dangerous pollutants, as well as the greenhouse gas carbon dioxide, into the air.

> ## Key Facts
>
> ✓ Vehicles powered by fossil fuels release harmful substances called pollutants into the air.
>
> ✓ Fossil fuels are made of hydrocarbons, which produce pollutants when combusted.
>
> ✓ Examples of poisonous pollutants include carbon monoxide, sulfur dioxide, and nitrogen oxide.

Particulate pollution
Pollutant substances contain tiny pieces of solids or liquid droplets suspended in the air, such as this pollutant that contains methane and carbon.

Methane molecule

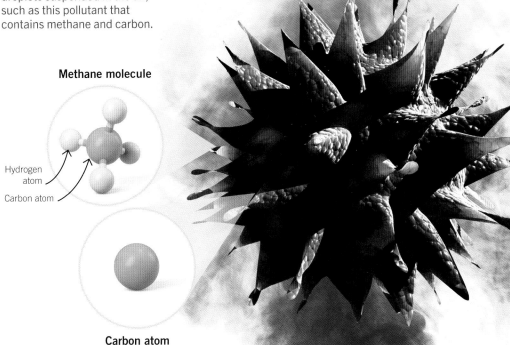

Hydrogen atom

Carbon atom

Carbon atom

🔍 Unburned Hydrocarbons

The main pollutants are the gases carbon monoxide, sulfur dioxide, and nitrogen oxides. If there is a low supply of air or oxygen, hydrocarbons in the engines of vehicles powered by fossil fuels may not combust properly. Unburned hydrocarbons can be just as harmful as these gases (see page 255).

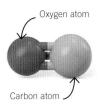

Oxygen atom

Carbon atom

Carbon monoxide

Sulfur atom

Oxygen atoms

Sulfur dioxide

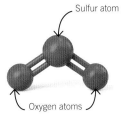

Nitrogen atom

Oxygen atom

Nitrogen monoxide

Pollution Problems

Pollutant particles in the air are toxic and can cause long-term health problems. They are dangerous because they are colorless, odorless, and typically can't be seen. They can impair our breathing and poison our blood. They may also darken buildings, block machinery, and some are flammable, presenting a fire risk.

Key Facts

✓ Pollutant particles are toxic and cause breathing problems.

✓ Pollutant particles are normally colorless and odorless gases, making them hard to detect.

✓ Pollutant particles may also cause physical damage to buildings.

Breathing problems

Hemoglobin is a protein (see page 225) in human blood that binds to oxygen which we breathe in, carrying it around our bodies. Carbon monoxide molecules also bind to hemoglobin, preventing it from carrying enough oxygen and causing us to feel drowsy, become unconscious, or even die.

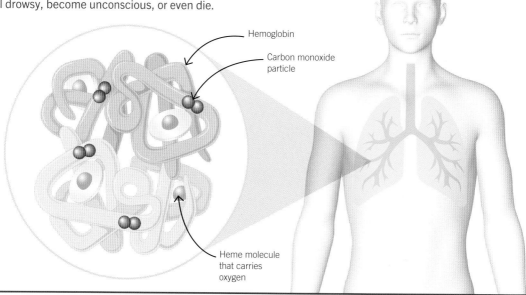

Hemoglobin

Carbon monoxide particle

Heme molecule that carries oxygen

🔍 Global Dimming

Tiny pollutant particles that are released into the Earth's atmosphere block the Sun's light. Over time, this has led to less light passing through the atmosphere, especially in cities and industrial areas, leading to global dimming.

Acid Rain

Natural rain contains a small amount of dissolved carbon dioxide, so it is slightly acidic. However, some parts of the atmosphere are polluted with gases such as sulfur dioxide and nitrogen dioxide from combustion (see page 163) of impurities in fossil fuels. When these gases dissolve in rainwater, they make rain even more acidic, creating acid rain.

Key Facts

✓ Rainwater is naturally acidic because of dissolved carbon dioxide.

✓ Acid rain is even more acidic because of sulfur and nitrogen dioxide.

✓ Acid rain can be natural, but is more potent when caused by human pollution.

Eroded statue
When acid rain falls on statues made of limestone, it reacts with calcium carbonate in the rock and erodes it.

Some parts of the statue have not been affected by acid rain.

Limestone corrodes and stains when exposed to acid rain.

🔍 Effects of Acid Rain

Acid rain can occur naturally in areas where volcanoes erupt or plants decompose. Both release carbon dioxide gas, which makes rainwater acidic. However, the most damaging acid rain is caused by human activity. Industrial plants such as power stations pump large amounts of gases, such as sulfur dioxide, into the atmosphere.

1. Acid rain reacts with metals, rocks, and other materials. This damages and erodes buildings made of these materials.

2. Acid rain is poisonous to plants. Acid rain damages leaves, reducing the rate of photosynthesis and reduces root growth, preventing the absorption of nutrients.

3. If lots of acid rain falls in rivers or lakes, it raises the acidity of the water. Most animals can't survive in acidic conditions.

Ceramics

Ceramics are nonmetallic materials, such as china, bricks, and glass. Their atoms are held together by covalent and/or ionic bonds (see pages 80 and 74). They are made by heating their components to very high temperatures. Ceramics all have a similar set of useful properties: they have high melting points, they are stiff, brittle, and strong, and they are good insulators.

Pottery
Different types of clay are heated to 1,832°F (1,000°C) and then molded into pottery. Chemical reactions occur during heating and cooling that bond the molecules in the ceramic together.

Bricks
Clay that contains impurities (see page 38) is molded, dried, and then heated to 2,192°F (1,200°C). Different impurities will produce different colored bricks.

Soda-lime glass
A mixture of the compounds silicon dioxide, sodium carbonate, and calcium carbonate is heated to 2,912°F (1,600°C) to create soda-lime glass. It is the cheapest form of glass.

Key Facts

✓ Ceramics are made of nonmetals that have covalent and/or ionic bonds.

✓ Ceramics are made from heating substances at high temperatures.

✓ Ceramics can contain metals bonded to nonmetals with ionic bonds.

✓ Ceramics have high melting points, resist heat, and are unreactive.

✓ Ceramics are stiff, brittle, strong, and good insulators.

Borosilicate glass
A mixture of the compounds silicon dioxide and boron oxide is heated to create borosilicate glass. This type of glass can withstand rapid heating and cooling, which makes it useful for experiments.

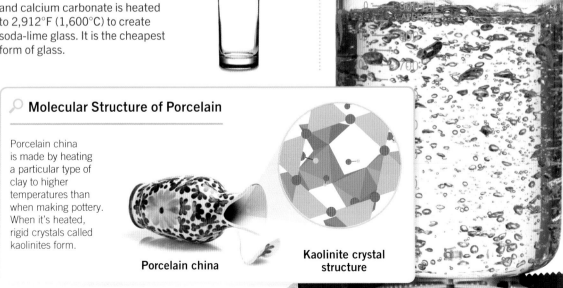

Molecular Structure of Porcelain

Porcelain china is made by heating a particular type of clay to higher temperatures than when making pottery. When it's heated, rigid crystals called kaolinites form.

Porcelain china

Kaolinite crystal structure

Composites

Composites are materials made of one substance enmeshed in another substance's fibers. Each substance has different properties. A composite usually has a combination of the properties of each of its components. Together, these properties make the composite suited for a particular use.

Key Facts

✓ Composites are materials made of one substance enmeshed in another substance's fibers.

✓ A composite's properties depend on the substance it is made from.

✓ Some artificial composites are made for specific purposes.

Fiberglass and carbon fiber

Glass or carbon fibers can be embedded in a polyester resin to create a strong composite. Fiberglass is easily shaped, strong, light, and slightly flexible. Carbon fiber is stronger and lighter than fiberglass, but costs much more to make.

Outer layer of resin

Layers of fibers made of either carbon or glass.

Plastic core for insulation and shock absorption.

Paralympic racing wheelchair

Concrete

Made of sand, cement, and aggregate (small pieces of rock), concrete is a strong composite often used in buildings. Reinforced concrete has steel rods added to make it even stronger.

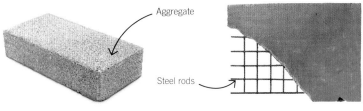

Aggregate

Steel rods

Concrete

Reinforced concrete

Natural composite

Cellulose fibers (see page 226) embedded in a natural polymer called lignin in wood is an example of a natural composite. This combination is much stronger than the separate substances on their own.

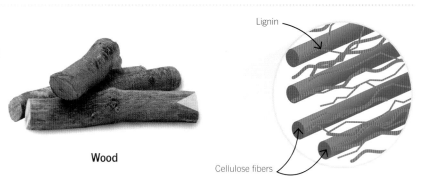

Lignin

Cellulose fibers

Wood

Synthetic Polymers

Synthetic polymers are artificial long chain molecules, made by joining many monomers together. These polymers are used to make a wide range of items, equipment, buildings, tools, and clothes. Synthetic polymers are made to fit whatever purpose they need to fulfil.

Key Facts

✓ Synthetic polymers are made by joining together lots of small molecules called monomers.

✓ Synthetic polymers are strong, light, flexible, and good insulators of heat and electricity.

Low-density polyethylene
Plastic bags are made using polymers called low-density polyethylene, also called LDPE. It is strong, non-toxic, and very flexible.

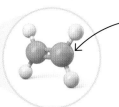

Long chains of hydrocarbons called ethylene that contain carbon and hydrogen atoms covalently bonded together make up low-density polyethylene.

High-density polyethylene
Drain pipes are made using polymers called high-density polyethylene, also called HDPE. It is strong, rigid, and waterproof.

Long chains of hydrocarbons that contain carbon and hydrogen atoms make up high-density polyethylene.

Polyvinyl chloride (PVC)
Electrical wiring is made using polymers called polyvinyl chloride because it is strong, hard wearing, and a good insulator of electricity.

Long chains of hydrocarbons that contain carbon, hydrogen, and chlorine atoms make up PVC.

Spandex
Sportswear is made using polymers called spandex, or Lycra, which is strong, durable, and stretches to fit.

Long chains of the repeated monomer urethane (containing oxygen, carbon, hydrogen, and nitrogen atoms) bonded together make up spandex.

Nylon
Toothbrushes are made using polymers called nylon that are strong, flexible, and hardwearing.

Long chains of oxygen, carbon, hydrogen, and nitrogen atoms make up nylon.

Making Polymers

Condensation polymers (see page 222) form when two monomers bond together by releasing a small molecule, such as water. These monomers have atoms called functional groups that facilitate reactions between monomers that keep joining together to form long chains. Nylon is an example of a condensation polymer.

Making nylon

Nylon can be formed as a continuous chain. As each layer is removed, the chain continues to form as more monomers in the solution bond to the end of the chain. This will continue until all of the monomers have reacted, forming a long chain of nylon.

Nylon

The top layer of the reaction solution is a chemical called hexanedioyl dichloride dissolved in cyclohexane.

Nylon forms between the two layers.

The bottom layer of the reaction solution is a chemical called 1,6-diaminohexane dissolved in water.

Key Facts

✓ Condensation polymers are formed by releasing a small molecule, such as water.

✓ Monomers for condensation polymerization have two functional groups.

✓ Nylon is an example of a condensation polymer.

Types of Plastics

Plastics are made of polymers. There are two different forms of plastic, depending on whether their chains are covalently bonded or not (see page 80).

Thermosoftening plastics, such as plastic bags, don't have covalent bonds between their chains. This means they melt easily and can be recycled (see page 268).

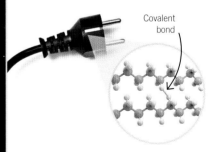

Covalent bond

Thermosetting plastics, such as plugs, have covalent bonds between their chains. This means they don't melt easily, which is useful for electrical appliances that may easily get hot.

Alloys

An alloy is a mixture (see page 32) of a metal with tiny amounts of other metals or nonmetals (see pages 56–57). Alloys can be more useful than the pure metals they are made of because they have new and useful properties. Bronze, an alloy of copper and tin, is much stronger than either of the pure metals alone. The structure of alloys compared to pure metals is shown on page 89.

> **Key Facts**
>
> ✓ Alloys are mixtures of metals with other elements.
>
> ✓ Alloys often have more useful properties than the pure metals.
>
> ✓ Alloys can be stronger, harder, lighter, or less likely to corrode.

Magnesium-silicon alloys
Bicycle frames are made from an aluminum alloy with combined magnesium and silicon that make them very light and strong.

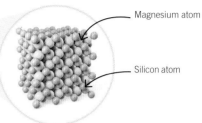

Magnesium atom

Silicon atom

Copper-zinc alloys
Trumpets are made of copper-zinc alloys called brass that are hard wearing and resist corrosion.

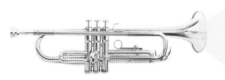

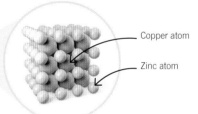

Copper atom

Zinc atom

Titanium-gold alloys
Watches and jewelry are made of titanium-gold alloys that are stronger and harder than pure gold.

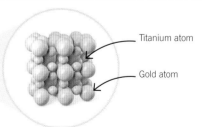

Titanium atom

Gold atom

Stainless steel
Utensils are made from stainless steel, an alloy of iron and chromium that resists corrosion (see page 264).

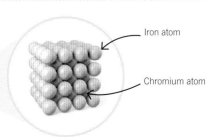

Iron atom

Chromium atom

Sustainability

A sustainable way of life aims to conserve finite resources (see page 266) so there are enough for future generations to use. Sustainability also considers resources that may never run out as sources of energy (see page 267). Many companies are now trying to be as sustainable as possible, by developing alternative methods to minimize their use of finite materials.

(see page 266) (see page 267)

Key Facts

✓ **A sustainable way of life is about preserving finite resources.**

✓ **Being sustainable means planning for the future.**

✓ **Bioleaching and phytomining are sustainable ways to collect copper.**

Bioleaching
Bacteria can be used to extract copper from low-grade ores (rocks with tiny amounts of copper in them). This costs less money and is less damaging to the environment than extracting copper from high-grade ores (rocks with lots of copper in them). This is bioleaching, and it's more sustainable because it extracts copper from sources that don't require mining.

Phytomining
Plants grown in copper-rich soils absorb the copper into their roots, which is then transported to their leaves. The copper can be extracted by burning the leaves and collecting the ash, which contains soluble copper compounds. This method is called phytomining, and is both economical and sustainable as it uses little energy and none of the natural reserves of copper ores.

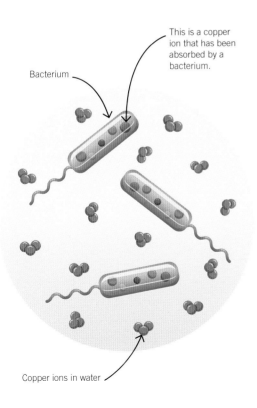

This is a copper ion that has been absorbed by a bacterium.

Bacterium

Copper ions in water

This is a copper ion that has been absorbed by the plant.

Copper ions in soil

Corrosion

Most metals form a dull coating on their surface when left out in the air. The coating is produced by a reaction between the metal's surface and a gas in the air (usually oxygen). The reaction is called corrosion. For instance, the reactive metal sodium corrodes quickly, forming a dull coating of sodium oxide around it. Silver, which is less reactive, corrodes slowly to form a black surface layer of silver oxide.

Key Facts

✓ Corrosion is the reaction of a metal surface with substances around it.

✓ More reactive metals corrode more quickly.

✓ The corrosion of a metal in air often forms a layer of metal oxide.

Corrosion over time
Our atmosphere contains small amounts of different gases. Over time, iron nails react with oxygen to form a layer of rust made of iron oxide.

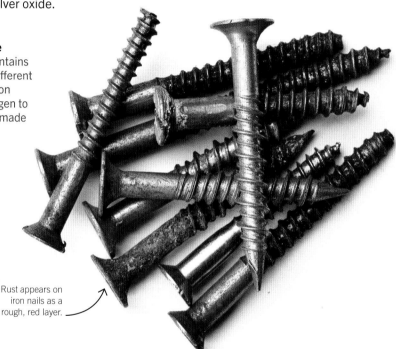

Rust appears on iron nails as a rough, red layer.

⚙ How Aluminum Corrodes

Aluminum also reacts with oxygen in the air and forms a layer of aluminum oxide. However, this form of corrosion does not crumble or erode like rust does. The layer sticks to aluminum, preventing further corrosion.

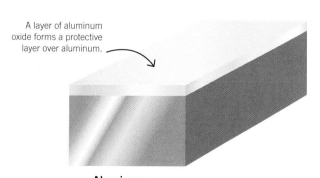

A layer of aluminum oxide forms a protective layer over aluminum.

Aluminum

Preventing Corrosion

Corrosion can destroy metals, which have to be replaced. Replacing metals can be expensive. The easiest way to prevent corrosion is to coat metals with a substance to block out air and moisture. Different coatings work best for different objects. For example, machines and tools are coated in oil or grease, whereas cars are painted.

Key Facts

✓ Corrosion damages metals and costs money.

✓ Coatings prevent corrosion by keeping out air and water.

✓ Types of coating include: oil and grease, paint, tin plating, and electroplating.

Preventing iron from rusting

You can set up an experiment to show how different environments affect the amount of rust produced on an iron nail. To prevent iron from rusting, you need to remove either water or oxygen.

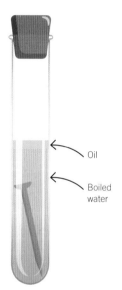

← Oil

← Boiled water

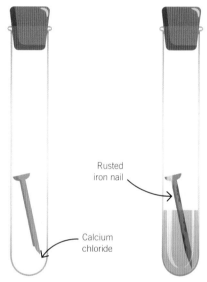

Rusted iron nail

Calcium chloride

An iron nail in a test tube of boiled water won't rust—the layer of oil stops air reaching it.

An iron nail in a test tube with calcium chloride will not rust, because calcium chloride absorbs water vapor from the air.

An iron nail will rust if placed in a test tube containing both water and air.

⚙ Protecting Metal

Materials such as steel can be coated with another material to protect them from rusting. Steel factories often spray their metal products with a powder containing pigments and resin to prevent rusting.

Finite Resources

A finite resource is a useful substance that is in limited supply, and may eventually run out. Most manufacturing processes use finite resources such as fossil fuels, metal ores, and other minerals. Fossil fuels like oil are not only used as sources of energy, but can also supply raw materials for the chemical industry.

Key Facts

✓ Finite resources are in limited supply and will run out.

✓ Fossil fuels, metal ores, and minerals are all finite resources.

✓ Fossil fuels are sources of energy and chemicals.

✓ Mining operations for finite resources have pros and cons.

Copper mines
Bingham Canyon mine in the US is one of the largest copper mines on Earth.

Trucks carrying rocks produce lots of noise, disturbing local people.

This copper mine is 3,900 ft (1,200 m) deep.

🔍 Extraction

The rate at which we use fossil fuels such as oil and natural gas means we will run out in about 50 years. Supplies of coal will last just over 100 years. Mining and drilling operations for fuels, minerals, or ores can have advantages and disadvantages. However, unless we can find an alternative product, or stop using a particular substance, we will just have to minimize the problems associated with their extraction and continue to search for new sources.

Pros	Cons
Creates useful products	Uses up energy sources
Provides jobs	Damages habitats
Improves local infrastructure	Produces waste material
Extracts lots of fossil fuels	Expensive

Renewable Resources

Renewable resources are substances that can be used and will not run out in our lifetime. This is because we can make more in a short amount of time, or because it is a natural energy source. For example, alcohol is made by fermenting sugars from plants, and is used widely in the chemical industry. More plants can always be grown to make more sugars, so alcohol is a renewable resource. Renewable resources provide an effective alternative to using finite resources.

Key Facts

✓ Renewable resources are substances that will not run out.

✓ Renewable resources can be made from plants.

✓ Renewable energy supplies conserve fossil fuels.

Renewable energy
There are many types of renewable resources. Natural processes are the most reliable sources of energy, as we do not have to make them.

Fermenting plant material (biomass) can be used to produce methane gas for fuel.

Wind turns turbines to make electricity.

Hydroelectric power stations use the stored energy in the water behind dams to make electricity.

Solar panels transform the Sun's light into electrical energy.

High temperatures below Earth's surface can be used to heat water that turns turbines.

Underwater turbines produce electrical energy from the movement of water in rivers and tides.

Recycling

Recycling is the process of transforming finite resources (see page 266) into new products. Materials are collected, sorted, and recycled—this can be a difficult process, but it means we do not depend on finite resources as much. Recycling often uses less energy than sourcing finite resources.

> ## Key Facts
>
> ✓ Recycling means using materials more than once.
>
> ✓ Recycling means we don't use up finite resources.
>
> ✓ Recycling can save energy and fossil fuels.

Recycling glass
Glass is easy to collect and sort for recycling. Recycling glass saves time and money, and the recycled product is almost identical to the original.

1. Glass is collected at recycling points.

2. The glass is sorted by color and type, and crushed.

6. The recycled glass bottles are ready to be used again.

3. The crushed glass is mixed together and heated until it melts.

5. The glass sheets are then shaped into bottles.

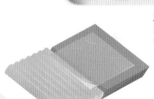

4. The glass is formed into sheets.

⚙ **Recycling Metals**

Metals are recycled in a similar way as glass. They are melted and molded into a different shape. Sometimes, they need to be treated with chemical processes to remove impurities.

Aluminum is rolled into sheets that can be shaped into new products.

Aluminum is crushed into blocks.

Life Cycle Assessment

A life cycle assessment (LCA) looks at the environmental impact of a product at every stage of its life. Gathering information for a full LCA can be time-consuming; however, it can help people make decisions about what products they use, how efficient they are, and whether they should be using alternative products instead.

Key Facts

✓ A life cycle assessment (LCA) considers a product's impact on the environment.

✓ There are four stages to an LCA; obtaining materials, manufacturing, uses, and disposal.

✓ An LCA helps to make decisions on how to design, make, and recycle products.

LCA stages
There are four stages to an LCA; assessing what materials are used to make the product, the process of making the product, using the product, and disposing of the product.

LCA for plastic bags
Although making plastic bags uses up finite supplies of crude oil and energy, LCA studies have shown that they have less effect on the environment than some alternatives.

LCA for paper bags
Paper bags are made from trees, which are a renewable resource (see page 267), so they may appear to be a "greener" alternative to plastic bags. However, manufacturing paper bags uses a lot of energy.

The main raw material needed is crude oil, which is finite.

A lot of energy is needed to make polyethylene from crude oil.

Most plastic bags are not easily disposable and end up on landfill sites.

Plastic bags are reusable.

The main raw materials needed are wood and water, which are renewable.

Large amounts of energy are used when making paper bags.

Paper products can be recycled.

Paper bags break easily and are less likely to be reused.

Potable Water

The water that we drink is called potable water. Most of this water comes from rivers, lakes, and aquifers (underground rocks that hold water). This water contains impurities, such as stones, leaves, mud, and dissolved substances such as salts, fertilizers, and microorganisms. Water is stored in reservoirs and treated to remove these impurities before it's ready to drink.

Key Facts

✓ Water from rivers, lakes, and aquifers is stored in reservoirs.

✓ Natural water contains insoluble solids, soluble substances, and bacteria.

✓ Potable water is water that is safe to drink.

✓ There are four main stages to creating potable water: grids, filtration, chlorination, and storage.

How water is treated
A clean, safe water supply is essential. The water from reservoirs is treated through a number of processes to make it potable.

1. The water passes through grids and sedimentation tanks to remove large objects such as twigs.

Impure water

Fine gravel

Sand

Charcoal

Clean water

2. A filtration bed of gravel, sand, and charcoal removes small solid particles from the water.

Pure and Drinking Water

Drinking water has all solid particles and microorganisms removed; however, it's not pure—it may still contain dissolved substances, such as salt. Distillation can be used to produce pure water (see page 271), which only contains water molecules.

Water molecule

Water molecule

Impurities

Pure water

Impure water

Disinfectant

Chlorine gas

3. Chlorine gas and disinfectant is bubbled through the water to kill bacteria. This is called chlorination.

4. Within storage tanks, fine, tiny particles settle at the bottom.

Storage tank

Drinking water

5. Drinking water is then piped to homes.

Seawater

About 97% of Earth's water is in the oceans. This water isn't drinkable because it contains too much salt. Seawater can undergo a process called desalination to make it drinkable. Desalination can take place in industrial plants that pass seawater through membranes to remove the salt, or may involve simple distillation (see page 49).

Desalination
Hot countries that don't have easy access to water set up desalination plants near the coast to produce drinkable water.

Key Facts

✓ We can't drink seawater because it contains too much salt.

✓ The process of turning seawater into pure water is called desalination.

✓ Desalination involves evaporating the seawater and then condensing the water vapor.

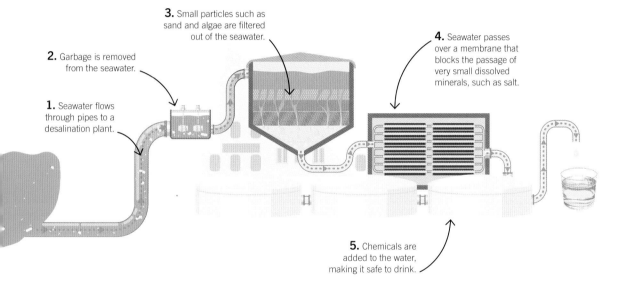

3. Small particles such as sand and algae are filtered out of the seawater.

2. Garbage is removed from the seawater.

4. Seawater passes over a membrane that blocks the passage of very small dissolved minerals, such as salt.

1. Seawater flows through pipes to a desalination plant.

5. Chemicals are added to the water, making it safe to drink.

⚙ Distillation in the Lab

Distillation can be performed in the laboratory (see page 49) to remove the salt from seawater.

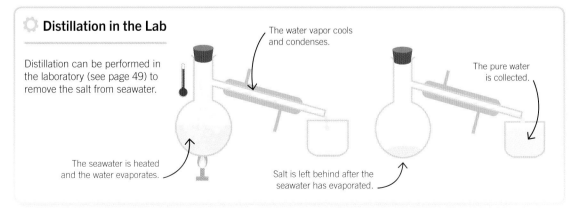

The water vapor cools and condenses.

The pure water is collected.

The seawater is heated and the water evaporates.

Salt is left behind after the seawater has evaporated.

Wastewater

Water is used every day, but a lot of it is wasted. Billions of liters of wasted water ends up in drains and sewers. Wastewater from industry, agriculture, or homes contains harmful substances—for example, wastewater from homes containing bacteria that can cause disease.

Key Facts

✓ Water contains harmful substances.

✓ Wastewater comes from the home, industry, and agriculture.

Human wastewater
Water from our showers, baths, and toilets can contain harmful nitrogen compounds, such as ammonia.

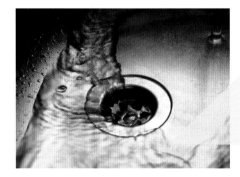

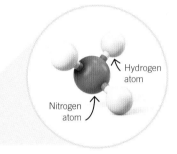
Hydrogen atom
Nitrogen atom

Ammonia molecule

Industrial wastewater
Wastewater that comes from factories can contain hydrocarbons such as butane and other toxic substances. This can flow into rivers and lakes, poisoning local wildlife.

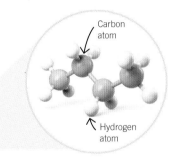
Carbon atom
Hydrogen atom

Butane molecule

Agricultural wastewater
Water that flows from farms can contain fertilizers, causing algae in lakes to grow over the water surface. This disturbs local ecosystems by blocking sunlight from reaching the lake bed, causing plants and animals to die.

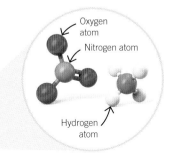
Oxygen atom
Nitrogen atom
Hydrogen atom

Ammonium nitrate molecules

Treating Wastewater

Water from bathrooms contains solid waste, chemicals, and microorganisms that are carried by drainpipes to larger sewage pipes. The water is then collected and treated to ensure that it is safe before it is released into the environment.

Key Facts

✓ Wastewater is taken to sewage treatment centers to be purified.

✓ The treatment removes solids, chemicals, and harmful bacteria.

✓ After treatment, the wastewater can be released into the environment.

✓ The main steps in sewage treatment are screening, clarification, biological treatment, aeration, and chemical treatment.

Sewage treatment

The main stages in sewage treatment are screening and grit removal, clarification, biological treatment, aeration to break down sludge, and a final round of chemical treatment. After this, the water can be released into rivers, lakes, or the sea.

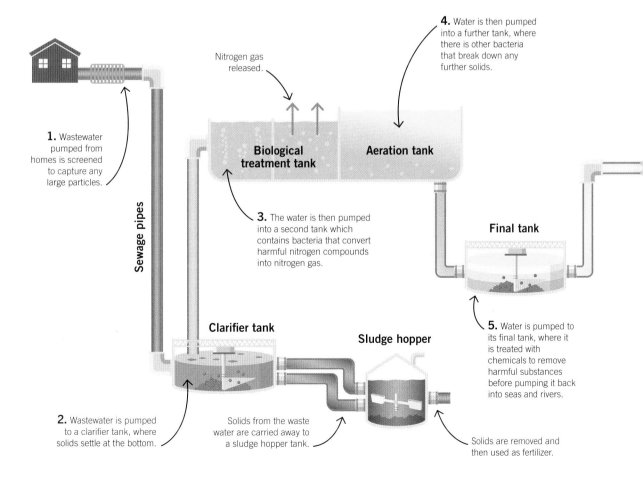

4. Water is then pumped into a further tank, where there is other bacteria that break down any further solids.

Nitrogen gas released.

1. Wastewater pumped from homes is screened to capture any large particles.

Biological treatment tank

Aeration tank

Sewage pipes

3. The water is then pumped into a second tank which contains bacteria that convert harmful nitrogen compounds into nitrogen gas.

Final tank

Clarifier tank

Sludge hopper

5. Water is pumped to its final tank, where it is treated with chemicals to remove harmful substances before pumping it back into seas and rivers.

2. Wastewater is pumped to a clarifier tank, where solids settle at the bottom.

Solids from the waste water are carried away to a sludge hopper tank.

Solids are removed and then used as fertilizer.

The Haber Process

Ammonia (NH_3) is a very important compound (see page 33) in the production of fertilizers, plastics, and dyes. It contains the elements nitrogen and hydrogen. Nitrogen is an unreactive gas, so the process to create ammonia requires a catalyst (see page 184). The Haber process uses iron as a catalyst to make nitrogen and hydrogen react with one another to create ammonia.

Key Facts

✓ Ammonia is an important industrial chemical.

✓ The Haber process makes ammonia using nitrogen in the air and hydrogen in methane.

✓ A catalyst of iron is used to speed up the reaction.

✓ The ammonia is separated by cooling, and the unreacted nitrogen and hydrogen are recycled.

How the Haber process works

The Haber process is an industrial method of making liquid ammonia from nitrogen and hydrogen gases.

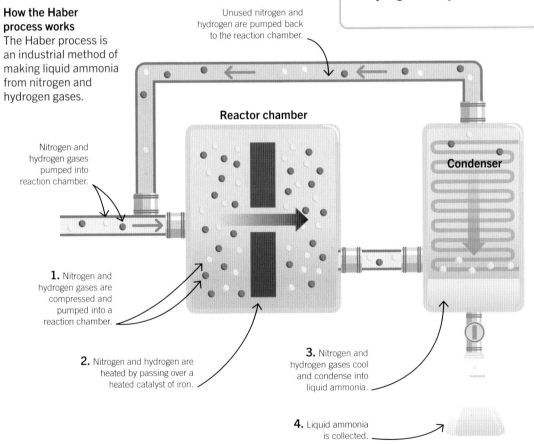

Unused nitrogen and hydrogen are pumped back to the reaction chamber.

Reactor chamber

Condenser

Nitrogen and hydrogen gases pumped into reaction chamber.

1. Nitrogen and hydrogen gases are compressed and pumped into a reaction chamber.

2. Nitrogen and hydrogen are heated by passing over a heated catalyst of iron.

3. Nitrogen and hydrogen gases cool and condense into liquid ammonia.

4. Liquid ammonia is collected.

Equation

The reaction is reversible, so only some of the nitrogen and hydrogen is converted into ammonia.

$$N_{2(g)} + 3H_{2(g)} \rightleftharpoons 2NH_{3(g)}$$

Reaction Conditions

The chemical industry tries to produce as much product as quickly as possible, with the aim of making money. This is called product yield. The Haber process is an efficient, reversible reaction that is slow and does not produce much ammonia. However, scientists can still improve this by changing the conditions for the reaction.

Choosing conditions

The graph shows that the highest yield of ammonia is obtained at lower temperatures and high pressures. The conditions chosen for Haber plants are a compromise between speed of the reaction, yield, and cost.

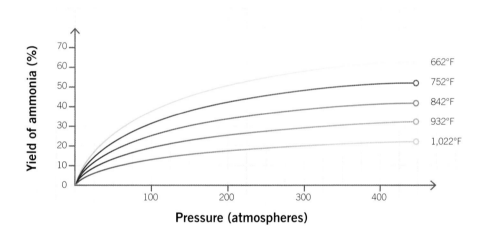

- 662°F
- 752°F
- 842°F
- 932°F
- 1,022°F

Industrial Catalysts

Catalysts are often used in industrial reactions as they speed up the rate of reaction by providing an alternative pathway (see page 184). They keep costs down because catalysts are not changed by the reaction so can be used over and over again. Vanadium oxide crystals are sometimes used in the Haber process as catalysts.

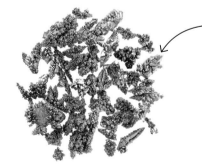

The catalyst is broken up into small pieces to get the largest surface area on which the reaction can occur (see page 183).

Vanadium oxide crystals

Fertilizers

Plants absorb certain elements in the soil that are used to help them grow. Over time, these elements are used up, so farmers and gardeners have to add them back into the soil. They add chemical substances called fertilizers, which contain soluble compounds that include the elements needed by the plants.

Fertilizer compounds
Artificial fertilizers contain different ratios (amounts) of the elements nitrogen, phosphorus, and potassium. These elements are absorbed by plants in the form of soluble compounds. They are called NPK fertilizers after their constituent elements' symbols (see pages 52–53), and their colors vary depending on the amount of each element in them.

Element	Function
Nitrogen	Growth
Magnesium	Photosynthesis
Potassium	Opens and closes stomata
Phosphorus	Photosynthesis and respiration

Key Facts

✓ Plants use elements in the soil to grow.

✓ The three most important elements are nitrogen, potassium, and phosphorus.

✓ Fertilizers need to be soluble and supply the essential elements.

✓ Many fertilizers are ionic compounds.

 How Fertilizers Work

On some farms, fertilizers are deposited into the soil by machines. The soil is then watered so the fertilizers can dissolve and release elements into the soil. As plants grow, their roots begin to take up nutrients from the soil, including these essential elements.

Nitrogen in the soil

Essential element being taken up by plant root

Producing Fertilizers

Fertilizers can be made in the laboratory using simple equipment, or in industry. Giant vats (steel containers) hold the exothermic reaction needed to produce fertilizers. Heat released by the reaction is used to evaporate water from the fertilizer to make it even more concentrated (potent). However, making fertilizers in the laboratory is on a much smaller scale.

Making fertilizers in the laboratory
To make ammonium sulfate (a type of fertilizer), you need a conical flask, a titration tube, and either a Bunsen burner or a water bath to heat your mixture.

Key Facts

✓ Fertilizers can be made in industry or in the lab.

✓ Fertilizers produced in industry are more concentrated and in greater quantity.

✓ Fertilizers can be made in the lab using titration and crystallization.

1. Measure 25 cm³ of ammonia solution using a measuring cylinder, and pour it into a conical flask.

2. Add two drops of methyl orange indicator. The solution will turn yellow, telling you it is alkaline.

3. Using a titration tube, add dilute sulfuric acid slowly until the solution turns orange.

4. Record the amount of sulfuric acid added. Dispose of the solution in a chemical waste container.

5. Repeat the experiment with the same volumes of ammonia and sulfuric acid. Now that you know the amount of sulfuric acid needed, you don't need to use the indicator.

6. Crystallize (see page 47) the ammonia sulfate solution. The crystals are the fertilizer.

ammonia + sulfuric acid $\longrightarrow$ ammonium sulfate

$$2NH_{3(aq)} + H_2SO_{4(aq)} \longrightarrow (NH_4)_2SO_{4(aq)}$$

Glossary

Accurate A measurement taken in an experiment is accurate if it is close to the true value that you need to measure.

Acid A compound that has a pH value less than 7, contains hydrogen, and releases ions of hydrogen when it is dissolved in water.

Acidic A word used to describe a substance that has the properties of an acid.

Activation energy The minimum amount of energy that particles must have for them to react.

Addition reaction A chemical reaction in which two reactants combine to make a single product.

Agent A substance that prompts an effect by interacting with another substance.

Alcohol A homologous compound with the functional group –OH.

Algae Simple, plantlike organisms that live in water and make their food by photosynthesis.

Alkali A compound that has a pH value greater than 7 and produces OH⁻ ions when dissolved in water.

Alkaline A word used to describe a substance that has the properties of an alkali.

Alkane A hydrocarbon with no carbon–carbon double bonds in its molecules.

Alkene A homologous hydrocarbon with carbon–carbon double bonds in its molecules.

Alloy A material made by mixing a metal with other metals or nonmetals.

Alpha particle A particle containing two protons and two neutrons with a 2+ charge (a helium nucleus).

Amino acid A smaller molecule that makes up larger protein molecules.

Anhydrous A compound (usually a crystal) that doesn't contain water molecules.

Anion A negatively charged ion that is attracted to the positive electrode (anode).

Anode A positively charged electrode.

Aqueous solution A solution containing water and a dissolved substance.

Artificial A substance that doesn't exist in nature and is made by humans.

Atmosphere The mixture of gases that surrounds Earth.

Atom The smallest unit of an element. They are composed of protons, neutrons, and electrons.

Atomic number The number of protons in an atom of an element. Every element has a unique, unchanging atomic number.

Axis One of the two perpendicular lines showing measurements plotted on a graph.

Bacteria Microscopic single-celled organisms that make up one of the main kingdoms of life on Earth. Many bacteria are helpful but some cause disease.

Base A substance that can neutralize an acid.

Battery A device containing a collection of chemical cells that react to produce electrical energy.

Blood A fluid that circulates through the bodies of animals delivering vital substances to cells and removing waste.

Boiling point The temperature at which a liquid gets hot enough to change into a gas.

Bond The attraction between atoms that holds them together in an element or a compound.

Brittle A word that describes a hard solid that shatters easily.

Bromide A compound containing the element bromine and one or more elements.

Burette A piece of apparatus used to measure accurate volumes of liquids.

By-product An incidental substance created during a chemical reaction that isn't useful.

Carbon dioxide A gas found in air. Its molecules are made of one carbon atom and two oxygen atoms.

Carbonate A compound that contains carbon and oxygen atoms, as well as atoms of other elements. Many minerals are carbonates.

Carboxylic acids A homologous series of organic compounds that contain the functional group –COOH.

Catalyst A substance that speeds up chemical reactions but is not changed during the reaction.

Cathode A negatively charged electrode.

Cell (biological) A tiny unit of living matter. Cells are the building blocks of all living things.

Cell (electrochemical) A piece of equipment that produces electrical energy.

Charge The positive or negative electrical energy attached to matter.

Chemical Another word for a substance, generally meaning a compound made from several elements.

Chemist A scientist who studies the elements, the compounds, and chemical reactions.

Chemistry The scientific study of the properties and reactions of the elements.

Chloride A compound that contains the element chlorine and one or more elements.

Coal *See* fossil fuel.

Compound A chemical consisting of two or more elements whose atoms have bonded.

Concentrated A word used to describe a high amount of one substance in relation to other substances, particularly in a solution.

Concentration A measure of the amount of solute dissolved in a solution.

Concentration gradient The difference between the concentration of a substance in one area and its concentration in another area. A large (steep) concentration gradient results in a fast rate of diffusion.

Condensation A process in which a substance changes from a gas into a liquid.

Condense To change from a gas to a liquid.

Conductor A substance that lets heat or electricity flow easily through it.

Corrosion A chemical reaction that attacks a metal, or other solid object, usually due to the presence of oxygen and water.

Corrosive The way of describing a substance that causes corrosion.

Covalent bond A bond that forms between two atoms that share two electrons between them.

Cracking A reaction that breaks down large hydrocarbon molecules into smaller, more useful alkanes and an alkene.

Crude oil *See* fossil fuel.

Crystal A naturally occurring solid substance that has atoms arranged in a regular three-dimensional pattern.

Data A collection of information, such as numbers, facts, and statistics, gathered during an experiment.

Decompose To break down into simpler substances.

Delocalized electrons Electrons that are free to move between the atoms of certain substances.

Density The amount of matter held within a known volume of a material.

Diatomic A molecule that consists of two atoms.

Dilute A word used to describe a substance, usually a liquid, that is found in small amounts within a solution.

Dioxide A compound containing two atoms of oxygen in its molecule.

Displacement A chemical reaction in which a more reactive element displaces a less reactive element from its compound.

Dissolve To become completely mixed into another substance. In most cases, a solid, such as salt, dissolves in a liquid, such as water.

Distillation A method of separating liquids from a solution.

Drug A chemical taken into the body in order to alter the way the body works. Most drugs are taken to treat or prevent disease.

Electrode An electrical contact in an electric circuit. Electrodes can have a positive or negative charge.

Electrolysis The use of an electrical current to split compounds into elements.

Electrolyte A molten substance or dissolved solution that undergoes electrolysis.

Electrons A negatively charged particle inside an atom. Electrons orbit the atom's nucleus in layers called shells. They are exchanged or shared by atoms to make bonds that hold molecules together.

Electronic configuration The way electrons are arranged in an atom.

Electrostatic attraction The force of attraction between negative electrons and positive nuclei within atoms.

Element A pure substance that can't be broken down into a simpler substance.

Endothermic reaction A chemical reaction that takes in energy, usually in the form of heat. *See also* exothermic reaction.

Energy A force that makes things happen. It can be stored, used, or transferred from one form to another.

Enzyme A protein made by living cells that speeds up a chemical reaction.

Equilibrium A state where the forward reaction happens at the same speed as the backward reaction.

Ester A homologous series of compounds that contain the functional group –COO–.

Ethene A compound containing two carbon and four hydrogen atoms. Ethene is usually found as a gas produced by plants and serves as a hormone that triggers the ripening of fruit.

Evaporate To change from a liquid to a gas.

Evaporation A process in which a substance changes from a liquid to a gas.

Exothermic reaction A chemical reaction that transfers energy to the surroundings, often in the form of heat.

Experiment A controlled situation set up by scientists in order to test whether a hypothesis is true or not.

Filter paper A type of paper that blocks the passage of insoluble substances but lets liquids pass through it.

Filtrate The liquid that has passed through a filter.

Filtration A method of separating a liquid from an insoluble solid.

Flammable A word used to describe a material that catches fire easily.

Fluoride A compound in which the element fluorine is bonded with one or more elements.

Formula (chemical) A chemical formula shows the actual number of atoms in a chemical compound.

Formula (mathematical) A mathematical formula is a rule or relationship written with mathematical symbols.

Fossil fuel A fuel derived from the fossilized remains of living things. Coal, crude oil, and natural gas are fossil fuels.

Freezing point The temperature at which a liquid turns into a solid.

Functional group An atom, group of atoms, or bond in an organic compound responsible for its properties.

Gas A state in which the particles of matter (atoms or molecules) aren't attracted to each other and can move freely. A gas can flow, take any shape, and fill any container.

Gene An instruction encoded in the molecule DNA and stored inside a living cell. Genes are passed from parents to their offspring and determine each living thing's inherited characteristics.

Group A set of elements in a column on the periodic table. Elements in a group have similar properties because each element has the same number of electrons in their outer shell.

Halogen The elements in Group 7 of the periodic table.

Homologous A word used to describe functional groups that are the same.

Hormone A chemical produced by a gland in the body that travels through the blood and changes the way certain target organs work, often with powerful effects.

Hydrated A way of describing a compound that has bonded with water molecules.

Hydrocarbon A compound containing only hydrogen and carbon atoms joined together by covalent bonds.

Hydroxide A type of compound containing hydrogen, oxygen, and normally a metallic element.

Hypothesis A scientific idea or theory.

Indicator A substance that changes color when placed in acidic or alkaline conditions.

Insoluble The inability to dissolve in a liquid.

Insulator A substance that doesn't let heat or electricity flow through it easily.

Iodide A compound containing the element iodine and one or more elements.

Ion When atoms lose or gain electrons, they become ions.

Ionic bond A bond that forms between two atoms of a metal and a nonmetal that involves electrostatic attraction.

Isotopes Two forms of an element with different numbers of neutrons.

Lattice The ordered structure of atoms.

Limiting reactant The reactant that is completely used up first in a reaction.

Liquid A state in which the particles of matter (atoms or molecules) are only loosely attached to each other and move freely. A liquid can flow and take any shape, but has a fixed volume.

Magnetic A word used to describe an object that produces a magnetic field, which attracts certain materials to it and can attract or repel other magnets.

Mass The amount of matter in an object.

Matter The material that makes up everything around us.

Mean (average) A measure of average found by adding up a set of values and dividing that by the total number of values.

Melting point The temperature at which a solid gets hot enough to turn into a liquid.

Membrane A thin lining or barrier that stops some substances from passing through it but allows others to cross.

Metals A group of elements that share many similar properties.

Microorganism A tiny organism that can be seen only with the aid of a microscope.

Microscope A scientific instrument that uses lenses to make small objects appear larger.

Mineral A naturally occurring inorganic chemical, such as salt, often found in rocks or dissolved in water. Some minerals are essential to life.

Mixture A collection of substances that fill the same space but aren't connected by chemical bonds.

Model A simplified representation of a real object or system that helps scientists understand how the object or system works.

Mole The same amount of particles as there are atoms in exactly 12g of carbon-12.

Molecule A group of two or more atoms joined by strong chemical bonds.

Molten A word used to describe a substance that is usually solid but has become a liquid after it has been heated to high temperatures.

Monomer A small molecule that can combine to form larger molecules called polymers.

Neutral A word used to describe something that has neither a positive or negative charge. Or a solution with a pH value of 7 that is neither acidic or alkaline.

Neutralization A chemical reaction between an acid and a base.

Neutron A particle with no charge in the nucleus of an atom.

Nitrate A salt containing nitrogen and oxygen anions.

Nonmetal A type of element that is likely to react with another element by acquiring electrons in the outermost shell of its atoms.

Nuclei Plural of nucleus.

Nucleus The central part of an atom, made up of protons and neutrons.

Nutrients Substances that animals and plants take in and that are essential for life and growth.

Ore A rock or mineral from which a useful element such as a metal can be purified and collected.

Organic Derived from living organisms or a compound based on carbon and hydrogen atoms.

Organism A living thing.

Oxidation A reaction in which oxygen is added to a substance or atoms in a substance lose electrons.

Oxide A compound in which oxygen is bound to one or more other elements.

Oxygen An element in Group 6 that is a gas at room temperature. It makes up 21 percent of air.

Particle A tiny bit of matter, such an atom, molecule, or ion.

Period A set of elements in a row on the periodic table.

Periodic table A table that identifies all known elements.

pH A scale used to measure how acidic or alkaline a solution is.

Photosynthesis The process by which plants use the Sun's energy to make food molecules from water and carbon dioxide.

Pipette A piece of apparatus used to transfer liquids.

Plastic A type of polymer that has a wide range of useful properties.

Poisonous *See* toxic.

Polymer A carbon compound with long, chainlike molecules made of repeating units. Plastics are examples of polymers.

Precipitate A collection of small, solid particles that form in solutions after a reaction between a substance dissolved in a solution and a substance added to the solution.

Precise A word used to describe a measurement made with a large number of significant figures. A precise measurement may not be accurate.

Pressure A measure of how hard a force pushes on a surface. Pressure depends upon the strength of the force and the area of the surface to which the pressure is applied.

Product A new substance that forms after a chemical reaction takes place between reactants.

Property A particular characteristic of an element or a compound, such as color or reactivity.

Protein An organic substance that contains nitrogen and is found in foods such as meat, fish, cheese, and beans. Organisms need proteins for growth and repair.

Protons A positively charged particle in the nucleus of an atom. Protons attract negative electrons that circle the nucleus.

Pure A word used to describe a substance that is composed of only one type of element or one compound.

Radiation An electromagnetic wave or a stream of particles emitted from a source of radioactivity.

Reactant A substance that chemically reacts with others to form products.

Reactive A word used to describe a substance that reacts (loses its electrons) easily with others.

Reduction When atoms in a substance gain electrons.

Relative atomic mass (A_r) The average mass of an element's atoms, including all of its isotopes compared to $\frac{1}{12}$ the mass of a carbon-12 atom.

Relative formula mass (M_r) The total mass of a compound's atoms compared to $\frac{1}{12}$ the mass of a carbon-12 atom.

Respiration The process by which living cells transfer energy from food molecules.

Room temperature 68°F (20°C).

Rusting The corrosion of iron.

Salt A compound that forms when an acid reacts with an alkali.

Sample A small portion of a larger substance that is tested.

Saturated (organic compounds) A word used to describe a molecule that only contains single covalent bonds.

Saturated (solutions) A solution is described as saturated when no more solute can be dissolved in it.

Shell The pathway an electron orbits around a nucleus.

Solid A state in which the particles of matter (atoms or molecules) are bound to each other, so they remain in fixed positions. A solid has a fixed shape and volume.

Soluble The ability to dissolve in a liquid.

Solute A substance that dissolves in a solvent to form a solution.

Solution A mixture in which the molecules or ions of a solute are evenly spread out among the molecules of a solvent.

Solvent A substance (usually a liquid) in which a solute dissolves to form a solution.

Strong acid An acid where most of the hydrogen ions from the acid dissolve in water.

Structural formula A type of formula that uses symbols and straight lines to show the bonds between atoms in molecules.

Sublimation A process in which a substance changes from a solid to a gas without becoming a liquid first.

Substance A single compound or a mixture of compounds.

Sugar A carbohydrate with a small molecule.

Sulfate A compound containing sulfur and oxygen anions.

Sulfide A compound containing the element sulfur and one or more other elements.

Surface area The total area of the exterior of a solid object expressed in square units.

Symbol (chemical) A unique one- or two-letter indicator that represents an element.

Synthetic A material made by humans to serve a specific purpose.

Temperature A measure of how hot or cold something is.

Theory A well established scientific idea that explains some aspect of the real world and has been tested by experiments.

Toxic A word used to describe a substance that is harmful.

Universal indicator A mixture of dyes that turns a certain color along the pH scale when it comes into contact with substances.

Universe The whole of space and everything it contains.

Vaccine A safe way of presenting the antigens of a disease to the body so that if the real disease appears, the body is primed to fight it.

Vapor A gas that can easily be changed back to a liquid, by cooling it or putting it under pressure.

Volume The amount of space an object takes up.

Weak acid An acid where only a few of the hydrogen ions from the acid dissolve in water.

x-axis The horizontal axis of a graph.

y-axis The vertical axis of a graph.

Index

Acknowledgements

The publisher would like to thank the following people for their assistance in the preparation of this book: Sam Atkinson, Edward Aves, and Alexandra Di Falco for editorial help; Nicola Erdpresser, Joe Lawrence, Daksheeta Pattni, and Sammi Richiardi for design help; Steve Crozier for picture retouching; Martin Payne for proofreading; Helen Peters for the index.

Smithsonian Enterprises:
Kealy E. Gordon, Product Development Manager;
Ellen Nanney, Senior Manager, Licensed Publishing;
Jill Corcoran, Director, Licensed Publishing;
Brigid Ferraro, Vice President, Education and Consumer Products; Ed Howell, Senior Vice President, Retail Group; Carol LeBlanc, President

Smithsonian's National Museum of Natural History:
Jeffrey Post, Department of Mineral Sciences, Chair
Michael Ackerson, Research Geologist

The publisher would like to thank the following for their kind permission to reproduce photographs:
(Key: a-above; b-below/bottom; c-center; f-far; l-left; r-right; t-top)

1 Science Photo Library: Martyn F. Chillmaid. 2 Dorling Kindersley: Ruth Jenkinson / RGB Research Limited (background). 3 Dorling Kindersley: Ruth Jenkinson / RGB Research Limited (bl, bl/sodium, bc, br, br/Caesium). 5 Dreamstime.com: Okea (br). 6 Science Photo Library: (bl); Martyn F. Chillmaid (bl/Strong Acid, c/Weak Acid). 7 Science Photo Library: (br). 8 Science Photo Library: Martyn F. Chillmaid (br). 12 Dreamstime.com: Katerynakon (c). iStockphoto.com: E+ / bymuratdeniz (c). 15 Alamy Stock Photo: sciencephotos (bc). Dreamstime.com: Robert Davies (ca). iStockphoto.com: Ranta Images (cr). Science Photo Library: Andrew Lambert Photography (cb). 16 Science Photo Library: Martyn F. Chillmaid (c). 20 Dreamstime.com: Dmitrii Kazitsyn (cra). Fotolia: Fotoedgaras (cr). Science Photo Library: Martyn F. Chillmaid (cla). 22 Dorling Kindersley: Clive Streeter / The Science Museum, London (c/used 2 times). 30 Dorling Kindersley: Ruth Jenkinson / RGB Research Limited (fcl, cra); Colin Keates / Natural History Museum, London (c). 31 Dorling Kindersley: Ruth Jenkinson / RGB Research Limited. 32 Alamy Stock Photo: studiomode (cl). iStockphoto.com: E+ / Turnervisual (c). Science Photo Library: Martyn F. Chillmaid (cr). 33 Alamy Stock Photo: studiomode (cl). iStockphoto.com: E+ / Turnervisual (c). Science Photo Library: Editorial Image (c). 35 Science Photo Library: Martyn F. Chillmaid (br/used 2 times). 36 Science Photo Library: (tc). 38 Alamy Stock Photo: Evgeny Karandaev (clb). Science Photo Library: Vitaliy Belousov / Sputnik (br); Martyn F.

Chillmaid (crb). 39 iStockphoto.com: E+ / Mitshu (r). 40 Science Photo Library: Turtle Rock Scientific (r). 41 Science Photo Library: (c). 42 Science Photo Library: Giphotostock (c). 43 Science Photo Library: Giphotostock (cra). 44 Science Photo Library: Giphotostock (b/used 2 times). 45 Science Photo Library: Giphotostock (bl). 46 Science Photo Library: (c). 47 Alamy Stock Photo: Stocksearch (c). 48 Science Photo Library: Giphotostock (c). 50 Science Photo Library: (c/used twice). 54 Getty Images: Science & Society Picture Library (c). 56 123RF.com: photopips (crb). Dorling Kindersley: Ruth Jenkinson / RGB Research Limited (cb). SuperStock: Science Photo Library (cl). 57 Dorling Kindersley: Ruth Jenkinson / Holts Gems (cla). Dreamstime.com: Laurenthive (fcla); Dmitry Skutin (cra). Science Photo Library: Ian Cuming / Ikon Images (bc). 58 Dorling Kindersley: Ruth Jenkinson / RGB Research Limited (fbr, br, bl/sodium, fbl/Lithium, bc). 59 Getty Images: Moment Open / (c) Philip Evans (bl). 60 Dorling Kindersley: Ruth Jenkinson / RGB Research Limited (cb, clb, cr, c, cl). 61 Dorling Kindersley: Ruth Jenkinson / RGB Research Limited (crb, cb, cr, c, cl). 62-63 Science Photo Library: Andrew Lambert Photography (b). 64 123RF.com: cobalt (bc); Oleksandr Marynchenko (bl). Dorling Kindersley: Ruth Jenkinson / RGB Research Limited (crb, cb, clb, cr, c, cl, cra, ca, cla). Fotolia: efired (fbr). 65 Dorling Kindersley: Ruth Jenkinson / RGB Research Limited (br). Science Photo Library: US Department Of Energy (bl); Dirk Wiersma (crb). 66 Dreamstime.com: Pavel Naumov (fbr). 67 123RF.com: scanrail (bc). Dorling Kindersley: Ruth Jenkinson / RGB Research Limited (crb, clb, cr, cl). SuperStock: Science Photo Library (c). 68 Dorling Kindersley: Ruth Jenkinson / RGB Research Limited (cb, clb, c, cl). 69 Dorling Kindersley: Ruth Jenkinson / RGB Research Limited (br, bl, crb, cl). 70 Dorling Kindersley: Ruth Jenkinson / RGB Research Limited (cr, cl, cl/fluorine, ca). 71 Dorling Kindersley: Ruth Jenkinson / RGB Research Limited (cr, cb, clb, cr, c, cl). 79 Science Photo Library: Charles D. Winters (c). 83 Dorling Kindersley: Ruth Jenkinson / RGB Research Limited (c). 84 Alamy Stock Photo: Mediscan (c). 85 Alamy Stock Photo: Phil Degginger (br). 86 Dreamstime.com: MinervaStudio (clb); Eduard Bonnin Turina (bc). Fotolia: apptone (c). 88 Alamy Stock Photo: Yuen Man Cheung (br). 89 Dorling Kindersley: Ruth Jenkinson / RGB Research Limited (cl). 91 Dreamstime.com: Grafner (c). 93 Dreamstime.com: Bblood (c). 96 Dreamstime.com: Andreykuzmin (c); Romikmk (crb); Nikkytok (crb/Dense steam); Valentyn75 (clb). 98 Science Photo Library: Turtle Rock Scientific (c). 100 SuperStock: Science Photo Library (c). 102 Alamy Stock Photo: James King-Holmes (clb). JOHN ROGERS/UNIVERSITY OF

ILLINOIS AT URBANA-CHAMPAIGN: (crb). Science Photo Library: Steve Gschmeissner (cb); National Cancer Institute (b). 103 Science Photo Library: David Parker (c). 104 Science Photo Library: Giphotostock (cl). Shutterstock: xiaorui (c). 105 iStockphoto.com: Sashul9 (l). 107 Science Photo Library: (ca). 109 Science Photo Library: (b). 111 Science Photo Library: Andrew Lambert Photography (cl, cr). 112 Science Photo Library: Science Source (cr, c, cl). 115 Science Photo Library: Turtle Rock Scientific / Science Source (c). 116 Science Photo Library: Trevor Clifford Photography / Science Photo Library (r). 127 Science Photo Library: Martyn F. Chillmaid (cr). 130 123RF.com: maksym yemelyanov / maxxyustas (cl); mrtwister (c). Dreamstime.com: Denira777 (c). 131 123RF.com: imagepixels (c). Dreamstime.com: Puripat Khummungkhoon (cl); Winnipuhin (cr). Science Photo Library: (tc). 132 Science Photo Library: Andrew Lambert Photography (l). 133 Science Photo Library: (c). 134 Science Photo Library: (cra); Turtle Rock Scientific (br, cr). 135 Science Photo Library: Giphotostock (cr, cl). 136 Science Photo Library: Charles D. Winters (r). 137 Science Photo Library: Martyn F. Chillmaid (c, c/Strong Acid). 138 Science Photo Library: Giphotostock (cr, cl). 140 Science Photo Library: (c). 145 Science Photo Library: Martyn F. Chillmaid (c). 146 Science Photo Library: (cr); Charles D. Winters (c/sodium); Turtle Rock Scientific (fcl, c/Lithium). 147 Science Photo Library: Martyn F. Chillmaid (c). 152 Science Photo Library: Giphotostock (b). 156 Dreamstime.com: Ekaterina Semenova / Ekaterinasemenova (bc). 158 Science Photo Library: (b). 163 Science Photo Library: Lewis Houghton (r). 164 Science Photo Library: (c). 165 Science Photo Library: Turtle Rock Scientific / Science Source (c). 166 123RF.com: Romolo Tavani (c). 167 Science Photo Library: Giphotostock (r). 173 Alamy Stock Photo: Independent Picture Service (bc/fruit battery). Science Photo Library: (r). Shutterstock: Alexander Konradi (bc). 174 Science Photo Library: (c). 175 Dreamstime.com: Yudesign (c). 176 Science Photo Library: Giphotostock (c). 177 Science Photo Library: Mikkel Juul Jensen (c). 179 123RF.com: Romolo Tavani (br). Dreamstime.com: Anest (c). Science Photo Library: Giphotostock (bc); Paul Rapson (bc/crude oil). 181 Science Photo Library: Martyn F. Chillmaid (c). 182 Science Photo Library: Giphotostock (c). 183 Science Photo Library: Turtle Rock Scientific (c). 184 Science Photo Library: Trevor Clifford Photography (c). 187 Science Photo Library: sciencephotos (c). 188 Alamy Stock Photo: sciencephotos (c). 191 Science Photo Library: Martyn F. Chillmaid (cr, c). 192 Science Photo Library: Turtle Rock Scientific / Science Source (c). 193 Science Photo Library: Giphotostock (cr, cl).

194 Science Photo Library: Turtle Rock Scientific / Science Source (b). 196 Science Photo Library: Giphotostock (r). 201 Dreamstime.com: Gualtiero Boffi (cb). Science Photo Library: (c). 202 Science Photo Library: Spacex (c). 203 Science Photo Library: Crown Copyright / Health & Safety Laboratory (crb). 205 123RF.com: Scanrail (tr). Alamy Stock Photo: Nathan Allred (cra). Dreamstime.com: Ilfede (crb). PunchStock: Westend61 / Rainer Dittrich (cr). Science Photo Library: Paul Rapson (cr/Kerosene); Victor De Schwanberg (br). 206 Science Photo Library: Paul Rapson (c). 211 Science Photo Library: Martyn F. Chillmaid (r). 216 Science Photo Library: Andrew Lambert Photography (bc); Martyn F. Chillmaid (cb); Turtle Rock Scientific / Science Source (ca). 217 Alamy Stock Photo: David Lee (cr). Dreamstime.com: R. Gino Santa Maria / Shutterfree, Llc (cra). Science Photo Library: Andrew Lambert Photography (crb). 218 Getty Images: Brand X Pictures / Science Photo Library - Steve Gschmeissner (cr). Science Photo Library: Martyn F. Chillmaid (c). 225 Dreamstime.com: Pglazar (c). 226 Science Photo Library: Dennis Kunkel Microscopy (c). 232 Science Photo Library: (c). 233 Science Photo Library: Giphotostock (c); Turtle Rock Scientific / Science Source (c). 234 Science Photo Library: Giphotostock (tr). 235 Science Photo Library: (tl/Silver nitrate, ftl/Chloride ions, tc/Iodide ions). 236 Science Photo Library: Martyn F. Chillmaid (b). 237 Science Photo Library: (br); Martyn F. Chillmaid (c). 241 Dorling Kindersley: Arran Lewis / NASA (c). 242 Alamy Stock Photo: Naeblys (c). 243 Dorling Kindersley: Colin Keates / Natural History Museum, London (bc). 254 Science Photo Library: 201010 LTD (c). 255 123RF.com: Nikolai Grigoriev / grynold (bc). 256 Alamy Stock Photo: Ryan McGinnis (c). 258 Dorling Kindersley: Cloki (cb). Dreamstime.com: Design56 (bc); Subodh Sathe (ca). Science Photo Library: Turtle Rock Scientific (br). 259 Dorling Kindersley: Gary Ombler / Universal Cycle Centre (c). 260 Dreamstime.com: Georgii Dolgykh / Gdolgikh (bc); Gemenacom (cb). 261 123RF.com: Aleksey Poprugin (c). Dreamstime.com: Ib Photography / Inbj (crb). Science Photo Library: Giphotostock (l). 262 Dreamstime.com: Yifang Zhao (c). 264 123RF.com: Nik Merkulov (c). 265 Dreamstime.com: Dingalt (b). 266 123RF.com: Dmytro Nikitin (cr). 269 123RF.com: Aleksey Poprugin (bl). 272 Alamy Stock Photo: Robert Brook / Science Photo Library (cb). Science Photo Library: Robert Brook (bc). Shutterstock: dkingsleyfish (ca). 275 Dorling Kindersley: Ruth Jenkinson / RGB Research Limited (bc). 276 Science Photo Library: Martyn F. Chillmaid (c)

All other images © Dorling Kindersley
For further information see: www.dkimages.com